WEB DESIGN I

3

WEB DESIGN INDEX

3

Compiled by Günter Beer

THE PEPIN PRESS / AGILE RABBIT EDITIONS
AMSTERDAM AND SINGAPORE

With special thanks to Magda Garcia Masana from LocTeam S.L., Barcelona

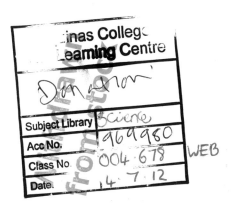
Compiled and edited by Günter Beer
www.webdesignindex.org
Compilation and CD content copyright © 2002 Günter Beer

Cover, CD label and book design by Pepin van Roojen
Layout and CD master by Kathrin Günter

Introduction by Günter Beer and Pepin van Roojen
Translations by LocTeam, Barcelona (German, Spanish, French and Italian),
and Mitaka, Leeds (Japanese).

ISBN 90 5768 045 9

Agile Rabbit Editions
c/o The Pepin Press BV
P.O. Box 10349
1001 EH Amsterdam
The Netherlands

Tel +31 20 4202021
Fax +31 20 4201152
mail@pepinpress.com
www.pepinpress.com

Printed in Singapore

Web Design Index

In this third edition of the highly successful Web Design Index,
another 1,002 outstanding web pages are presented. With each
design, the URL is indicated, followed by the names of those involved
in the design and programming of the site concerned.
The following codes have been used:

D = design
C = coding
P = production
A = agency
M = designer's mail/contact

The purpose of the Web Design Index is to provide a source of inspiration and reference, and a means of communication for designers
and others with an interest in web design. Should you be inspired by
designs in this book, please observe that all designs are copyright,
and that copying is not permitted. Most designers who made work
available for this book can be contacted as indicated, and for easy
reference the designers and agencies are listed in the back of the
book.

The principal criteria on which the index's selection is based are
design quality and innovation, and the page's effectiveness. No
attempt has been made to classify the selection, other than arrange
and group the designs on principal colour.

The internet's technical possibilities, language of navigation, and
users' perception are in a constant state of flux; all of which have a
profound effect on web design. So pages designed not that long ago
may already look dated. Since we selected them for the index, some
pages may have changed, or even disappeared from the net. This
being the case, this book and CD-Rom give an accurate and lasting
overview of the state of the art in current web design.

In the inside back cover, you will find a CD-ROM containing almost
all designs, arranged according to their location in this book. You can
view them on your monitor with a minimum of loading time, and
access the internet to explore the selected site in full.

Submissions
The Web Design Index is published annually. Should you wish to
submit or recommend a design for consideration for the next edition
of the Web Design Index, please access the submission form at
www.webdesignindex.org.

The Pepin Press/Agile Rabbit Editions
The Pepin Press/Agile Rabbit Editions publishes a wide range of
books and CD-ROMs with visual reference material and ready-to-use
images for designers, for internet applications as well as high-resolu-
tion printed media. For more information visit www.pepinpress.com.

Index de modèles de sites Web

Cette troisième édition de l'Index de modèles de sites Web, dont la première avait obtenu un franc succès, présente 1.002 nouvelles pages Web exceptionnelles. Pour chacune d'elles sont indiqués son adresse URL ainsi que le nom des personnes ayant collaboré à sa conception et sa programmation.
Les codes ci-après ont été employés :

D = conception
C = codage
P = production
A = agence
M = coordonnées/adresse électronique du concepteur

L'Index de modèles de sites Web sert de source d'inspiration, de référence et représente un moyen de communication pour les concepteurs et toute personne intéressée par la conception de pages Web. Si certaines des conceptions de ce recueil vous inspirent, sachez qu'il est formellement interdit de les reproduire car elles sont protégées par des droits d'auteur. La plupart des concepteurs ayant participé à la réalisation de ce livre peuvent être contactés comme indiqué. Pour trouver facilement leurs références, reportez-vous à la liste des concepteurs et agences indiquée au dos du livre.

Les principaux critères de sélection de cet index ont été la qualité des images, le degré d'innovation et les performances de la page. Les conceptions n'ont été classées et regroupées qu'en fonction de leur couleur dominante.

La technologie d'Internet, le langage de navigation et la perception des pages Internet par les utilisateurs sont en perpétuelle évolution. Ces éléments ont un effet considérable sur la conception de pages Web. Ainsi, les pages conçues il y a pas peu peuvent déjà paraître dépassées. Certaines des pages apparaissant dans cet index ont peut-être déjà été modifiées, ou peuvent avoir disparu de la toile. Cela étant dit, ce livre et son CD-ROM donnent un aperçu précis et actuel de ce qui se fait de mieux en conception de pages Web.

À l'intérieur du livre, vous trouverez un CD-ROM contenant la quasi totalité des pages Web, classées selon leur emplacement dans ce livre. Vous pouvez les télécharger en un minimum de temps afin de les visualiser sur votre écran d'ordinateur et accéder à Internet pour explorer le site sélectionné dans son intégralité.

Propositions de sites :
L'Index de modèles de sites Web est publié annuellement. Si vous souhaitez soumettre ou recommander un site Web pour la prochaine édition de l'Index de modèles de sites Web, complétez le formulaire à l'adresse : www.webdesignindex.org

Les éditions Pepin Press/Agile Rabbit
Les éditions Pepin Press/Agile Rabbit publient un vaste éventail de livres et de CD-ROM comportant du matériel de référence visuel et des images prêtes à l'emploi destinées aux concepteurs et aux applications Internet, ainsi que des supports imprimés à haute résolution. Pour en savoir plus, visitez le site : www.pepinpress.com

Web Design Index

In dieser dritten Ausgabe des höchst erfolgreichen Web Design Index, werden eintausendundzwei aktuelle, herausragend gestaltete Webseiten vorgestellt.

Qualität des Designs, Innovation, Handhabbarkeit und Verständlichkeit der Navigation sowie die Gesamtwirkung einer Seite bestimmten die Auswahl für diesen Index. Die Reihenfolge der Abbildungen spiegelt keine Wertung wieder, sortiert wurde nur nach dem Farbeindruck.

Der Web Design Index will zu Qualität bei der Gestaltung von Websites anregen und Kontakt zu exzellenten Web-Professionals herstellen. Die Gestaltungsideen sind geistiges Eigentum der jeweiligen Designer. Bitte respektieren Sie das, wenn Sie sich inspirieren lassen.

Zu jedem Design sind der URL-Link sowie Namen und Kontaktadresse der Designer angegeben. Die Buchstaben haben folgende Bedeutung:

D = Design
C = Programmierung, Code Erstellung
P = Produktion
A = Agentur
M = Mail oder Website des Designers

Schneller als bei anderen Medien ändert sich die Formen- und Bildsprache des Internets. Aus diesem Grund können Seiten, die vor zwei Jahren gestaltet wurden, heute bereits altmodisch oder altbacken erscheinen. Auch kann es sein, dass nach Fertigstellung des vorliegenden Indexes manche Seiten geändert worden oder sogar ganz aus dem Internet verschwunden sein werden. So behält diese auf CD-ROM konservierte Momentaufnahme des aktuellen Webdesigns bleibenden Wert.

Im inneren Rücktitel finden Sie ein CD-ROM die fast die fast sämtliche im vorliegenden Buch vorgestellten Sites in der Reihenfolge ihrer Präsentation enthält. So können Sie so bequem offline das jeweilige vorgestellte Design auf ihrem Bildschirm sehen.

Vorschlagen einer Website:
Der Web Design Index wird jährlich herausgegeben. Wenn Sie für die nächste Ausgabe eine Site vorschlagen wollen, wenden Sie sich bitte an unsere Website: www.webdesignindex.org. Dort finden Sie ein Formular.

Die Pepin Press/Agile Rabbit Editions
The Pepin Press/Agile Rabbit Editions verlegt eine breite Palette an Büchern und CD-ROMs mit Bildreferenzmaterial und gebrauchsfertigen Bildern für Designer, Internetanwendungen sowie hochauflösende Druckmedien. Nähere Informationen erhalten Sie unter: www.pepin-press.com.

L´Indice del Disegno Web

In questa terza edizione del L´Indice del Disegno Web vengono presentate altre 1.002 straordinarie pagine web. Con ogni modello viene indicata l'URL, seguita dai nomi di coloro che hanno partecipato alla creazione e alla programmazione del sito in questione. Sono stati usati i seguenti codici:

D = disegno
C = codificazione
P = produzione
A = agenzia
M = mail/contatto dell'autore

Lo scopo del L´Indice del Disegno Web è quello di offrire una fonte di ispira-zione e di riferimento, nonché un mezzo di comunicazione per autori di pagine web ed altre persone interessate alla creazione di siti web. Se doveste trarre ispirazione dai modelli di questo libro, tenete presente che sono tutti copyright e che ne è proibita la riproduzione. La maggior parte degli autori che hanno messo a disposizione il loro lavoro per questo libro si può contattare come indicato –per comodità gli autori e le agenzie sono elencate sul retro del libro.

I principali criteri su cui si basa la selezione dell'indice sono la qualità del design e l'innovazione, nonché l'impatto della pagina. Le pagine selezionate sono state classificate raggruppando i modelli unicamente in base al colore dominante.

Le possibilità tecniche di internet, il linguaggio di navigazione e la percezione degli utenti sono in costante trasformazione, e tutto ciò incide considerevolmente sulla creazione di pagine web. Ecco perché pagine create non molto tempo fa possono apparire obsolete. Da quando le abbiamo selezionate per l'indice, alcune pagine possono essere cambiate, o addirittura scomparse dalla rete. In questo caso, il libro e il CD-Rom offrono una panoramica accurata e durevole delle ultime novità nella creazione di pagine web attuale.

All'interno della penultima di copertina troverete un CD-Rom che contiene quasi tutti i modelli, organizzati in base alla loro collocazione nel libro. Potete visualizzarli sul monitor in pochi istanti ed accedere ad Internet per esplorare il sito scelto in tutte le sue parti.

Proposte
Il L´Indice del Disegno Web viene pubblicato annualmente. Se desiderate presentare o raccomandare il design di una pagina da prendere in consi-derazione per la prossima edizione del Web Design Index, accedete al modulo di presentazione all'indirizzo www.webdesignindex.org.

La Pepin Press/Agile Rabbit Editions
La Pepin Press/Agile Rabbit Editions pubblica un'ampia gamma di libri e CD-ROM con materiale di riferimento visuale ed immagini pronte per disegnatori, applicazioni Internet e mezzi stampati ad alta risoluzione. Per maggiori informazioni visitate il sito www.pepinpress.com

Índice de diseño de páginas web

En esta tercera edición del exitoso Índice de diseño de páginas web se presentan otras 1.002 magníficas páginas web. Junto a cada una de ellas se indica el URL, seguido de los nombres de quienes han participado en el diseño y la programación del sitio en cuestión.
En este libro se han utilizado los siguientes códigos:

D = diseño
C = codificación
P = producción
A = agencia
M = correo electrónico del diseñador

El objetivo del Índice de diseños de páginas web es proporcionar una fuente de inspiración y de referencia, y un medio de comunicación a los diseñadores y a aquellas otras personas interesadas en el diseño de páginas web. Si le inspira alguno de los diseños que aparecen en este libro, por favor, tenga en cuenta que todos ellos tienen derechos de autor y que, por lo tanto, está prohibida su copia. Si lo desea, puede ponerse en contacto, tal como le indicamos, con la mayoría de los diseñadores que han participado en la elaboración de esta obra. Para mayor comodidad, al final del libro aparece una lista con el nombre de los diseñadores y las agencias.

Los principales criterios de selección en los que se basa este índice son la calidad y la innovación del diseño y la eficacia de la página web. Para clasificar las páginas seleccionadas, los diseños se han ordenado y agrupado teniendo en cuenta únicamente el color principal de los mismos.

Las posibilidades técnicas de Internet, el lenguaje de la navegación y la percepción de los usuarios cambian continuamente, y todo ello queda reflejado en el diseño de páginas web. De este modo, algunas páginas web diseñadas no hace mucho tiempo pueden parecer anticuadas. Desde que realizamos la selección para incluirlas en el índice, es posible que algunas páginas hayan cambiado o incluso desaparecido de la red. En cualquier caso, este libro y CD-Rom ofrecen una visión de conjunto precisa y permanente del arte en el diseño actual de páginas web.

En el interior de la contracubierta encontrará un CD-ROM que contiene casi todos los diseños, ordenados según aparecen en este libro. Si lo desea, puede verlos en su monitor (el tiempo de descarga es mínimo) o acceder a Internet para explorar en su totalidad el sitio web seleccionado.

Sugerencias
El Índice de diseños de páginas web se publica cada año. Si desea sugerir o recomendar un diseño para que se tenga en cuenta para la próxima edición del Índice de diseños de páginas web, por favor, rellene el formulario de sugerencias que aparece en la dirección www.webdesignindex.org.

The Pepin Press/Agile Rabbit Editions
The Pepin Press/Agile Rabbit Editions publica una gran variedad de libros y CD-ROMs con material de referencia visual e imágenes destinados a diseñadores, aplicaciones de Internet y medios de impresión de alta resolución. Para más información visite www.pepinpress.com.

ウェブ設計インデックス

ウェブ設計インデックスは非常に好評を博し、その第 2 版には、更に 1,002 の素晴らしいウェブページを掲載しています。各設計と共に、まずホームページ、次にそのホームページの設計者とプログラマーの名前を表示しています。その際、下記のコードを使用しています。

D: 設計
C: コード
P: 生産
A: 担当代理店
M: 設計者のメールアドレス/連絡先

設計者、およびウェブ設計に興味のある方々の意思疎通の手段として、示唆と参照の源をご提供することが、このウェブ設計インデックスの目的です。本書に掲載している設計からインスピレーションを受けた場合には、すべての設計には著作権があり、コピーは許可されていませんので、その旨お気をつけください。この本に掲載しているほとんどの設計者に連絡を取ることができます。また、設計者や設計代理店も本書の後ろに挙げていますので、簡単に参照になれます。

このインデックスへの採用基準は、設計の品質と革新性、およびページの効果です。主な色合いでグループ化した以外には、採用したウェブページの分類は実施していません。

インターネット技術の可能性、操作言語、ユーザーの認識が、常に流入してきます。これらはすべてウェブの設計に大きな影響があります。そのため、最近作成したページも、時代遅れに見えることがあります。このインデックスに採用した後に、変更されたウェブページ、またはインターネットから消えたウェブページもあるかもしれませんが、本書と CD-ROM では、現在のウェブ設計の正確で最新の概要をお伝えしています。

裏表紙の内側に、ほぼすべての設計が場所順に入っている CD-ROM があります。最小の読み込み時間で画面に表示でき、インターネットへのアクセスにより選択サイトをすべて探索できます。

出版
ウェブ設計インデックスは、毎年発行しています。次回のウェブ設計インデックスに掲載する設計、または掲載を推奨する設計がある場合、www.webdesignindex.org にアクセスをお願い申し上げます。

The Pepin Press/Agile Rabbit Editions
The Pepin Press/Agile Rabbit Editions は、幅広い書物と CD-ROM を発行しています。これらには、設計者やインターネットの用途に、すぐに使用できる画像や視覚的な参照資料、高解像度の印刷データが記載されています。詳細は、www.pepinpress.com へお越しください。

WWW.TOUCHEE.DE
D: WALTER MÖSSLER, **C**: PACO LA LUCA, **P**: BAMBOO PRODUCTIONS
A: TOUCHEE, **M**: INFO@TOUCHEE.DE

WWW.MATTSINDALL.COM
D: FREDERIC BONTEMPS
M: FRED_BONTEMPS@HOTMAIL.COM

WWW.ANTIGIRL.COM
D: TIPHANIE BROOKE
M: TART@ANTIGIRL.COM

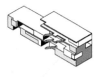

on/off

WWW.STUDIO-TSUNAMI.COM
D: ANTHONY BUSI
A: STUDIO-TSUNAMI, **M:** ANTHONY@STUDIO-TSUNAMI.COM

0   50   0   50   100   150   200   250   300   350   400

STIMUL8.NET : VIEW SOURCE, LEARN, DRINK COFFEE, REPEAT.

	NEWS	BIO	PROJECTS

CSS

zeldman
a list apart
the noodle incident
bluerobot
glish
designflea

XML

tech-nique
topxml
w3schools

DESIGN

net diver
the best designs

06.01.02

Back to the basics...CSS validates 100% :)

05.01.02

New project.

WWW.STIMUL8.NET
D: TEODOR DIMITROV
A: STIMUL8, **M:** T13@MYREALBOX.COM

SEC. 1

◁ GO ▷

Lucas Huffman

Switch backside 3

MENU

WWW.UNREALFACTORY.COM
D: DAVID BOLEAS GUTIERREZ
A: UNREALFACTORY, **M:** DBOLEAS@YAHOO.COM

about   Johannes Wohnseifer - lives and works in Cologne

Museum Fridericianum, Kassel

1995 spindy
neugerriemschneider, Köln

spindy b
Künstlerhaus Bethanien, Berlin

1996 MOMAS-Guard
Museum of Modern Art Syros

10 Portraits
Bundesverkehrsministerium, Bonn

publications

1997 Psylocibyn Experience
Nice Fine Arts, Nizza

videos

WWW.WOHNSEIFER.COM
D: DIRK BOSBACH
A: STUDIO ORANGE, **M:** DIRK@STUDIOORANGE.DE

miniml

ABOUT
CONTACT
DESIGN
FONTS
LINKS

NEWS

June Update~
I'm going to be very busy this month. I'm
rebuilding miniml (with JD Hooge) to make
it even more enjoyable to use. I'm planning to
relaunch on July 2, but don't set that in stone.

I'm also planning on releasing new fonts when I
relaunch with a bunch of new content. But, being
summer, I also plan on cruising around Milwaukee
in my recently acquired '76 GMC Sprint. Oh yeah!

In the meantime, keep sending me links, and have
some fun...

WWW.MINIML.COM
D: CRAIG KROEGER, **C:** JD HOOGE
M: CRAIG@MINIML.COM

|X|

Irriverente
sull'interpretazione dei nuovi scenari del paesaggio digitale.

incoscienza, La mente artificiale che
inventa, e morphizza in modo naturale quella che Novak ha definito come
. Architettura della Quarta Dimensione: l'Architettura **Liquida.**
wireless.e **non un bordo entro cui contenersi**
un processo di **colonizzazione** che crea relazioni spaziali

media space proietta l'utente dalla condizione locale a quella condivisa
sulla rete. l'apprendimento collaborativo necessita di un clima collaborativo favorevole. dorsale/flusso
s p a z i o   s o c i a l e   a c c r e s c i u t o

l a n d s c a p e

NURBS.MTGC.NET
D: ANDREA SCIARRETTA
A: MT GLOBAL CONSULTING, **M:** ANDREA@MTGC.NET

WWW.DB-DB.COM
D: FRANCIS LAM
M: FRANCIS@DB-DB.COM

@ DESIGNUEBERFALL.............................

HOME   ANFANG   SERVICE   PROJEKTE   WEB   KONTAKT   LINKS   NEWS   FIN

WILLKOMMEN IN DER GALERIE MIT WECHSELRAHMEN. SIE BESCHREIBT MIT NEUN BILDERN DEN ZYKLUS DES LEBENS.

WWW.DESIGNUEBERFALL.DE
D: TOBIAS IMMEL
A: DESIGNUEBERFALL, **M:** POST@DESIGNUEBERFALL.DE

@ - Moquette Bar

http://www.moquettebar.com

info@moquettebar.com   Moquette via dell'Asta I7 Forli tel (0543)92751

WWW.MOQUETTEBAR.COM/MOQUETTE.HTM
D: LUCA SANTOLAMAZZA
A: LSDESIGN, **M:** ELLESSE_D@LIBERO.IT

HTML ONLY   26 - 27 RIDING HOUSE STREET   LONDON   W1W 7DU   TEL +44 (0)20 7323 9933   FAX +44 (0)20 7323 9930   E-MAIL info@passion-pictures.com

WWW.PASSION-PICTURES.COM
D: BEN HIBON
A: UNIT9, **M:** UNIT9@UNIT9.COM

GALGO

I Home
I Judge this website
I Suggestion box
I Technical consultations
I News
I The company
I Selection screen
I Sampler

WWW.GALGO.COM
D: I. BURGUI
A: DIMENSION_INTERACTIVA, **M:** INFO@DIMENSIONINTERACTIVA.COM

Presentation 05   Issues June 2002

XIMERALABS
Randomness Collected.

WWW.XIMERALABS.COM
D: TOM MULLER
M: TOMM@XIMERALABS.COM

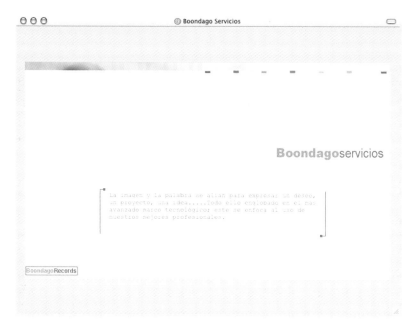

WWW.BOONDAGO.COM
D: PEPE VERA
A: BOONDAGO, **M:** PEPEVERA@BOONDAGO.COM

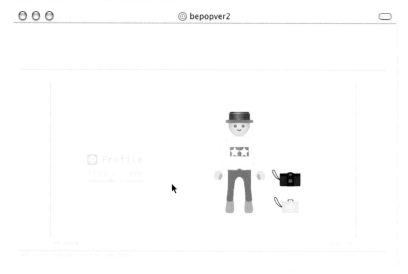

WWW.MAX.HI-HO.NE.JP/ASTRONAUT2001
D: TADASHI MINEMURA
M: ASTRONAUT2001@MAX.HI-HO.NE.JP

WWW.HEIKESTOECKER.COM
D: HEIKE STOECKER
M: HEIKE_STOECKER@HOTMAIL.COM

16

MAYO 2002

WWW.BACKFOLDER.COM
D: ABEL MARTÌNEZ FORONDA, **C:** VÌCTOR SAN VICENTE BORALLA
A: DIFERNET, **M:** WENCES@BACKFOLDER.COM

MondoRondoDigitalDesignV3

/portfolio

WWW.MONDORONDO.COM
D: PHILIP CLARK
M: CLARK@MONDORONDO.COM

SSJ EXPERIMENTAL

WWW.JJJJJJJJJJJJJJJJJJJJJJJJJJJJJJJJJJJJJJJJJJJJJJJJJJ.COM
D: P.J.MEDDA
M: PAOLOJACM@FLASHMAIL.COM

AGENCE**NANCY**

AGENCE**METZ**
metz@projetp40.com

95 RUE MAZELLE F-57000 METZ, FRANCE
TEL 00 33 (0)3 87 36 14 40 / fax 00 33 (0)3 87 36 14 93

© PROJETP40 - juin 2000 - réalisation I-spheres webdesign - illustrations Thierry Badet

WWW.PROJETP40.COM
D: JEAN-LOUIS BUR, **C:** OLIVIER KAUTZ
A: I-SPHERES, **M:** WWW.PROJETP40.COM

WWW.PUSULA.COM/JSP
D: NUMAN PEKGOZ
M: NUMANPEK@HOTMAIL.COM

cartoon

ulrike krappen
design

kontakt   intro   referenzen

WWW.MAD-KLOSE.DE/UKRAPPEN/HOME.HTML
D: ULRIKE KRAPPEN
A: ECHTERNACHT NEW MEDIA, **M:** UKRAPPEN22@COMPUSERVE.DE

18

WWW.HEYNDELS.EASYNET.BE
D: DANY JPR HEYNDELS
M: DANYJPR@EASYNET.BE

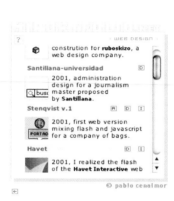

WWW.MIPORTFOLIO.NET
D: PABLO CENALMOR
A: RUBOSKIZO, **M:** INFO@MIPORTFOLIO.NET

WWW.YUNGOKI.COM
D: DANY KWINTNER
A: YUNGOKI DOT COM, **M:** DANY@YUNGOKI.COM

@ Jorge Eduardo Eielson

signo / poética   la dignidad humana   poemas no recogidos   primeras versiones   referencias   galería

jorge eduardo eielson

+ presentación   + contáctenos   + índice

arte
contemporáneo

textiles
precolombinos/
arquelogía

costa del
perú

ciencia (ficción)/
matemáticas/
ecología

roma

joyce

jazz

jorge
eduardo
eielson

viajes/
mar
natación

místicos
castellanos/
zen

rf more ferarum + agradecimientos +   + créditos +

WWW.EIELSON.PERUCULTURAL.ORG.PE
D: CHRISTIAN ARAKAKI, **C:** FAUSTO CARDENAS, **P:** FUNDACION TELEFONICA
A: TELEFONICA DATA, **M:** CHRISTIAN@TSI.COM.PE

○ ○ ○   @ TRANSFLOW

HOME   COMPANY   SERVICES   REFERENZEN   NEWSROOM

PHILOSOPHIE
STRUKTUR
TECHNOLOGIE
CAREERS
KONTAKT
SITEMAP

Vergessen Sie den Heuhaufen !

WWW.TRANSFLOW.COM
D: WALTER MÖSSLER, **C:** PACO LA LUCA, **P:** BAMBOO PRODUCTIONS
A: TOUCHEE, **M:** INFO@TOUCHEE.DE

○ ○ ○   @ Flash

HOME PROBLEME BIKE PHOTOS FLASH LINKS CONTACT

Here are a few test I made in Flash, to get to know the program.
In the future I'm planning to make complete films with this program,
especially because the program offers a range of possibilities. It's
really nice to work with.

"Wies' birthday" 1 MB / 37 sec.
part of a small film I made for the 2nd
birthday of Wies, the son of my best
girlfriend Riam

"Bee in a meadow" 196 kB / 6 sec.
the first thing I made in Flash
to test how the motion path works

"Little piggy" 121 kB / 6 sec.
here I tested the use of a photographic
background

"Save the deer" 466 kB / 35 sec.
an interactive test I made to test button action

WWW.FATMANINBERLIN.DE
D: MARK VAN DER MAAREL
M: M_V_D_M@YAHOO.COM

20

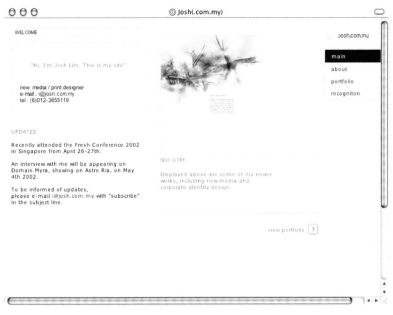

WWW.JOSH.COM.MY
D: JOSH LIM
A: JOSH.COM.MY, **M:** I@JOSH.COM.MY

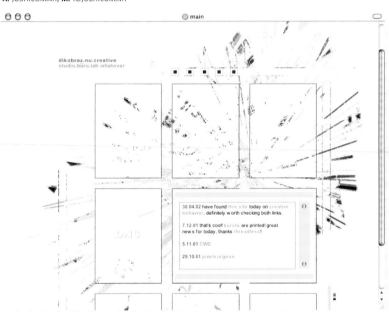

WWW.DIKOBRAZ.COM
D: GEORGE NAZIROV
M: G.D@DIKOBRAZ.COM

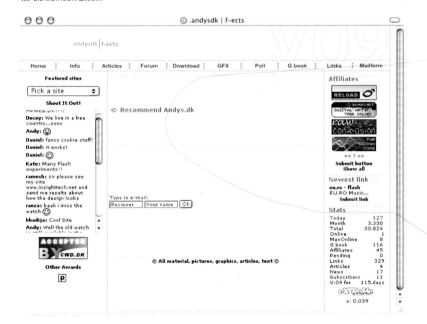

WWW.ANDYS.DK
D: ANDY SØRENSEN
M: ANDY@ANDYS.DK

Tipografia CRESPI *Piazza* San Bartolomeo **4** Trezzo sull'*Adda* (MI)

Tipografia CRESPI *Piazza* San Bartolomeo **4** Trezzo sull'*Adda* (MI)

WWW.TIPOGRAFIACRESPI.COM
D: MARIO DONADONI
A: MD IMMAGINI, **M:** MD@MDIMMAGINI.COM

3 sehenswert

Das kann sich sehen lassen. Und so sind wir schon ein bisschen stolz, was wir für unsere Kunden bisher realisiert haben.

Textilverband Baden-Württemberg
Stuttgart
Konzeption eines neuen Corporate Designs Geschäftsausstattung, Jahresbericht, Konzeption, Text und Layout von Werbemitteln

Baden-Württembergische Bank AG
Stuttgart
Weiterentwicklung des Corporate Designs Konzeption, Text und Layout von Werbemitteln

Fahrschule Bauer & Walcher
Stuttgart-Vaihingen
Entwicklung eines neuen Corporate Designs Logoüberarbeitung, Geschäftsausstattung, Konzeption, Text und Layout von Werbemitteln

Bischoff GmbH, Büroplanungen
Stuttgart
Konzeption, Text und Layout von Werbemitteln

Bullinger GmbH u. Co, Spedition
Stuttgart-Vaihingen

vandervelden.de   kontakt

WWW.VANDERVELDEN.DE
D: JOE LANDEN
A: TWINPIX MEDIA LAB, **M:** LANDEN@TWINPIX.DE

Hennessy PUREWHITE籍此機會，恭喜贏取
PUREWHITE巴黎繽紛之旅2001的幸運兒

▶ 以上得獎者及其貴賓將可於2002年6月享有夢境之旅。請於7月期
間瀏覽我們的網頁，分享他們於巴黎的繽紛旅程。

◀••• 重播得獎者名單

PURE**WHITE**
Hennessy

PUREWHITE Hennessy Privacy Policy Terms & Conditions

WWW.PUREWHITE.COM.HK
D: GARY CHAN, **C:** KENNY TSANG, **P:** CONNIE HO
A: OGILVY INTERACTIVE WORLDWIDE (HK), **M:** FLETCH.WONG@OGILVY.COM

WWW.SKIPINTRO.NL
D: YACCO VIJN, **P:** HANS VAN DIJK,
A: SKIPINTRO, **M:** YACCO@SKIPINTRO.NL

WWW.ARABIANSONLINE.NET
D: EYAD ABUTAHA, **C:** TIM CHIPMAN, **P:** MUHAMAD ABDELKADER
A: WWW.EYAD.COM, **M:** INFO@ARABIANSONLINE.NET

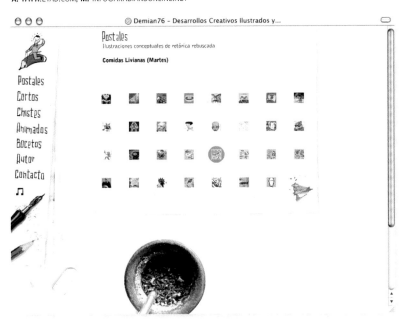

WWW.DEMIAN76.COM.AR
D: MATIAS GILLI
M: DEMIAN76@CIUDAD.COM.AR

FUNNY   NEWS   PRODUCTION   GALLERY   RESEARCHES   WRITINGS   SPECIAL   WEB

WWW.IRSBURGER.COM
D: JUKKA KESKIAHO
M: JUKKA@SNPP.COM

OPUS wurde 1998 in Herzebrock im Herzen von Ostwestfalen gegründet. Ziel war es von Anfang an, eine modische Hose - mit sehr guter Passform, sehr gutem Preis- Leistungsverhältnis und immer dem Zeitgeist entsprechend zu entwickeln. Die Umsetzung dieser Ziele sind vom ersten Tag an mit Erfolg belohnt worden. Durch die partnerschaftliche Zusammenarbeit mit den führenden Mode- Fachhändlern im In- und Ausland gibt es genügend Input für eine innovative, junge Hosen Kollektion.
Nachdem die Organisation 2001 komplett neu -dem Erfolg entsprechend- organsiert wurde ist OPUS fit für die Zukunft.

WWW.OPUS-HOSEN.DE
D: MARQUE LEEWE
A: [WERK01.DE], **M:** MARQUE@WERK01.DE

WWW.MUTABOR.DE
D: JOHANNES PLASS
M: INFO@MUTABOR.DE

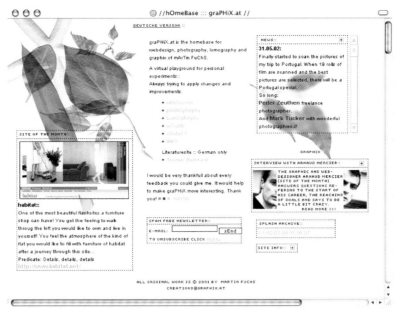

WWW.GRAPHIX.AT
D: MARTIN FUCHS
M: MARTIN.FUCHS@GRAPHIX.AT

WWW.GEOLOGO.COM
D: JOHNNIE MANEIRO
A: GRAFF.NET, **M:** JOHNNIEMANEIRO@MAC.COM

WWW.CORESOLUTIONS.COM
D: MARC SCOTT
A: CORESOLUTIONS, **M:** THREE@NME.COM

sin y con | **método** | contacta | portfolio

sinyconpapel s|u c|p

WWW.SINYCONPAPEL.COM
D: ALMUDENA ROYO, **C:** JORGE ORTUNO MUNOZ
A: SINYCONPAPEL, **M:** JORIS@SINYCONPAPEL.COM

@ ..:: Pixelfreak.com ::..

WWW.PIXELFREAK.COM
D: RENE HERNANDEZ
M: RENE@PIXELFREAK.COM

@ Elince Networks, soluciones globales en progr...

elince networks

PRAC t i c o s

| Misión | Empresa | Alianzas | Proyectos | Trabajo | E. N. Media | Contacto |

WWW.ELINCENETWORKS.COM
D: MIRIAM CAMPILLO, **C:** DENIS DUREUX
A: ELINCE NETWORKS S.L., **M:** MCAMPILLO@ELINCENETWORKS.COM

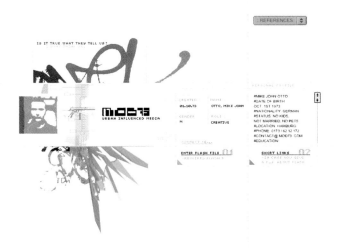

WWW.MOD73.COM
D: MIKE JOHN OTTO
A: MOD 73 - URBAN INFLUENCED MEDIA, **M:** MOTTO@MOD73.COM

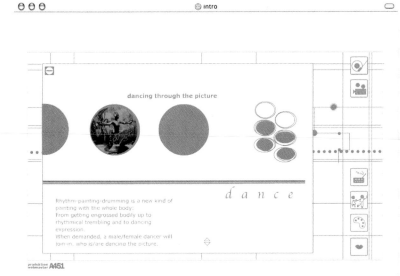

WWW.EYECANHEARIT.DE
D: KARIN GEURTZ
M: KARIN.GEURTZ@T-ONLINE.DE

WWW.LINDENLIFE.DE
D: NIELS BUENEMANN
A: FORM ONE - VISUELLE KOMMUNIKATION, **M:** INFO@FORM-ONE.DE

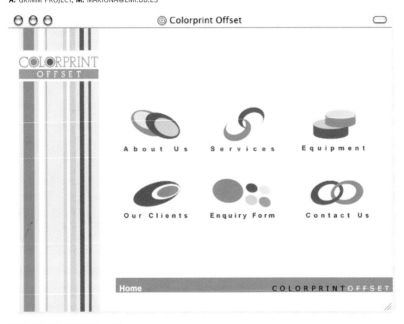

WWW.XINXETA.COM
D: MIGUEL ANGEL MURAS, **C:** TERESA OLLOQUI
A: GRIMM PROJECT, **M:** MARIONA@LMI.UB.ES

WWW.CPO.COM.HK/INDEX_2.HTM
D: TOBY YEUNG, **C:** TAKA CHAN
A: CUBEMEN STUDIO, **M:** TOBY@DG21.COM

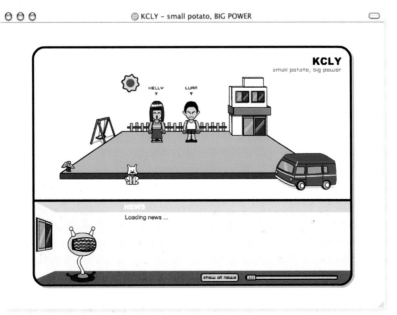

WWW.LUAR.COM.HK
D: LUAR YEN, **C:** KELLY CHUNG
M: LUAR@LUAR.NET

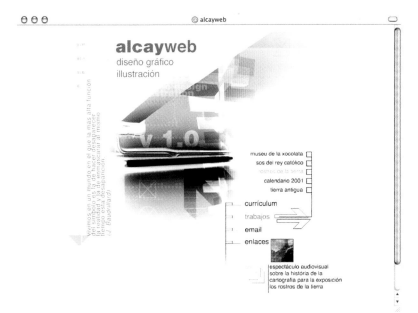

alcayweb
diseño gráfico
ilustración

vivimos en un mundo en el que la mas alta función
del símbolo es la de hacer desaparecer
la realidad y a la de enmascarar al mismo
tiempo esta desaparición
(J. Baudrillard)

museu de la xocolata ☐
sos del rey católico ☐
rostro de la tierra ☐
calendario 2001 ☐
tierra antigua ☐

curriculum
trabajos
email
enlaces

espectáculo audiovisual
sobre la história de la
cartografia para la exposición
los rostros de la tierra

WWW.ALCAYWEB.COM
D: JORDI ALCAY
A: ALCAYWEB, **M:** INFO@ALCAYWEB.COM

menu

oud
nieuw
ontwerp

www.mooiefoto.nl
www.rawstainless.com
www.borealis-light.com
intranet - deheemde.nl
www.cannabiscam.nl
www.francistenhove.com
www.mystrez.nl
www.artofthefuture.com
www.everthommink.nl
www.freakssportiefskatewear.nl
www.fransvantzpoor.nl

WWW.LUAP.NL
D: PAUL REMMELTS
A: LUAP WEBMEDIA, **M:** LUAP@HOME.NL

Kubori Kikiam

101 home   953 **salamat kina**

Pahinga muna anak   **November 15, 2001**
   Kung meron man akong natutunan sa pag gawa at
pag mimintina ng website, ito 'yon: mahirap. Isa din ay ang
kaylangan mo itong paglaanan ng oras...at yun ang kasalu-
kuyang kinakapos kami. Kaya pahinga muna sa Kubori site.
Anong ibig sabihin ng pahinga: wala munang updates (puta,
parang may tumitingin nitong site na 'to, ah).
   Hopefully by December marami nang bago dito sa
Kubori but I doubt it. Give us April next year para maka-
bawi. In the meantime mag surf (or purchase) nalang kayo
ng hentai (Silky Whip, Slut Girl, Countdown Sex Bombs-highly
recommended) Again, sa lahat ng tumutulong at sumusuporta
sa site na ito maraming salamat! Tulog muna tayo! **[-Kanal]**

huling updates: **Ryanski**, dumaan ng office hindi nanlibre!!!

WWW.GEOCITIES.COM/KUBORIKIKIAM
D: MICHAEL DAVID
M: NAKAKABUR@YAHOO.COM

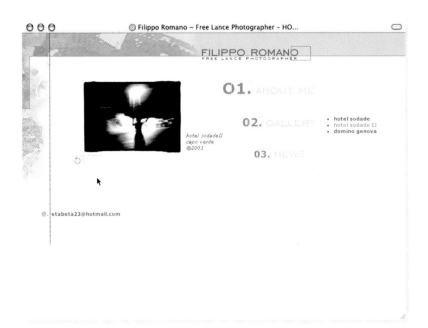

WWW.FILIPPOROMANO.COM
D: ALESSANDRO AMODIO
A: ALCHIMEDIA S.R.L., **M:** AAMODIO@ALCHIMEDIA.COM

WWW.A-LISTONLINE.COM
D: AFRA AMIRSANJARI
A: A-LIST ONLINE, **M:** AMIRSANJARI@A-LISTONLINE.COM

WWW.DIEICH.COM.MX
D: DIEGO HERRERA
A: DIEICH.COM, **M:** DIEICH@MAIL.COM

welcome
w3d: edition 2002

W3d è un piccolo laboratorio di idee nel quale prendono forma
pensieri, intuizioni e sensazioni.

INSPIRATION | WHO's WHO | FAQ | PRESSROOM | CONTACT

JAN	1		3	4	5		8							
FEB					7			12	13	16	18	19		28
MAR		3				10			15				29	30
APR	1			6		9		14			21	23	27	
MAY		4		7					18	19		25		
JUN					8	9	10							
JUL														
AUG														
SEP														
OCT														
NOV														
DEC														

Play more
image 83kb

WWW.W3D.IT
D: LUCA MARCHETTONI
M: LUCA@W3D.IT

Macein
colchoneria

- Principal
- Quien somos
- Contacte
- Mapa situacion

colchones   canapes   somieres   sofas   literas y plegatines   muebles

C/ Doctor Calero nº 42
Majadahonda, Madrid
Tel: 916 380 757
e-mail: **macein@maceinweb.com**

diseño web: molomace@hotmail.com

WWW.MACEINWEB.COM
D: JOSE JUAN MACEIN
M: MOLOMACE@HOTMAIL.COM

New entry
Nuova entrata nel reparto LAB/MULTI con il
progetto Homo Sapiens Marsupialis (nudi con le
mani in tasca) di Massimo Cremagnani. Un
divertente, raffinato e intrigante lavoro
antropologico.

Web newz
Il sito Linkdup in continuo aumento andatelo a
visitare troverete interessantissimi siti legati al
mondo della grafica e del multimedia.

Il mitico Josh Ulm riapre the remedi project
con una nuova veste (non bella come la prime) con
una particolare interfaccia interattiva.

Concorso
Online Flash Film Festival (OFFF)
Barcellona. Termine di iscrizione 31 marzo
2001. Sono accettati solamente lavori non
commerciali realizzati in Flash o Director.
Le categorie a disposizione sono:
arte
documentario
scienza
interattività
cartoni
clip musicali

DeskTopPicture:
scaricati i desktop picture di artificio.
Formato 1024 x 768.
Download page

WWW.ARTIFICIO.COM
D: CONRAD DEMIAN, **P:** ARTIFICIO
A: POINTPIXEL | COMMUNICATION DESIGN, **M:** INFO@POINTPIXEL.COM

Welcome to Atelier CoCoRo & ...on web.
You are 18434 th visitor

(C) Copyright 2000-2002
Atelier CoCoRo &... all right reserved
e-mail mail@a-cocoro.com

HOME | カタログ | お店紹介 | アンケート | サイトマップ | ご注文方法

仲間と一緒に時間と空間
の中で、
CoCoRo の豊かさを
積み重ねることのお手伝
い。
ぬくもりのある仲間達。
手に、耳に、目に、環境
に、
そしてCoCoRo にもやさ
しい
木製、布製、紙製の
品々。

———————

アトリエ CoCoRo & ...
は、

Green has Come !
GWはいかが過ごされましたか？
季節の風も日々心地よく気持ちいいものに
なってきました。木々の緑もいちだんと鮮や
かになってきています。CoCoRoにも、あた
らしい仲間たちがぞくぞくとやってきます。
お楽しみに！

→CHECK

What's new

2002.05.10
カタログ更新
2002.3.13～19
千里阪急「近所で見つけた素
敵なお店バザール」出店
2002.01.19

It's new arrival !
カタログを更新します。

WWW.A-COCORO.COM
D: HIROAKI OHTA
A: MARBLE.CO, **M:** OSTH@MARBLE-CO.NET

Over ons | Verzekeringen Partikulieren | Verzekeringen Ondernemingen | Sparen & Beleggen | Tips & Links

CLAES
VERZEKERINGEN

Home | Sitemap

Sparen en Beleggen ...

Naast verzekeringen biedt Claes Verzekeringen ook verschillende spaar-
en beleggingsformules aan.

Dankzij de samenwerking met verscheidene kredietverstrekkers zijn wij
het best geplaatst om u de beste formule aan te boeden tegen de meest
gunstige voorwaarden.

Keuze

U kunt kiezen uit de volgende formules:

- Pensioensparen
- Levensverzekering
- Overlijdensverzekering
- Verzekeringsbon

Vragen ?

Vindt u niet onmiddelijk wat u zoekt?
Heeft u een vraag over een verzekeringsformule?
Of wenst u een offerte aan te vragen?

Vul uw gegevens hier in en wij contacteren u zo snel mogelijk !

Nl | Fr

(c) by Dyncell – Encounters Mediascience - www.encounters.be

WWW.CLAESVERZEKERINGEN.BE
D: SVEN GODIJN, **C:** JAN BOLS
A: ENCOUNTERS MEDIASCIENCE, **M:** INFO@ENCOUNTERS.BE

E-Mail: KUFO-Hamburg

Unser Service:

Aktuell
LinkListe
KunstTermine
GästeBuch
Unser Forum
Umfrage
Adressen

Das KUFO - Hamburg übernimmt
keine Verantwortung für die ein-
getragenen Beiträge. Tina Meier
(Impressum)

Besucher Online: 7 (1)(1)

» Beiträge Musik

Martina Meier Schattenrand

Diese CD beinhaltet 39 vertonte Gedichte und ist ca. 20 Min.
lang - 20,- DM incl. Versand
Viel Spaß (MP3 Beispiel)

Produktion Januar 99
STIL: Gedichte musikalisch untermalt

Martina Meier wagt auf dieser CD die Annäherung zwischen Wort und Ton. Durch
dezente Untermalung ihrer Gedichte mit Musik ergibt sich eine Athmosphäre von
Meditation und Ruhe

Flamingo X

Diese CD beinhaltet 8 Songs und ist ca. 30 Min. lang - 20,-
DM incl. Versand.
Viel Spaß (MP3 Beispiel)

Produktion Juni 98
STIL: Rock/Pop Deutsch

Produktion mit dem im Raum Hamburg/Berlin bekannten Sänger Frank "ZSA
ZSA" Schmidt. Produzent Uli Pahlke.

HOME | LYRIK | MALEREI | MUSIK | FORUM | GÄSTE | LOG IN | IMPRESSUM

K U F O | KunstForum Hamburg

WWW.KUNSTFORUM-HAMBURG.DE
D: ULI PAHLKE
A: SCREENGRAPHICS, **M:** WEBMASTER@SCREENGRAPHICS.DE

Grupo Aldeasa
Prensa
Accionistas
Tiendas aeroportuarias
Palacios y Museos
Empleo
Contacto
Tiendas online : libroarte.com
Ofertas y Promociones :

WWW.ALDEASA.ES
A: DOUBLEYOU, **M:** DCOMUNICACION@ALDEASA.ES

🗎 **Why Should I Hire 37signals?**(PDF, 46K): World-class experience, real results, straight talk, and more.

design **usability reviews** **training** our work resources news contact home

37signals simple for sale

We design web sites, conduct usability reviews, and educate people about the real-world advantages of simplicity and clarity online.

Interface Design	**Usability Reviews**	**Teaching Simplicity**
We offer a range of visual interface design services for web sites, intra/extranets, and web-based applications. Our focus on simplicity, usability, and clarity will make your customers happy.	Our unique scenario-based Contingency Plan and Reality Check usability reviews provide an honest, unbiased take on your site's usability and customer experience issues.	Our hands-on seminars will teach your staff how to simplify and improve your web business. We also make educational presentations to conferences and universities.
Learn more	Learn more	Learn more

About 37signals Q&A

How is 37signals different than other web firms?
We're a small, honest, agile team of experts with tons of experience (we've all been working on the

37signals highlights

Recent client projects
• Kicksology: Shoe fetish
• Tenzing: In-flight email interface

WWW.37SIGNALS.COM
D: JASON FRIED
A: 37SIGNALS, **M:** JASON@37SIGNALS.COM

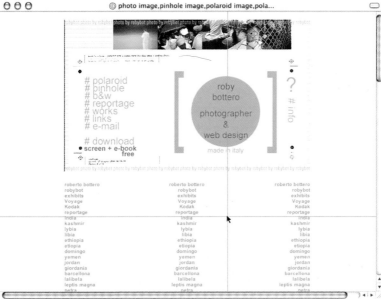

WWW.SPACE.TIN.IT/ARTE/ROBBOT
D: ROBERTO BOTTERO
M: ROBYBOT@YAHOO.COM

WWW.MARKALITE.COM
D: HAMZA AYTAC
A: HAMZA AYTAC CREATIVE SOLUTIONS, **M:** HAMZAYTAC@YAHOO.COM

WWW.RETINENE.COM
D: DALE RETINENE
M: DALE@RETINENE.COM

WWW.GIGIGRASSO.COM
D: JAC, **P:** ERIKA MARQUEZ
M: ERIKA_MARQUEZ_99@YAHOO.IT

COMPANY PROFILE   SITI INTERNET   AREA SOFTWARE   CD MASTERING

WWW.FOTOCOMPOSISTEM.COM
D: OLIVER MICHALAK
A: [WERK01.DE], **M:** OMICH@WERK01.DE

random features industries

design   photography   illustration   contact   ftp location   links   bonus

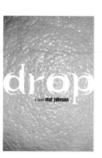

001   002   003   [004]   005   006   007   008

logo | identity | art direction | brand development | publishing | promotion /
marketing | advertising

WWW.RANDOMFEATURES.COM
D: VINCENT GIAVELLI
A: RANDOM FEATURES INDUSTRIES, **M:** CASEY@RANDOMFEATURES.COM

WWW.MILOMEDIA.CO.UK
D: GRANT FORREST
M: GRANT@MILOMEDIA.CO.UK

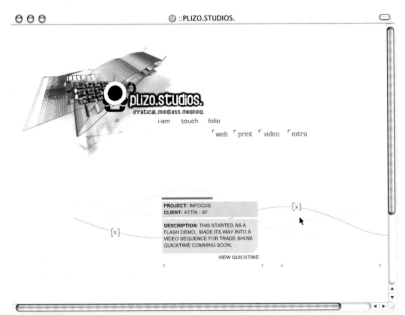

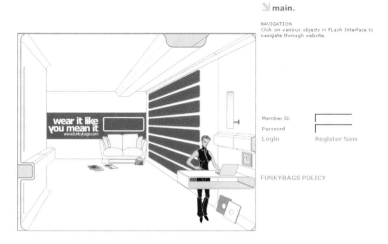

↘ **main.**

NAVIGATION
Click on various objects in FLash Interface to
navigate through website.

Member ID
Password
Login   Register Now

FUNKYBAGS POLICY

WWW.FUNKYBAGS.COM
D: EUGENE LOW
A: SUBLIMINAL INFLUENCE, **M:** EUGENE@SUBLIMINALINFLUENCE.COM

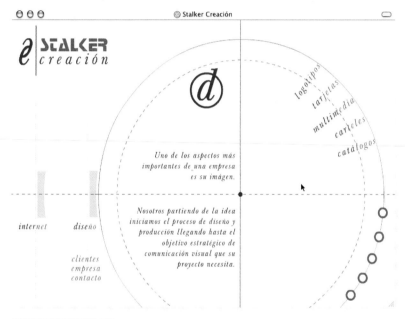

*Uno de los aspectos más
importantes de una empresa
es su imágen.*

*Nosotros partiendo de la idea
iniciamos el proceso de diseño y
producción llegando hasta el
objetivo estratégico de
comunicación visual que su
proyecto necesita.*

logotipos · tarjetas · multimedia · carteles · catálogos

internet · diseño
clientes · empresa · contacto

WWW.STALKERCREACION.COM
D: ELOY MORENO OLARIA
A: STALKER CREACION S.L., **M:** INFO@STALKERCREACION.COM

⊛ **ruboskizo**

NOSOTROS_   SERVICIOS_   CLIENTES_   TRABAJOS_   RUBOLAB_   CONTACTO_   NOTICIAS_

TRABAJOS_

▸ Medio digital
▸ Medio impreso
▸ 3D

[volver]

92

C/ VALLEHERMOSO 35 · 1º OF. 4 · 28015 MADRID · TLF. +34 91 446 93 63   FAX +34 91 446 93 63   EMAIL: INFO@RUBOSKIZO.COM

WWW.RUBOSKIZO.COM
D: PABLO CENALMOR
A: RUBOSKIZO, **M:** INFO@RUBOSKIZO.COM

WWW.JACKSONMENDOZA.COM/JACKSON.HTML
D: LUCA IONESCU
M: ACUL@OPTUSHOME.COM.AU

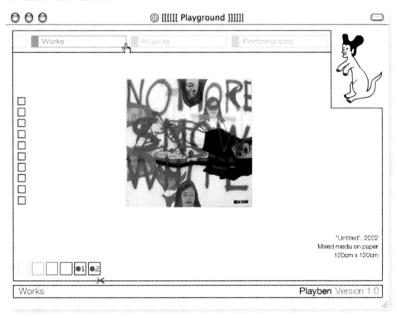

WWW.PLAYBEN.COM
D: GERARD TAN
M: PLAYBEN@HOTMAIL.COM

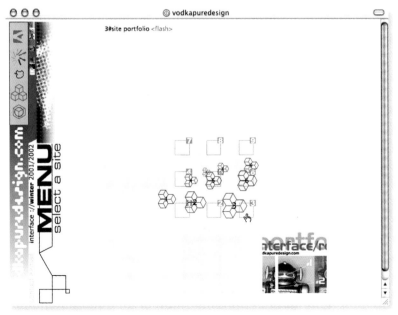

WWW.VODKAPUREDESIGN.COM
D: JOHN-PATRICK RACLE
M: VODKAPURE@FREE.FR

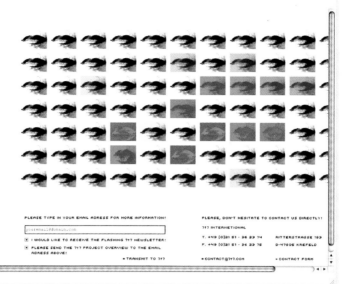

WWW.7T7.COM
D: STEFFEN OPPENBERG, **C:** SASCHA DEUTZMANN
A: 7T7, **M:** STEFFEN@7T7.COM

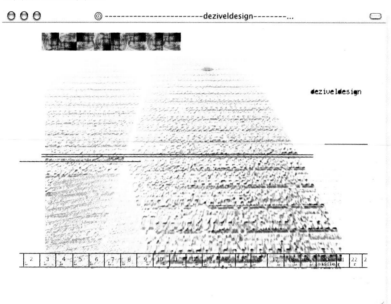

WWW.DEZIVELDESIGN.50G.COM
D: KARIN REYES
A: DEZIVEL DESIGN, **M:** PINION@OUTGUN.COM

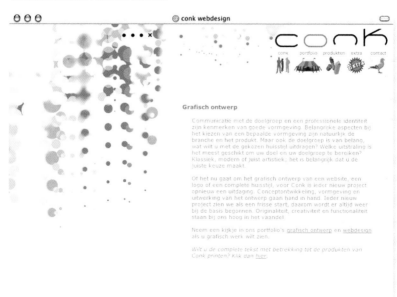

WWW.CONK.NL
D: DEBBY VAN DONGEN
A: CONK, **M:** INFO@CONK.NL

inicio
productos
servicios
empresa
situación

Nikon CoolPix 5000

PVPR: 1.225 € +
I.V.A./
203.823 ptas. + I.V.A.

Photoshop 7.0   Power Mac G4   Pinnacle Studio

Artículos Anteriores

Productos   Buscar

Petición de Presupuestos

Aviso de Averías

Simple Informática S.L. Taller: c/ Río Jarama, 32 Tienda: c/ Río Guadalquivir, 5 28913 Leganés (Madrid) España
Tel. (+34) 91 694 77 06 Fax. (+34) 91 693 66 01 servicios@simpleinformatica.es

WWW.SIMPLEINFORMATICA.ES
D: MANUEL ESTRADA
A: SIMPLE INFORMATICA, **M:** DIGITAL@MANUELESTRADA.COM

@ .SAKAMOTO™

SAKAMOTO

▸ SAKAMOTO™.SWF

▸ SAKAMOTO™ (SCSS)

(SCSS) TM Corporate Style System – (Download PDF) ▸

01 ▸ PROFIL
02 ▸ MEDARBEJDERPROFIL
03 ▸ REFERENCER
04 ▸ CASESTUDIES
05 ▸ DOWNLOADS

06 ▸ KONTAKT
07 ▸ FRAKTIONEN
08 ▸ PLAYGROUND

00 ▸

▸ UDVALGTE CASESTUDIES

▸ KOMPETENCER

Bifkids ▸ (web, brand, print, event)
Eventtur ▸ (web, brand, print, event)
SAKAMOTO™ ▸ (web, brand, print)
Skvulp ▸ (web, brand, print)

Kompetencer:

SAKAMOTO™ er et moderne hybrid-bureau med stærke
kompetencer indenfor branding, kommunikation og Internet-
løsninger.
Vi er eksperter i at udnytte synergien mellem forskellige
medier og vi er konstant på forkant med teknologien.

00 ▸
00 ▸

© 2002 SAKAMOTO™. ALL RIGHTS RESERVED.

WWW.SAKAMOTO.DK
D: CLAUS SCHACK
A: SAKAMOTO, **M:** CLAUS@SAKAMOTO.DK

@ aseptic404 simple version

aseptic404 simplified version

00
01
02
03
04
05   micromovies/microfilmati
06
07
08

micromovies/microfilmati
test yourself/testati
reactor bunny/coniglio reattore

the message/il messaggio
xmas
xperiseptic
happened
aseptic404 new headquarter

action coded 4/49/4
item description/descrizione articolo

"we are not alone", and Pippo
knows it very well/"non siamo
soli" e Pippo lo sa' molto bene

WWW.ASEPTIC404.NET
D: ALESSANDRO RANDI
A: ASEPTIC404, **M:** STERILE@ASEPTIC404.NET

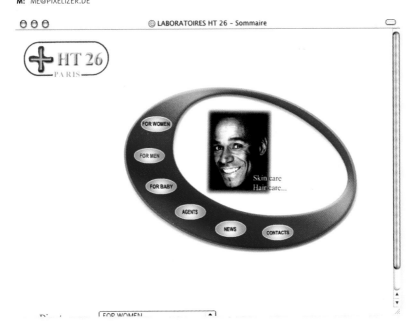

WWW.COAPI.ORG
D: SANTI SALLÈS
A: TUNDRABCN, **M:** INFO@TUNDRABCN.COM

WWW.PIXELIZER.DE
D: PIERRE BROST
M: ME@PIXELIZER.DE

WWW.HT26.COM

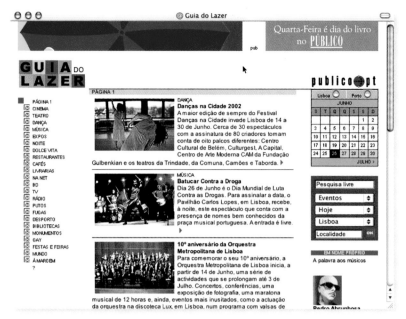

WWW.LAZER.PUBLICO.PT
D: MARIO CAMEIRA
A: PUBLICO.PT, **M:** MCAMEIRA@PUBLICO.PT

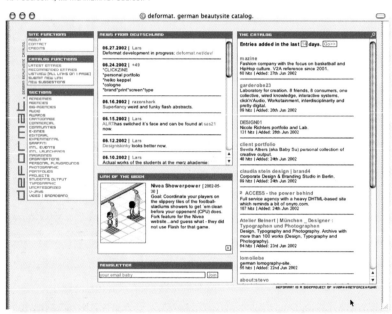

WWW.DEFORMAT.DE
D: LARS WOEHNING
A: V2A**NETFORCE**RUHR, **M:** LW@V2A.NET

WWW.LOCOMPREAQUI.COM
D: LEONARDO MONTERO, **C:** ADRIANA QUESADA, **P:** TICONET
A: TICONET, **M:** MARVIN@LOCOMPREAQUI.COM

DE SILVA ASSOCIATI

HISTORY   CURRICULUM   INFO   SYMBOLS   WORKS   ARTWORK

published later as comic strips for a magazine destined to make history not only in it's own field but in the world of custom as well: "L'Avventuroso" (the Adventurous).
As everyday experience teaches us, we know that great talent is not enough in our field. After the first spell of creative exuberance, de Silva had an intuition and turned into a communications wizard. He was able to create full-blown projects including graphics, architecture, industrial design and copy, as well as all the significant techniques that were needed in order to make the public understand products of every type, from automobiles to books. The rules that govern this delicate relationship are fortunately not very strict, and the "conveyor" with a strong personality is ready to bring them into question any day, or else to find new ones. The important thing is that the message comes through as original, leaving no room for clichés or anonymity.
These are all things that you learn with time and experience and that can luckily be passed down. Emilio entrusted these assets to his sons Giorgio and Walter, and as he was a man of clear ideas, he synthesized

WWW.DESILVAASSOCIATI.COM
D: UBALDO PONZIO
A: UBYWEB&MULTIMEDIA, **M:** UBALDO@PONZIO.IT

WWW.URBANDESK.FR.ST
D: CHRISTOPHE MALSERT
M: TWEN@SPRAY.FR

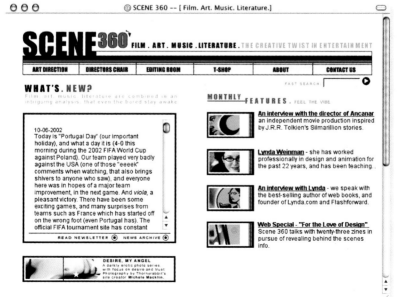

WWW.SCENE360.COM
D: ADRIANA DE BARROS
A: SCENE 360, **M:** CONTACT@SCENE360.COM

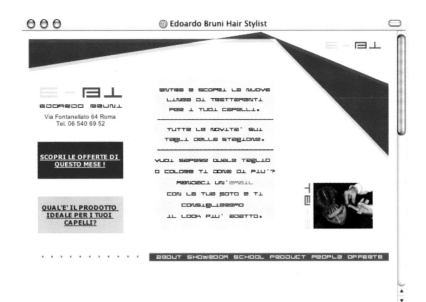

WWW.E-BI.IT
D: ROMINA RAFFAELLI, **C:** STEFANO MARINI
A: WINKLER & NOAH, **M:** INFO@WINKLER-NOAH.IT

WWW.QUINTAGENERACION.COM
D: ALFONSO LOPEZ REDONDO
A: QUINTA GENERACION, **M:** ALFONSO.LOPEZ@QUINTAGENERACION.COM

WWW.SANTILLANAFORMACION.COM
D: MARTIN BETO
A: HAIKU MEDIA TEAM, **M:** A@HAIKU-MEDIA.COM

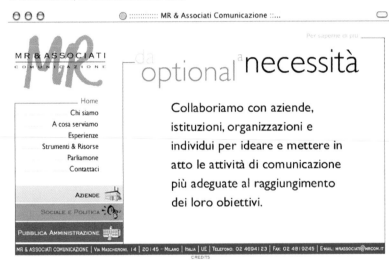

WWW.MALANA.COM
D: MAURIZIO SARTORE
A: MALANA DESIGN, **M:** WEBMASTER@MALANA.COM

WWW.MRCOM.IT
D: BEPPE DIENA
A: LOGICAL NET, **M:** GIUSEPPE@LOGICAL.IT

WWW.CANON.DE
D: MARIA TOMECZEK, **C:** WAGNER
A: TWMD, **M:** MT@TWMD.DE

ecole des maitres: il nuovo bando

adriatico: progetto di interazione teatrale

lachrymae debutta a colle umberto (treviso)
dopo il successo riscosso a roma, torna in scena il 15 giugno nel

conclusa la ventesima stagione di teatro contatto

maratona di new york nuove tappe in friuli

peteano trent'anni dopo

centro servizi e spettacoli di udine
teatro stabile di innovazione del friuli venezia giulia

4

WWW.CSSUDINE.IT/INTRO2.HTM
D: TASSINARI/VETTA, **C:** SARA PACOR, **P:** NICOLETTA BENVENUTI
A: INCIPIT SRL, **M:** INFO@INCIPITONLINE.IT

presentazione
catalogo
segnalazioni
contatti

eurisco'

Edizioni d'if
Si affaccia sul già affollato panorama editoriale una piccola casa editrice dal nome misterioso, ma che – a ripeterlo – fa venire in mente un luogo leggendario: il castello-prigione d'if, da cui evade il *Conte di Montecristo*, il personaggio più famoso di Alexandre Dumas e forse di tutta la narrativa popolare.

Uscire dal castello-prigione, scavare alla ricerca della luce e della libertà, scambiare segni, sogni e fisionomia, inventare giochi a rimpiattino tra ricchi e poveri – come a volte sanno fare bambini e ragazzi – sono metafore che ben rappresentano gli intenti programmatici delle Edizioni d'if...»

Le prime due collane: i coccogrilli e i pipistrilli
i coccogrilli, rivolta a una fascia di lettori dai 7 ai 12 anni, è la prima collana a debuttare...»

I libri sono corredati da schede interattive...»

Cataloghi delle Edizioni d'if
È possibile scaricare il catalogo delle Edizioni d'if come e-book e in formato pdf.

Segnalazioni
Nell'area denominata Segnalazioni trovi aggiornamenti sulle attività delle Edizioni d'if e link ad altri siti dedicati alla scrittura come www.lettoricreattivi o www.solotesto.

E-Book
Diffondere cultura e informazione in Internet non è mai stato così facile. Un e-book può contenere testi e foto proprio come un vero libro, con una leggibilità mai vista prima in Internet e con costi irrisori.
Un esempio di e-book è il catalogo delle Edizioni d'if. Per poter leggere gli e-book è necessario scaricare il programma gratuito:

Microsoft
Reader
with ClearType.

WWW.EDIZIONIDIF.IT
D: FRANCESCO E. GUIDA
A: STUDIO GUIDA, **M:** ERMGUIDA@UNINA.IT

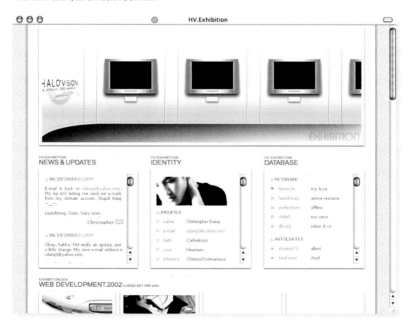

WWW.HALOVISION.ORG
D: CHRISTOPHER DANG
M: CDANG1@YAHOO.COM

WWW.INCREIBLE.DAMMBIER.ES
D: MARTIN BETO
A: HAIKU MEDIA TEAM, **M:** A@HAIKU-MEDIA.COM

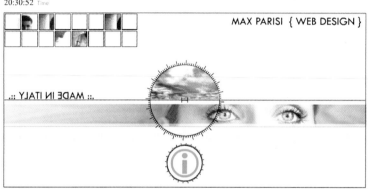

WWW.MAXPARISI.COM
D: MAX PARISI
M: MAXPARISI@MAXPARISI.COM

.Tripany   .Services   .Portfolio   .Medialab   **ENGLISH HOME**

Tripany BV Internet en Communicatie is gespecialiseerd in het ontwikkelen en beheren van database gestuurde internet oplossingen voor bedrijven en instellingen.

De nadruk ligt bij Tripany, naast de techniek achter websites, intranet en extranet, vooral ook op design. Door de combinatie van Flash en HTML komen wij tot zeer verrassende en gebruiksvriendelijke ontwerpen.

Ook dragen wij zorg voor de afhandeling van uw domeinnaam aanvraag en bieden we de bijpassende hosting services. Hierdoor kunnen wij onze klanten een gepaste totaal oplossing aanbieden.

.Nieuws

03-06-2002	5 DIM Mailings Dun & Bradstreet
21-05-2002	Business Plan 2002
17-05-2002	Multiplan Technical Support
10-05-2002	Intrum Justita Live
06-05-2002	Unique Vakantiepersoneel online

Tripany internet & communicatie :: T 070 381 64 62 :: F 070 381 64 63 :: E info@tripany.com

WWW.TRIPANY.COM
D: TRIPANY TEAM
A: TRIPANY INTERNET & COMMUNICATIE, **M:** INFO@TRIPANY.COM

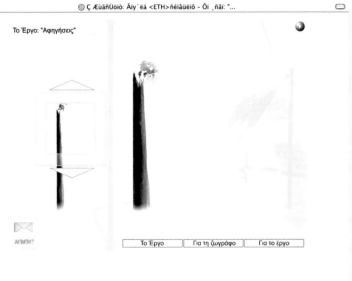

Το Έργο: "Αφηγήσεις"

| Το Έργο | Για τη ζωγράφο | Για το έργο |

WWW.PRIOVOLOU.GR
D: STEFANOS STEFANIDIS
A: WEB RELATION DESIGN, **M:** STEF@COMPULINK.GR

SCHNEIDER & SCHIFFER
Rechtsanwälte · Wirtschaftsprüfer · Steuerberater

ZUR STARTSEITE   UNSERE THEMEN   UNSER TEAM | KANZLEIPROFIL   STANDORTE

SCHNEIDER
& SCHIFFER

P+S TREUHAND UND
STEUERBERATUNGS
GMBH

KOMPETENZ UND PERSÖNLICHER STIL

Schneider & Schiffer ist durch das Zusammengehen der beiden
langjährigen Partnerschaften Antoine & Schneider sowie
Dr. Schiffer & Partner entstanden, letztere seit jeher assoziiert mit der
P+S Treuhand und Steuerberatungs GmbH. Ziel unseres Zusammenschlus-
ses war es, genügend groß zu sein, um als Allgemeinkanzlei alle
wichtigen Themen abzudecken, gleichzeitig aber auch unsere speziel-
len Kompetenzen weiter auszubauen.

In dieser Struktur können wir flexibel und mit kurzer Reaktionszeit
auf die Mandantenbelange eingehen. Durch den Verbund einer
überschaubaren Anzahl von Berufsträgern, die unter einem Dach eng
zusammenarbeiten, hat sich die Kanzlei ihren persönlichen Charakter
bewahrt. Jeder Partner versteht sich nicht nur als Bearbeiter eines
bestimmten Mandats oder Spezialgebietes, sondern behält auch die
Gesamtsituation des Mandanten im Auge. Persönlicher Kontakt und
gegenseitiges Vertrauen sind die Basis, auf der wir Ihnen unser
Know-how anbieten.

WWW.SCHNEIDER-SCHIFFER.DE
D: STEFAN BEHRINGER, **C:** SMARTIT
A: D:\SIGN CREATIVECONCEPTS, **M:** BEHRINGER@DSIGN.DE

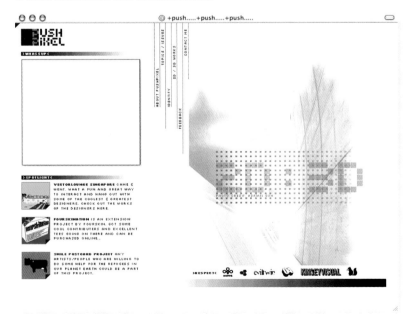

WWW.PUSHPIXEL.COM
D: MEDINA CHEN
M: INFO@PUSHPIXEL.COM

DESIGN. ABOUT. CONTACT.

Innovative Design Solutions

PhaseZero can be considered as a multi-cultural design symbiosis. We are only two designers, and our distinguished backgrounds and experiences are very diverse.

PhaseZero è una partnership tra designers dal curriculum lavorativo e dalle origini molto diverse. Siamo solo due, ma le nostre culture e i nostri sbb insieme ne formano mille altri.

PhaseZero kann als eine multikulturelle Design-Symbiose betrachtet werden. Wir sind nur zwei Designer und unsere Hintergründe und Lebenserfahrungen sind sehr vielfältig.

The purpose of this relationship is to solve design problems in an innovative and unique fashion. Simplicity equals beauty. That is what we believe.

Collaboriamo insieme per sviluppare problematiche di comunicazione attraverso soluzioni uniche ed innovative. Semplicità è sinonimo di bellezza. Questo è quello in cui crediamo.

Der Zweck dieser Beziehung ist die Lösung von Designproblemen auf eine innovative und einzigartige Weise. Schlichtheit ist Schönheit. Das ist was wir glauben.

INNOVATIVE DESIGN SOLUTIONS FOR PRINT & NEW MEDIA

We collaborate with:
www.tense.it

WWW.PHASEZERO.DE
D: KARSHAN PATEL, **C:** ALESSANDRA TAGLIABUE
A: WWW.PHASEZERO.DE, **M:** ALESSANDRA@PHASEZERO.DE

DA WIR NICHT AN MANGELNDEM SELBSTBEWUSSTSEIN LEIDEN, ABER AUCH NICHT ZU GRÖSSENWAHN NEIGEN, WISSEN WIR, DASS ES NICHT IMMER MÖGLICH IST SPEZIALISTEN AUS DEN EIGENEN REIHEN ZU STELLEN. AUS DIESEM GRUND ARBEITEN WIR SCHON SEID LANGEM MIT FREELANCERN ZUSAMMEN.

MIT DIESEN FREIBERUFLERN AUS ALLEN BEREICHEN UND NATIONEN BILDEN WIR DANN PROJEKT-, BUGDET- UND ZEITBEZOGEN DAS RICHTIGE TEAM. WEIL WIR NICHT BEREIT SIND AM FALSCHEN ENDE ZU SPAREN, WIRD BEI UNS DER PROJEKTABLAUF VON ANFANG AN, VON SORGFALT UND DESIGN BESTIMMT. ZUM WOHLE ALLER!

PROJEKTABLAUF

DAS ERSTE KENNENLERNEN...
DIESER WICHTIGE TERMIN DIENT IHNEN UND UNS ZUM GEGENSEITIGEN BESCHNUPPERN UND BEI POSITIVEN FEROMONSIGNALEN, ZUR KLÄRUNG ERSTER WICHTIGER FRAGEN. WIE Z.B. UM WAS FÜR EIN PROJEKT ES SICH HANDELN SOLL, WELCHE AUSGANGSIDEE IHNEN VORSCHWEBT, WAS SIE MIT IHRER VISION ERREICHEN WOLLEN UND WIE WIR SIE DABEI UNTERSTÜTZEN, ENTLASTEN ODER IHNEN HELFEN KÖNNEN UND DÜRFEN.

DIE KÖPFE RAUCHEN...
WIR ERSTELLEN EINEN VORENTWURF, AUF GRUNDLAGE DES BRIEFINGS, IHRER CORPORATE-IDENTITY (FALLS SIE NOCH NICHT ÜBER EIN CORPORATE-ID VERFÜGEN, WÜRDEN WIR DIESES GERNE FÜR SIE MITERSTELLEN) UND DER VON IHNEN ZUR VERFÜGUNG GESTELLTEN

WWW.SPRAFKE.COM
D: OLIVER SPRAFKE
A: SPRAFKEVISION, **M:** VISION@SPRAFKE.COM

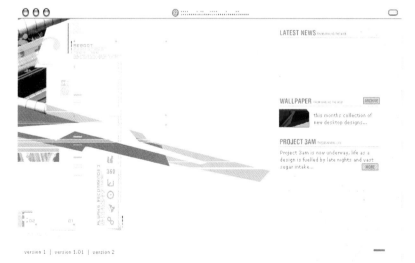

LATEST NEWS FROM AROUND THE WEB

WALLPAPER FROM AROUND THE WEB   ARCHIVE
this months collection of new desktop designs...

PROJECT 3AM THIS IS WHAT I DO
Project 3am is now underway. life as a design is fuelled by late nights and vast sugar intake...   MORE

version 1 | version 1.01 | version 2

WWW.THEDESIGNER.CO.UK
D: DAREN BACH
A: THEDESIGNER, **M:** DAREN@THEDESIGNER.CO.UK

VEDDAN design

@ ???. ?????

информация
— новости
— о студии
— технологии

услуги
web дизайнеру
портфолио
гостевая книга

10/
01/
02
Блюзовый фольклерный фестиваль Д
ельта Невы представляет ежемеся
чнрые концертные программы, инфо
рмацию о концертах, музыку и много
е другое можно увидеть на новом с
айте "Делта невы"

20/
10/
01
Подписано согл
ашение об участии в партнерской п
рограмме с Strela Systems ©

05/
09/
01
Запушен новый правозащитный про
ект посвященный проблемами взаи
модействия этничности и социальн
ости, "Этнологическое бюро"

10/
05/
01
НОВЫЙ !!! рекламоноситель в Петерб
ургском метрополитене. Рекл
ама на турникетах метро.

03/
03/
01
Рекламное Агентство "Зебра" откры
вает свое представляет свою стра
ницу и предл
агает широкий спектр услуг в обла
сти рекламы.

WWW.VEDDAN.RU
D: DANIEL VEDIN, **C:** VEDDAN & KASH, **P:** MARY V
A: VEDDAN ART STUDIO, **M:** VEDDAN@RAZEBRA.RU

@ ::::::::CAFE.LATINO.ONENIGHT.ONLINE::::::::

version 02
MUSIC
LIVE PERFORMERS
DANCERS
DJ'S
PEOPLE

DANCEROOM

WWW.CAFELATINO.IT
D: LORENZO CATTONI
A: CREASTILE, **M:** CATTONI@KATAMAIL.COM

@ Giò Forma

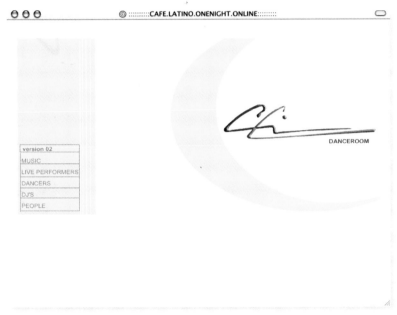

Giò Forma is formed by a group of international professionals that operate in a design studio based in Milan. Giò Forma is a specialist in design, architecture, stage and set fabrication, with over 10 years experience in the art and science of creating vanguard and innovative sets for music concert, tv show, television and more.

the studio
works
contact
clients

Taking advantage of the newest device in graphic, multimedia and design, mixed with his creativity, the studio

h   a   s
succeeded in reaching, over the years an important position in the italian design panorama. Some of the most important name on the business rely on Giò Forma for his professionality employed in the realization

website   works   private
the studio clients contact

WWW.GIOFORMA.COM
D: DAVIDE MARTELLI, **C:** FABRIZIO DANIELI
A: BBJ SRL, **M:** DESIGN@BBJ.IT

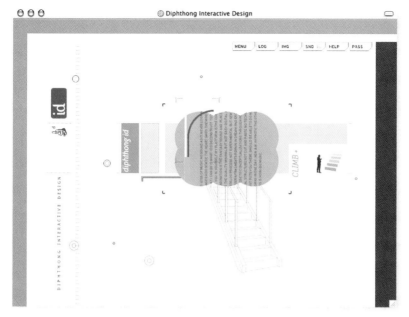

WWW.DIPHTHONG.COM
D: MAX HANCOCK
A: DIPHTHONG INTERACTIVE DESIGN, **M:** MAX@DIPHTHONG.COM

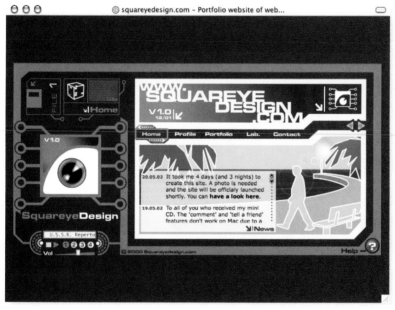

WWW.ZEROK.DE
D: KARSHAN PATEL
A: PHASEZERO.DE, **M:** KARSHAN@PHASEZERO.DE

WWW.AUGENAUF.NET
D: SCOTT-HENDRYK DILLAN
A: ZUCKERZEIT.COM INTERACTIVE, **M:** HENDRYK@AUGENAUF.NET

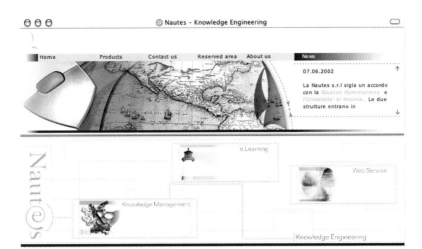

WWW.NAUTES-KE.IT
A: NAUTES SRL, **M:** INFO@NAUTES-KE.IT

WWW.DAGIN.COM
D: MARK VAN LAERE, **C:** FORTUNATO GEELHOED
A: WEB INZICHT, **M:** MARK@WEBINZICHT.COM

WWW.THREEOH.COM
D: JAMES WIDEGREN
A: THREE.OH - INSPIRATIONAL KINGDOM, **M:** JAMES@THREEOH.COM

WWW.COCQUYT.BE
D: KAAT FLAMEY, **C:** KOEN KEMSEKE
A: VANDEN BROELE, **M:** JODY.DUYCKP@VANDENBROELE.BE

WWW.FUNDACIOMALALTSMENTALS.ORG
D: JORDI GRANELL
A: PUKKAS WEB'S DESIGN S.L., **M:** INFO@PUKKAS.COM

WWW.PROCUREHERE.COM
D: NELSON GOUK
A: BIG TRUCK INTERACTIVE, **M:** ASHOK@PROCUREHERE.COM

spring-summer collection 2002

——— ANINOTO ———

contact

WWW.ANINOTO.COM
D: JORDI GRANELL
A: PUKKAS WEB'S DESIGN S.L., **M:** INFO@PUKKAS.COM

@ Clinica de Medicina Global

MEDICINA**GLOBAL**
acupuntura   medicina de familia

medicina de familia

Acupuntura
La medicina china concibe el funcionamiento del cuerpo
desde una óptica distinta a la de la medicina convencional.
Considera el enfermar como un desequilibrio y sus
tratamientos buscan recuperar el equilibrio perdido.
Esto permite resolver problemas de salud que a veces no
tienen muy buena solución en la medicina convencional.
▶ ¿Qué se puede tratar con acupuntura? ▶

WWW.CLINICAMEDICINAGLOBAL.COM
D: JUANJO LOPEZ ESPINOSA
M: JUANJOLORI@TELELINE.ES

@ Vicem Europe

Viçem
Yacht

Vicem Europe Ltd.· · · · · ▶ Credits

WWW.VICEMEUROPE.COM
D: JACOPO ROMEI
A: KOICHI.IT, **M:** JAKUZA@LIBERO.IT

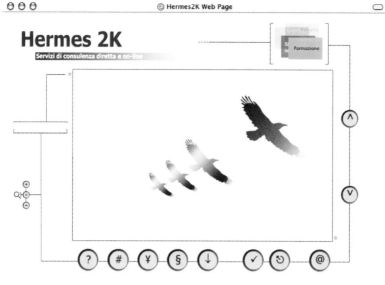

Hermes 2K
Servizi di consulenza diretta e on-line

Formazione

WWW.HERMES2K.IT
D: MICHELE VOLPE
A: HERMES2K, **M:** HERMES@HERMES2K.IT

Studio of
Pacific Architecture

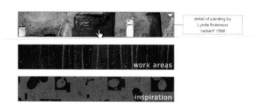

detail of painting by
Lynda Robinson
'radiant' 1998

work areas

inspiration

WWW.STUDIOPACIFIC.CO.NZ
D: ANDREW MAYFIELD, **C:** ANTHONY THORP
A: SPIKEFIN MOBILE WEB ARCHITECTURE, **M:** INFO@SPIKEFIN.COM

---

dev⑩design

emotion

>> Home   about us   services   process   portfolio   contact us

>> Tuesday, July 2, 2002

" The internet is fastest growing information network
on the world. Web designers across the globe are rising
to the challenge with a huge variety of groundbreaking
sites - online experiments in art, entertainment, education
and commerce that are revolutionizing the discipline
of design and our very notion of communication."

Liesbeth den Boer

dev⑩design

WWW.DEV10.COM
D: INDRA KUSUMA BEMBY
A: DEV 10, **M:** BPROTEAM@USA.COM

WWW.GREENPEACE-CHINA.ORG.HK/CHI
D: TOBY YEUNG, **C:** TAKA CHAN
A: CUBEMEN STUDIO, **M:** TOBY@DG21.COM

WWW.ROSARIO-FLORES.COM
D: LEONARDO VOLPE PRIGNANO
A: FVP DESIGN, **M:** QNLEO@HOTMAIL.COM

WWW.OVERVIEW.IT
D: GIANLUCA RECALCATI
A: MAGNETIKA, **M:** GREKA@MAGNETIKA.IT

WWW.PALLADIUM.TM
D: SAM SOHLBERG
A: LONEGÅRD & CO, **M:** SAM@LONEGARD.SE

@ CentroD onLine

WWW.CENTROD.IT
D: UBALDO PONZIO
A: UBYWEB&MULTIMEDIA, **M:** UBALDO@PONZIO.IT

@ LOFT - in der Brotfabrik

LOFT in der Brotfabrik ○ Kreuzstrasse 16 ○ 53225 Bonn

○ Start

WWW.BONNER-LOFT.DE
D: MARUSCHKA FLORCZYK
M: M.FLORCZYK@BONNER-LOFT.DE

Welcome to the site of Centertex,
a nationally leader company of knitted fabrics. Thanks to our
twenty-year experience and our high technology in addition to our
traditional better and better activity of manufacturing, today we can
offer you a consultation service for fabric research works and projects.
Our passwords are innovation, flexibility, reliability and quality.

COMPANY . SERVICES . QUALITY SYSTEM . CONTACTS .

servizi per il tessile   centertex   textile services

. SOCIETA' . SERVIZI . SISTEMA QUALITA' . CONTATTI   DIIE BY ALCHIMEDIA

Benvenuti nel sito di Centertex,
azienda leader a livello nazionale sul mercato dei tessuti a maglia.
Forti di un'esperienza ventennale e di tecnologie sempre
all'avanguardia, in aggiunta alla nostra tradizionale attività di
produzione, oggi più che mai migliorata e potenziata, offriamo
anche servizi di consulenza per la ricerca e progettazione
di tessuti. Le nostre parole d'ordine sono innovazione,
flessibilità, affidabilità e qualità.

WWW.CENTERTEX.IT
D: ALESSANDRO AMODIO
A: ALCHIMEDIA S.R.L., **M:** AAMODIO@ALCHIMEDIA.COM

XION
/solutions

simplifying success

About Us | Solutions | Process | Portfolio

Join Us | Contact Us

Today's thrive economy demands
ability with agility, that's timely too.
Information technology with its
collaborative efficiencies is vital for
surviving and thriving. At **Xion
Solutions,** we leverage technological
innovations for your continued growth.

We are a group of dynamic industry
experts focused on providing you with
interactive solutions that simplify
digital realities & harness
competencies.

Our Vision
"To transcend the frontiers
of imagination, innovation
& creation and
consistently delight our
clients with our best-of-
breed e-Catalysts".

2001
2002
Golden Web Award

Copyright ® 2001 Xion Solutions.

WWW.XIONSOLUTIONS.COM
D: PREETI GUPTA
A: XIONSOLUTIONS, **M:** SIGNET_35@HOTMAIL.COM

infinite ∞ light

360° pano-vr   Menu   contact   home

arquitectura contemporanea

WWW.INFINITE-LIGHT.NET
D: MARKUS BASSLER, BEAT MARUGG
A: INFINITE-LIGHT, **M:** INFO@M-FOTO.COM

WWW.LATINDOT.COM
D: ENRIQUE BUSTIOS, **C:** PABLO SALCEDO
A: LATIN DOTCOM, **M:** ASANMARTIN@LATINDOT.COM

WWW.TOBIASBAUR.DE
D: TOBIAS MAGNUS BAUR
A: BAUR, **M:** TMB@TOBIASBAUR.DE

WWW.ID10100.SAMSUNG.COM
D: SANG-A KIM, **C:** KI-YOUNG PARK, **P:** CHEIL COMMUNICATIONS
A: SUGARCUBE, **M:** IVORY@SAMSUNG.CO.KR

The Big Thumper
Version 1
Art devoted to Rock'n'Roll.

April 2002

Contact

WWW.MORE.AT/THUMPERLOUNGE
D: MISS THUMPER
M: MISS.THUMPER@LIBERTYSURF.FR

WWW.MILLWASH.COM
D: EVE, **C:** STEFANO MARINI
A: WINKLER & NOAH, **M:** INFO@WINKLER-NOAH.IT

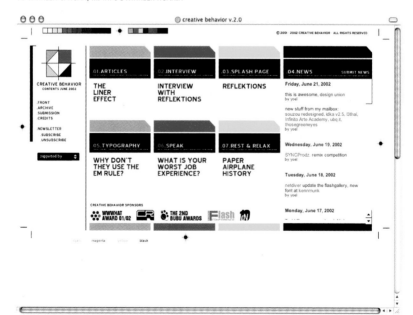

WWW.CREATIVEBEHAVIOR.COM
D: YOEL BURMAN KAREL
M: CREATIVE@CREATIVEBEHAVIOR.COM

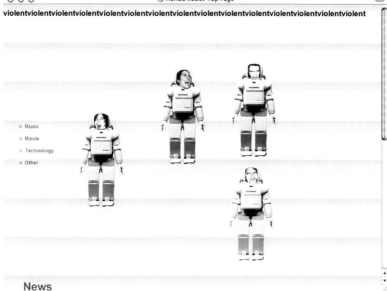

violentviolentviolentviolentviolentviolentviolentviolentviolentviolentviolentviolentviolent

□ Music
□ Movie
□ Technology
□ Other

News

WWW.VIOLENTPLASTIC.COM
D: CHRISTOPHER CALDWELL
A: VIOLENT PLASTIC, **M:** CHRIS@INTERNETICS.CO.UK

WWW.IZZYDESIGN.COM
D: CHRISTIAN SAYLOR, **C:** NATE LOKERS, **P:** CARRIE PALLAS
A: FUEL INTERACTIVE, **M:** ELOEHFELM@EARTHLINK.NET

WWW.WAREN-MIT-CHARME.DE
D: BERND SASSMANNSHAUSEN, **C:** STEPHAN HERCZEG
A: NETZRECHERCHE.DE, **M:** HERCZEG@NETZRECHERCHE.DE

WWW.EQUIS.YA.COM
A: X N O G R A F I C S, **M:** VICTOR@XNOGRAFICS.COM

WWW.HOPPE.JP
D: KOSHIRO TORISU
M: HELLO@TORISUKOSHIRO.COM

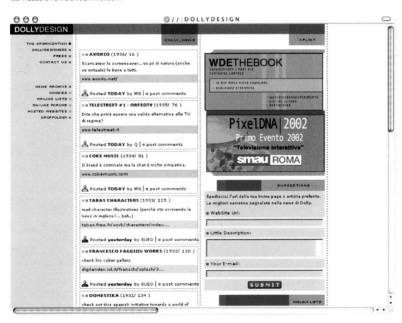

WWW.DOLLYDESIGN.COM
D: ANTONIO MORO
A: DOLLYDESIGN - THE ITALIAN WEBDESIGN COMMUNITY, **M:** INFO@DOLLYDESIGN.COM

WWW.BUILDLAB.COM
D: CRISTINA RIBEIRO, FRANCO PONTICELLI
A: LITEFARM SRL, **M:** PONTICELLI@LITEFARM.COM

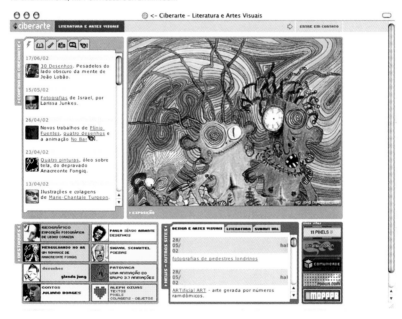

WWW.CIBERARTE.COM.BR
D: ALEPH OZUAS
A: CIBERARTE, **M:** ALEPH@CIBERARTE.COM.BR

WWW.PIXELICA.COM
D: DAVID SOTO
M: DSOTO@PIXELICA.COM

<factor**digital**>
soluções interactivas
para clientes exigentes

Um dia digital

Uma visão sobre a convergência dos meios ao alcance
das pessoas. A disponibilidade total da informação e
serviços para tornar a vida mais fácil para todos.
Na Factor Digital estamos a transformar

e-services em e-life,

uma visão natural sobre a revolução digital.

VER INTRODUÇÃO
SALTAR INTRODUÇÃO

A NOSSA VISÃO
info@factordigital.com
(+351) 21 453 99 51

Factor Digital renova Quadriga

Factor lança novo Web site da HCI Construções.

Factor reestrutura o site da Direcção Regional do
Ambiente de Lisboa e Vale do Tejo

Feedback | Mapa do Site
© 2001 Factor Digital - Todos os direitos reservados.

WWW.FACTORDIGITAL.COM
D: HUGO SILVA, **C:** MANUEL COSTA
A: FACTOR DIGITAL, **M:** HUGOS@FACTORDIGITAL.COM

WWW.APLIC2003.COM
D: KALINDA LOW, **C:** FOO YANLING
A: VOXMEDIA, **M:** KALINDA@VOXMEDIA.COM.SG

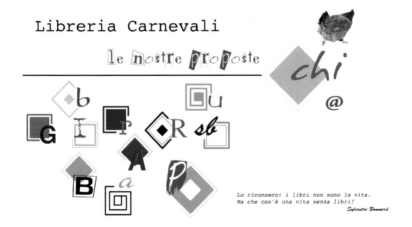

WWW.LIBRERIACARNEVALI.IT
D: ALESSANDRA COMPAROZZI
A: GRAFICHERO, **M:** INFO@GRAFICHERO.IT

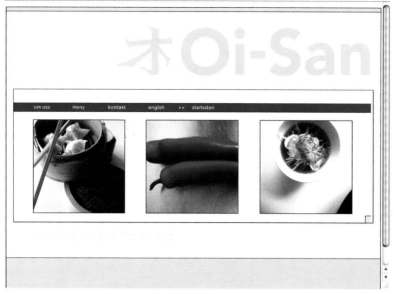

WWW.OI-SAN.COM
D: CHRISTIAN CHAMPAGNE
A: W2S INTERNET SERVICES, **M:** CHRIS@HELSINKIJAZZ.CO.UK

WWW.ZER09INE.COM
D: RAFAEL PAVON, **C:** MIGUEL COBIN
A: ZERONINE ACI, **M:** RPAVON@ZER09INE.COM

WWW.ARIANJEANS.NET
D: MONA AGHAYAN
A: MISAGH GRAPHIC, **M:** MONA@SMISAGH.COM

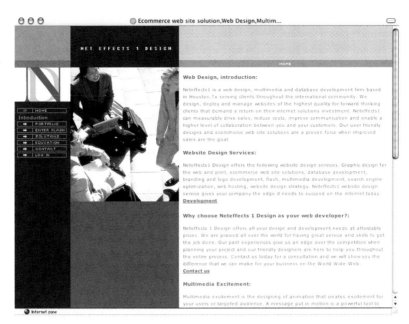

WWW.NETEFFECTS1.NET
D: KEVIN GENTRY, **C:** MISTY TRANG
A: NETEFFECTS 1 DESIGN, **M:** KEVIN@NETEFFECTS1.NET

WWW.E-BIZ4YOU.COM
D: GIRISH BABU
A: E-BIZ4YOU, **M:** GIRIBN@YAHOO.COM

WWW.TIPOCS.COM
D: STEFANO MARCHI
A: XTRAGROOVE-SSG CREATIVE FACTORY, **M:** STEFANO@XTRAGROOVE.COM

66

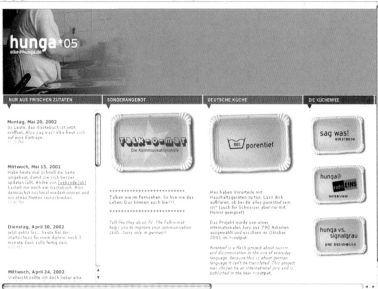

WWW.HUNGA.DE
D: ELKE SCHIEMANN
M: ELKE@HUNGA.DE

WWW.ADVENSA.COM
D: ALEXANDRA LEONOVA, **C:** VITALIY LEONOV
A: ADVENSA, **M:** INFO@ADVENSA.COM

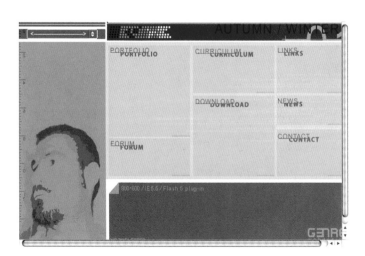

WWW.GENRE.FR.ST
D: MAXIME VAUTHIER
A: --=GENRE=--, **M:** MAXIME.VAUTHIER@LAPOSTE.NET

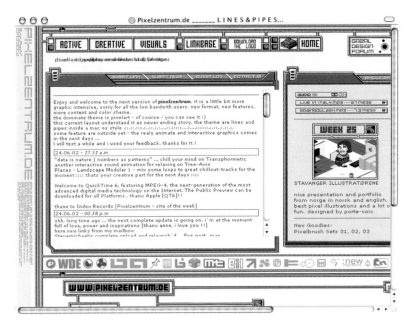

WWW.PIXELZENTRUM.DE
D: MAIK SANDER
M: PIXELZENTRUM@WEB.DE

WWW.REDCIENTIFICA.COM
D: DAVID NAVARRO GOMEZ
A: ENK3, **M:** NAVARRO@ENK3.COM

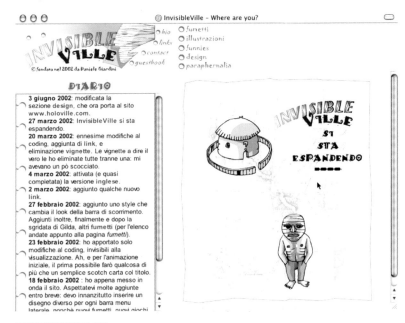

WWW.INVISIBLEVILLE.COM
D: DANIELE GIARDINI
M: DANIELEGIARDINI@HOTMAIL.COM

WWW.SEVENTY9.DE
M: ANNA@SEVENTY9.DE

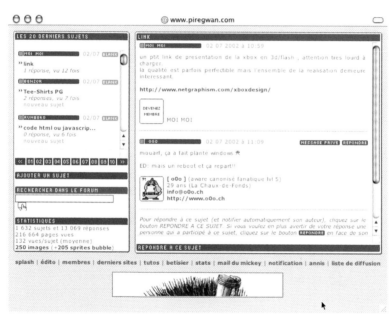

WWW.PIREGWAN.COM/FORUM2
D: DAVID ORSET
M: WEBMASTER@PIREGWAN.COM

WWW.HADEZ.BLOGALIA.COM
D: RENZO FERRER VÌA
M: RFERRER@ANWMP.COM

POLO

Polo de Fotografía:
BIG MAGAZINE
http://www.bigmagazine.com

Ya le hacía falta un lavado de cara
a la versión electrónica de la ya
célebre revista de fotografía BIG.
El resultado ha sido espectacular.
Si te gusta la fotografía, el diseño
y las tendencias contemporáneas,
entonces te gustará BIG. Contiene
proyectos propios y
complementarios a la edición en
papel.

⬎ POLO ES UN HELADO
ELECTRONICO. ES DE HIELO
Y SE DERRITE.

⬎ POLO NOS MUESTRA
TENDENCIAS EN LA RED
A TRAVES DE HIPERVINCULOS
ACTUALIZADOS. POR ESO ES DE
HIELO. PORQUE ESTA FRIO.
HELADO. PORQUE ES FRESCO.

⬎ POLO FUNCIONA CON
VARIABLES ALEATORIAS QUE
PERMITEN AL USUARIO VER
UN POLO DIFERENTE CADA VEZ
QUE LO VISITA. POR ESO SE
DERRITE. PORQUE DESAPARECE
CADA VEZ QUE EL BROWSER SE
ACTUALIZA O SE CIERRA.

"Polo de papel" por Eduardo de Felipe.

SPONSORED BY
CICLO HOUYHNHNMS

WWW.ELELEC.COM/POLO
D: EDUARDO DE FELIPE, **C:** HECTOR GARZON
A: ELEC, **M:** EDUARDO@ELELEC.COM

PRODUCTOS
Manillas para puertas

Manillas con rodamiento de bolas y fleje recuperador incluido en las rosetas o placas fijadas entre sí
mediante tornillos pasantes. Según DIN 18.255.

Erkoch

Haga click sobre la imagen del producto para ampliar su información. | 22 de 36 productos encontrados.

ver siguientes >>

| Empresa | Localización | Productos | Catálogo | | Pedido on-line |
| Manillas | Bisagras | Cerraduras | Pasadores | Barras Antipánico | Complementos | Felpudos | Contacto |

Erkoch Ibérica S.A. // Avenida Miraflores, 115, 3º - 48004 Bilbao (Vizcaya) // Tel. 94 412 49 00 // Fax. 94 411 42 00 // e-mail: info@erkoch.es

WWW.ERKOCH.ES
D: MIGUEL ZORRAQUINO, **C:** ALFREDO ALVAREZ
A: ZORRAQUINO DESIGN STUDIO, **M:** INFO@ZORRAQUINO.COM

INDEX ▧   IMAGE ▧   WORKS ▧   NEW ART ▧   POST PRO ▧

ALTEA'S INFO

ALTEA'S BORN IN ROME ON 1974
HER PASSIONS ARE INTERNET
WEB DESIGN, PLAY GUITAR,
AND SMALL RABBITS!

NOW SHE'S WORKING AS
FLASH MASTER IN A NET COMPANY
AND SHE MAKES THE POST-PRODUCTION
OF 33K RADIO.

use main menu on the top
to go to next page

WWW.PRNETWORK.IT
D: RICCARDO IANNARELLI
A: FORMAT C, **M:** RICCARDO@FORMATC.IT

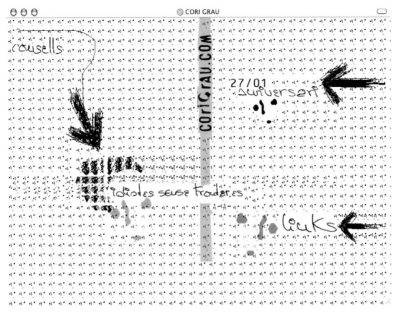

WWW.CORIGRAU.COM
D: CORI GRAU
M: CORI@CORIGRAU.COM

WWW.SPECTRE7.ORG
D: JENS WILDNER - ATOMIZER -
M: ATOMIZER@SPECTRE7.ORG

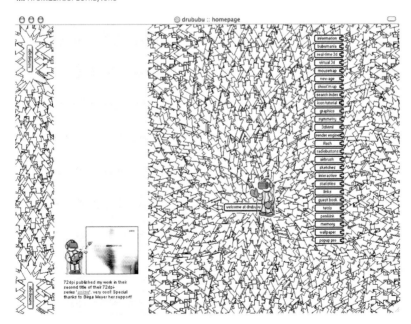

WWW.DRUBUBU.COM
D: ARJAN WESTERDIEP
A: DRUBUBU, **M:** ARJAN@DRUBUBU.COM

@ index

RESET

WWW.LOOPLOOPLOOP.COM
D: TANDA FRANCIS
A: LOOP, **M:** TANDAFRANCIS@HOTMAIL.COM

@ 1280PIXELS

PORTRAIT

LEN

LOGO

PHOTO

COUV'

03...
(...)
(...)

06...
Acne family
1280pixels

03...
(...)
(...)

03...
(...)
(...)

13...
Défense d'afficher
1280pixels

02...
(...)
(...)

04...
Elixirstudio
1280pixels

02...
(...)
(...)

02...
Charlotte
Alex de St-Victoret

12...
Gun
1280pixels

WWW.1280PIXELS.COM
D: SYLVAIN MESNARD
A: GRAPHISTE DA, **M:** CONTACT@1280PIXELS.COM

@ home

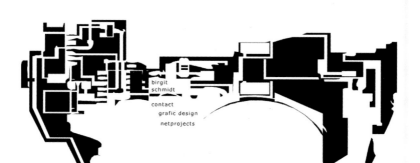

WWW.BIRGIT-SCHMIDT.DE
D: BIRGIT SCHMIDT
M: BSCHMIDT@TECO.EDU

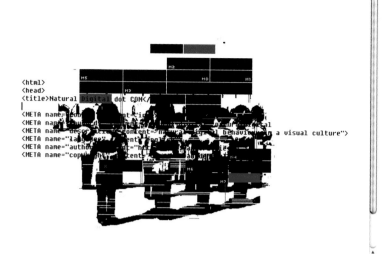

```
<html>
<head>
<title>Natural Digital dot COM</
|
<META name=
<META name=
<META name="des                    behavi    a visual culture">
<META name="la
<META name="auth
<META name="cop
```

WWW.NATURALDIGITAL.COM
D: CLEMENS VAN DER LELIE
M: CVDL@NATURALDIGITAL.COM

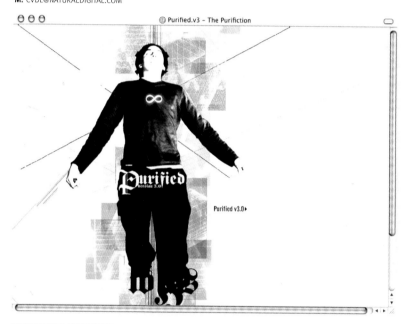

Purified v3.0▶

WWW.PURIFIED.ORG/VERSION3
D: BARD HOLE STANDAL
M: BARD@PURIFIED.ORG

WWW.MARKETMIND.NL
D: MONIQUE PRIEM, **C:** PETER DEKKER, **P:** GERARD VAN MELIS
A: MARKETMIND BV, **M:** GERARD@MARKETMIND.NL

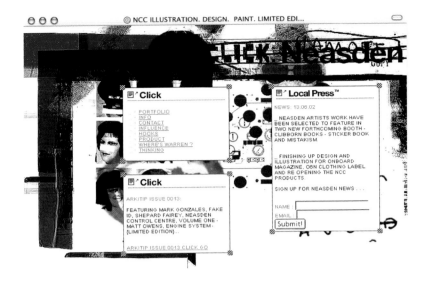

WWW.NEASDENCONTROLCENTRE.COM
A: NEASDEN CONTROL CENTRE, **M:** INFO@NEASDENCONTROLCENTRE.COM

WWW.DIESELSWEETIES.COM
D: RICHARD STEVENS
M: CLANGO@DIESELSWEETIES.COM

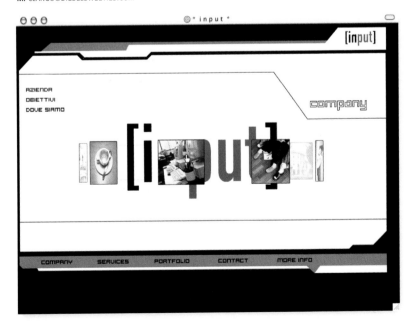

WWW.INPUT.VE.IT
D: ENRICO MANENTE, **C:** MARCO POGLIE, **P:** SIMONETTA DE SIMONE
M: INFO@INPUT.VE.IT

WWW.SHUTTLE-ADV.ORG/MANGAXOXO
A: MANGAXOXO, **M:** INFO@MANGAXOXO.COM

WWW.ASHERANDHOUSE.COM
D: ADELE CHAN
A: ASHER AND HOUSE, **M:** ADELE@ASHERANDHOUSE.COM

WWW.EMPTYDROME.COM
D: J.POU, **C:** MATHIEU
A: EMPTYDROME, **M:** ONABRAIN@EMAIL.COM

1974
1975
1976
1977
1978
1979
1980
1981
1982
1983
1984
1985
1986
1987
1988
1989
1990
1991
1992
1993
1994
1995
1996
1997
1998   Forma el grupo de rock acústico "Cien Mil Noches". Tambien forma con
1999   Fabrizio Sotelo "Kaktus Producciones", produciendo a grupos como
2000   "Silvio a la carta", "Cien Mil Noches", "Kuntur Wasi", entre otros.
2001
2002

WWW.LA-ROJA.COM
D: FABRIZIO SOTELO JIRON
A: KAKTUS, **M:** FSOTELO@CORREO.ULIMA.EDU.PE

⌐ ABOUT

⌐ PORTFOLIO

⌐ COLLECTIONS

⌐ PHOTOGRAPHY
     Digital
     SLR

⌐ LINKS
     Friends
     Cool

⌐ CALENDAR

WWW.NGARTE.COM
D: ADRIAN NG
A: PAPRIKA, **M:** ADRIAN@NGARTE.COM

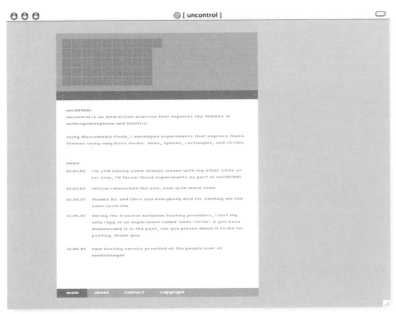

unCONTROL
uncontrol is an interactive exercise that explores the themes of
anthropomorphism and kinetics.

using Macromedia Flash, i developed experiments that express these
themes using only basic forms: lines, splines, rectangles, and circles.

news

01.01.02   i'm still having some domain issues with my other sites so
     for now, i'll throw those experiments as part of unCONTROL

01.01.02   official relaunched the site, now with more stuff

12.28.01   Thanks Ric and Chris and everybody else for sending me the
     semi circle file

12.05.01   during the transfer between hosting providers, i lost my
     only copy of an experiment called "semi-circle". if you have
     downloaded it in the past, can you please email it to me for
     posting. thank you.

12.05.01   new hosting service provided at the people over at
     mediatemple

main   about   contact   copyright

WWW.UNCONTROL.COM
D: MANUEL TAN
A: UNCONTROL.COM, **M:** MANNYTAN@UNCONTROL.COM

WWW.FIVEDAYS.TPU.FI
D: SAMI NIEMELÄ
M: FIVEDAYS@NEOCITE.COM

WWW.SKORPIO81.COM
D: MARTIN KLASSON
M: MARTIN@SKORPIO81.COM

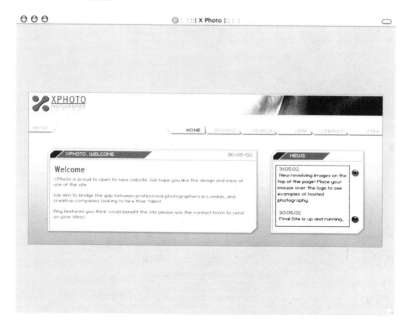

WWW.XPHOTO.CO.UK
D: NICK BRETT
M: JAMIESITH45@HOTMAIL.COM

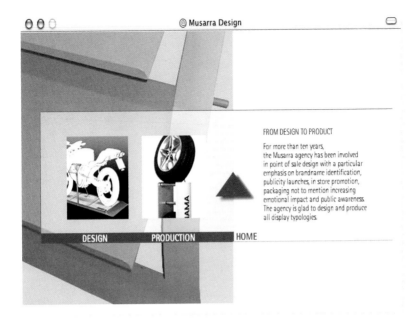

FROM DESIGN TO PRODUCT

For more than ten years,
the Musarra agency has been involved
in point of sale design with a particular
emphasis on brandname identification,
publicity launches, in store promotion,
packaging not to mention increasing
emotional impact and public awareness.
The agency is glad to design and produce
all display typologies.

DESIGN   PRODUCTION   HOME

WWW.MUSARRADESIGN.COM
D: PICCARDA DI MONTEREALE
A: PRISMA S.R.L., **M:** SUPERPIC@LIBERO.IT

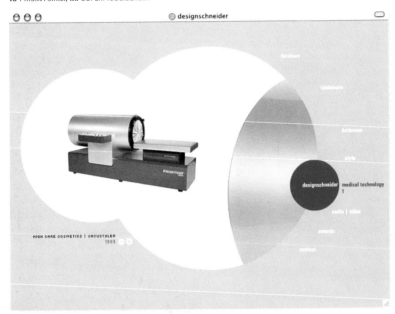

WWW.DESIGNSCHNEIDER.DE
D: JOERG WASCHAT, **C:** ANDREAS KUBANEK
A: DEFINIT, **M:** INFO@DEFINIT.ORG

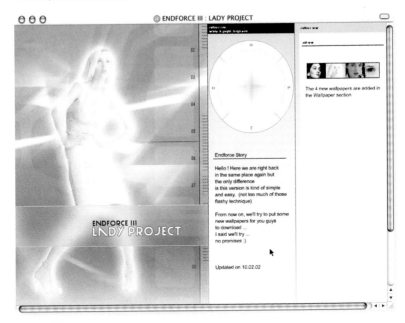

WWW.ENDFORCE.COM
D: GITTIRAT BOONKERTKAEW, **P:** NATTA CHARUMPORN
M: NOBODY@ENDFORCE.COM

78

es gibt eine theorie, die besagt,

wenn jemals irgendwer genau herausfindet,

wozu das universum da ist,

dann verschwindet es auf der stelle

und wird durch etwas noch bizarreres

und unbegreiflicheres ersetzt.

es gibt eine andere theorie,

nach der das schon passiert ist.

douglas adams · 1980

WWW.FORTYTWO.DE
D: AXEL BECKER
A: FORTYTWO-GRAFIK DESIGN, **M:** WEBKATALOG0987@FORTYTWO.DE

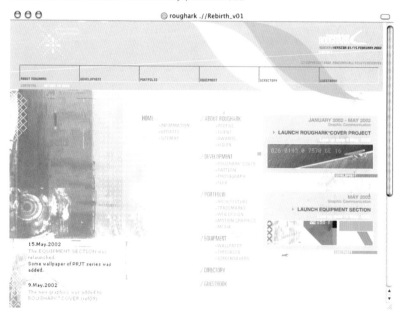

WWW.ROUGHARK.COM
D: TAKAYUKI SUGIHARA
A: ROUGHARK, **M:** INFO@ROUGHARK.COM

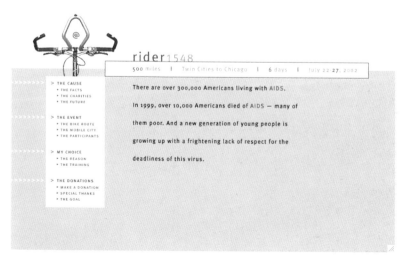

WWW.BRITTYNDEWERTH.COM
D: BRITTYN DEWERTH
M: BRITTYN@BRITTYNDEWERTH.COM

HOFFMANN REISER SCHALT DDB

QUER DENKEN – GERADE REDEN

04|INNENANSICHT

WWW.HRS.DDBN.DE
D: KATJA SCHÜLER
M: INFO@HRS.DDBN.DE

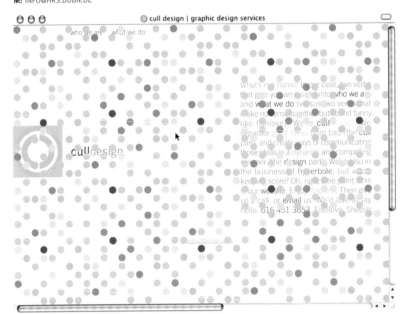

WWW.CULLDESIGN.COM
D: SCOTT MILLEN
A: CULL DESIGN, **M:** SCOTT@CULLDESIGN.COM

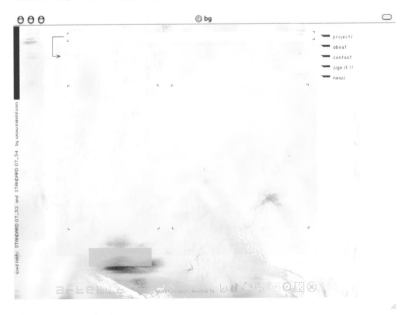

WWW.ARTETIC.COM
D: IRENE MARX
A: ARTETIC, **M:** IRENE@ARTETIC.COM

WELCOME
TITLE

GARP
GRUPPE AUTOREN, REGISSEURE, PRODUZENTEN
GROUPE AUTEURS, RÉALISATEURS, PRODUCTEURS
GRUPPO AUTORI, REGISTI, PRODUTTORI

ADRESS
DIENERSTRASSE 7 CH-8004 ZÜRICH
TEL: +41 (0) 1 241 16 56
FAX: +41 (0) 1 241 16 55
MAIL: INFO@GARP-CINEMA.CH

CONTACT   CREDITS

MENUE

1 HOME ▬▬   **2** NEWS   **3** ABOUT GARP   **4** MEMBERS   BENUTZER
PASSWORT
Go

LAST UPDATE:

WWW.GARP-CINEMA.CH/START.PHP
D: TRIX BARMETTLER
A: WEBLOTION, **M:** TAG@TAG-INN.CH

THREE BAGS
High-quality leather bags made in Finland since 1953.

Home	Products	Company	Contact
	Bags		
	Carrying cases		

© Copyright 2001 EJ-Laukku Oy   webdesign by AC-mainos

WWW.THREEBAGS.FI
D: KIMMO KUUSISTO, MISA KANNOS
A: AC-MAINOS, **M:** KIMMO@ACMAINOS.FI

STOLZUNDKUEHN.

• **gesehen**
• **geteilt**
• **geschenkt**

An Fortschritt glauben heisst nicht glauben, dass ein
Fortschritt schon geschehen ist. Das wäre kein Glauben.

Franz Kafka

gesehen.   geteilt.   geschenkt.

@ 2002 stolzundkuehn.

kontakt | hilfe | sitemap | webmaster

WWW.STOLZUNDKUEHN.DE
D: HANNES SUESS, MATTHIAS ZSCHALER
A: STOLZUNDKUEHN, **M:** INFO@STOLZUNDKUEHN.DE

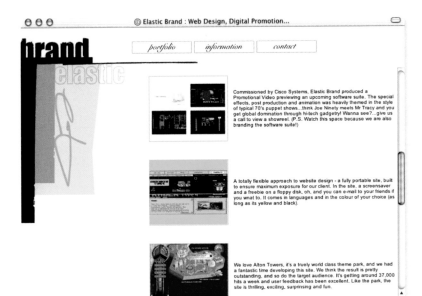

Commissioned by Cisco Systems, Elastic Brand produced a Promotional Video previewing an upcoming software suite. The special effects, post production and animation was heavily themed in the style of typical 70's puppet shows...think Joe Ninety meets Mr Tracy and you get global domination through hi-tech gadgetry! Wanna see?...give us a call to view a showreel. (P.S. Watch this space because we are also branding the software suite!)

A totally flexible approach to website design - a fully portable site, built to ensure maximum exposure for our client. In the site, a screensaver and a freebie on a floppy disk, oh, and you can e-mail to your friends if you want to. It comes in languages and in the colour of your choice (as long as its yellow and black).

We love Alton Towers, it's a truely world class theme park, and we had a fantastic time developing this site. We think the result is pretty outstanding, and so do the target audience. It's getting around 37,000 hits a week and user feedback has been excellent. Like the park, the site is thrilling, exciting, surprising and fun.

WWW.ELASTICBRAND.COM
D: NIK JORDAN, **C:** QASIM BUTT
A: ELASTIC BRAND, **M:** NIK@ELASTICBRAND.COM

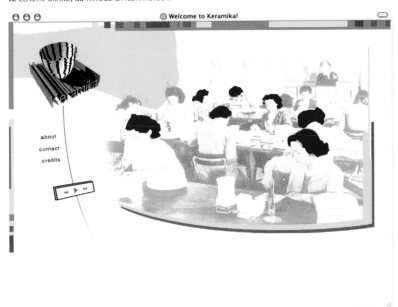

WWW.KERAMIKA.ORG
D: MANDY MCINTOSH
A: STUDIO HAM AND ENOS AND SINNFLUT, **M:** MANDYMCINTOSH14@HOTMAIL.COM

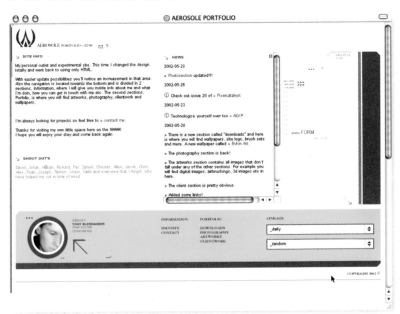

AEROSOLE.PLASTIQUEWEB.COM
D: TONY BLESSANDER
M: AEROSOLE@PLASTIQUEWEB.COM

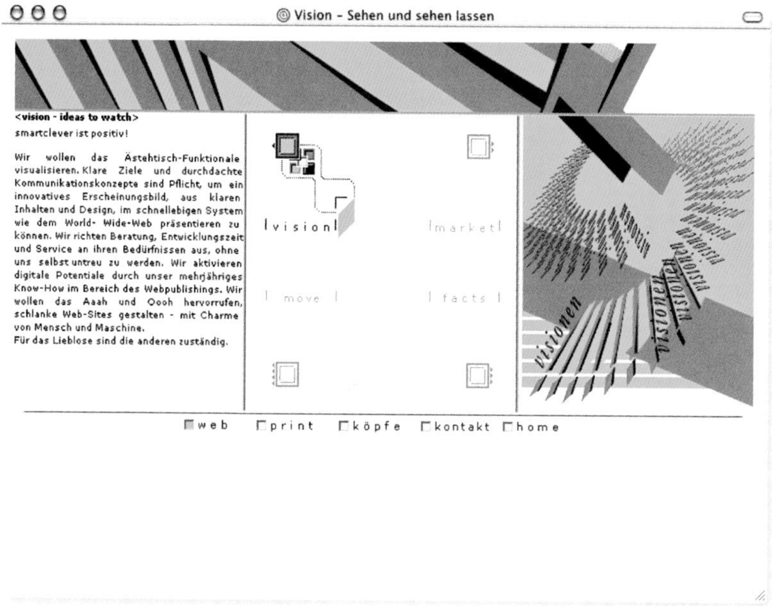
Vision - Sehen und sehen lassen
<vision - ideas to watch>
smartclever ist positiv!
Wir wollen das Ästehtisch-Funktionale visualisieren. Klare Ziele und durchdachte Kommunikationskonzepte sind Pflicht, um ein innovatives Erscheinungsbild, aus klaren Inhalten und Design, im schnellebigen System wie dem World- Wide-Web präsentieren zu können. Wir richten Beratung, Entwicklungszeit und Service an ihren Bedürfnissen aus, ohne uns selbst untreu zu werden. Wir aktivieren digitale Potentiale durch unser mehrjähriges Know-How im Bereich des Webpublishings. Wir wollen das Aaah und Oooh hervorrufen, schlanke Web-Sites gestalten - mit Charme von Mensch und Maschine.
Für das Lieblose sind die anderen zuständig.
|vision|
|market|
| move |
| facts |
web print köpfe kontakt home

WWW.SMARTCLEVER.DE
D: ROBERT RAJDA, **C:** BIRGIT HUTMACHER
A: DESIGNBÜRO SMARTCLEVER, **M:** KONTAKT@SMARTCLEVER.DE

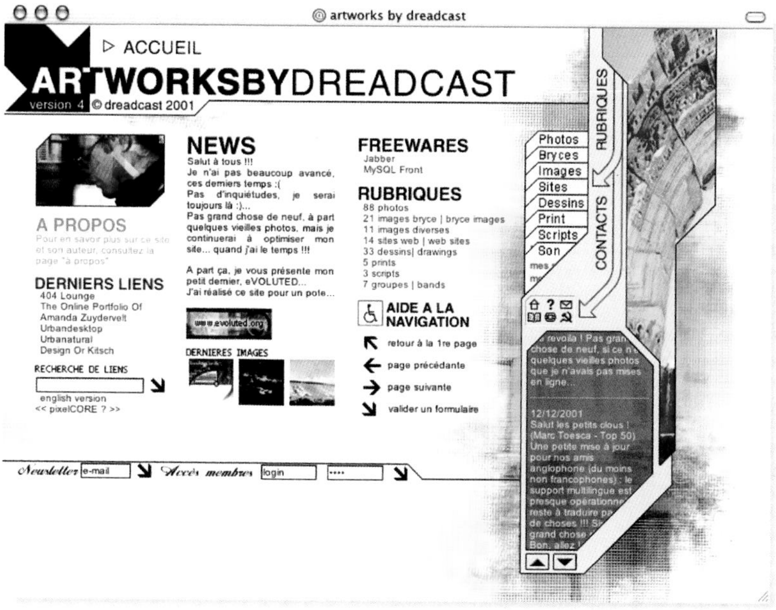
artworks by dreadcast
ACCUEIL
ARTWORKSBYDREADCAST
version 4 © dreadcast 2001
NEWS
FREEWARES
RUBRIQUES
A PROPOS
DERNIERS LIENS
AIDE A LA NAVIGATION
RUBRIQUES
CONTACTS
Photos
Bryces
Images
Sites
Dessins
Print
Scripts
Son

WWW.DREADCAST.COM
D: RAPH DREADCAST
A: PIMPMEDIA, **M:** WEBMASTER@PIMPMEDIA.NET

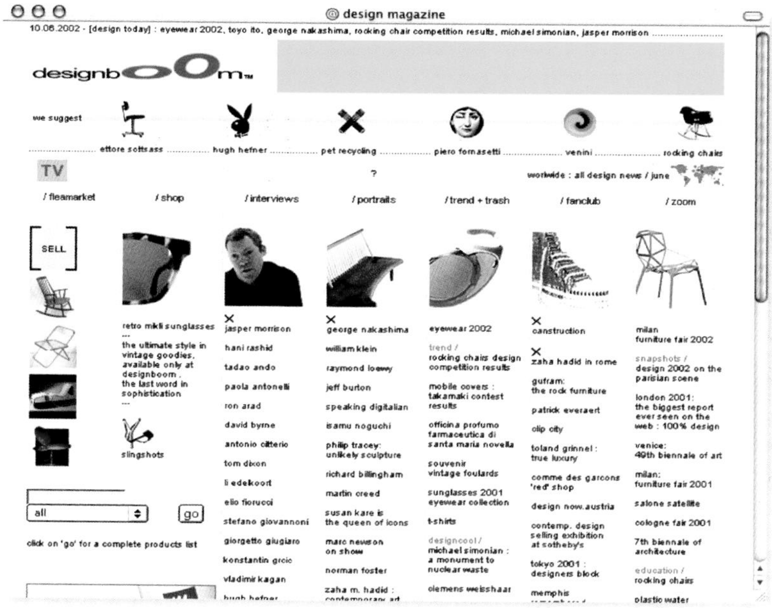
design magazine
designboom
TV
/ fleamarket
/ shop
/ interviews
/ portraits
/ trend + trash
/ fanclub
/ zoom
SELL

WWW.DESIGNBOOM.COM
A: DESIGNBOOM, **M:** MAIL@DESIGNBOOM.COM

THE MULTI-STANDARD PORTAL SOLUTION
FOR FINANCIAL MOBILITY

EVERY TIME
REAL TIME
EVERY MOBILE

F IN GO

designed by Distance Ultra Courte - D.U.C.

WWW.FINGO.COM
D: LAURENT CHARTIER
A: DUC - DISTANCE ULTRA COURTE, **M:** INFOS@D-U-C.COM

WWW.JIMMYTAN.COM
001WORKS
002CV

003THOUGHTS

004LINKS

001WORKS
A SELECTION OF OF MY WORK FOR YOUR
VIEWING. HOPE YOU ENJOY THEM AND PLS
FEEL FREE TO GIVE ME COMMENTS

CLICK ON ANY THUMBNAILS
TO VIEW A BIGGER IMG

COLOURS
NATIONAL SCHOOL OF DESIGN SCREENSAVER

VIEW QT 2.2MB

WWW.JIMMYTAN.COM
D: JIMMY TAN
M: JIMTAN@MAC.COM

DIGITALstudio

we take care of your web fashion (tm)

chi siamo

servizi

filosofia

contattaci

Benvenuti in DIGITALSTUDIO,
l'azienda che si prende cura di
voi e della vostra immagine sul
web. Seguiremo passo per passo
ogni vostro desiderio, curando
ogni aspetto per dare al vostro
prodotto, alla vostra società o al
vostro servizio, un impatto
visuale, sonoro ed espressivo
all'altezza della migliore
tradizione del design italiano e
della più moderna tecnologia.

WWW.DIGISTUDIO.IT
D: SERGIO GIOVANNINI
A: DIGITALSTUDIO, **M:** SERGIO@DIGISTUDIO.IT

CORPORATE ID	PRINT
CORPORATE LITERATURE	STATIONERY DESIGN
IDENTITY / LOGO DESIGN	ADVERTISEMENT DESIGN
CREATIVE CONSULTING	BROCHURE DESIGN
BRANDING	PACKAGING DESIGN
PUBLISHING	**WEB**
MAGAZINE	FLASH DESIGN / PRODUCTION
COFFEE TABLE BOOKS	HTML / ASP PROGRAMMING
GRAPHIC NOVELS	E-COMMERCE APPLICATION
ILLUSTRATIONS	BANNER ADVERTISMENT
	INTERACTIVE PRESENTATIONS

WWW.SNOW.COM.SG
D: JR PHUA
A: SNOW DESIGN, **M:** JR@SNOW.COM.SG

WWW.DMA2001.COM
D: LUCA IONESCU
M: ACUL@OPTUSHOME.COM.AU

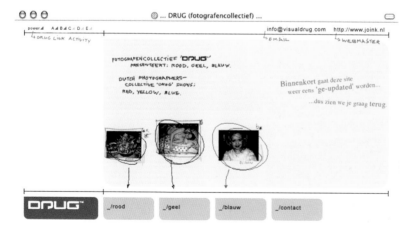

WWW.VISUALDRUG.COM
D: JOOST KUIJPERS
M: FRANK@VISUALDRUG.COM

WWW.CROSSMIND.DE
D: KIRILL BRUSILOVSKY, DIMITRI EICHHORN
A: CROSSMIND COMMUNICATIONS GMBH & CO. KG, **M:** KB@CROSSMIND.DE

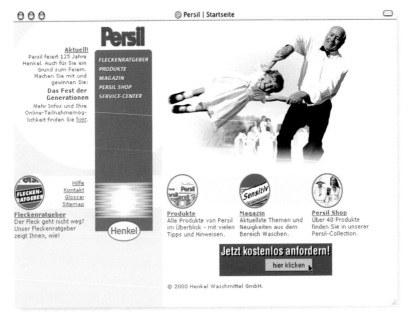

WWW.PERSIL.DE
D: JÖRG STAGGENBORG, **C:** KAY SCHEWE, **P:** HENKEL WASCHMITTEL GMBH
A: FLUXX.COM E-PRODUCTION GMBH, **M:** STAGGENBORG@FLUXX.COM

WWW.16-0-2.COM
D: AGNES TAN
A: JUNKFLEA, **M:** MAIL@16-0-2.COM

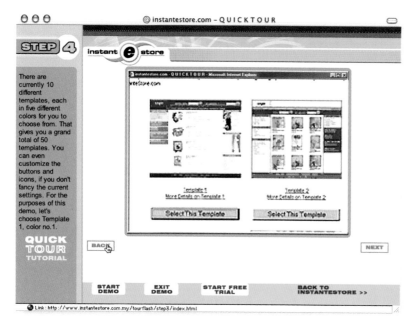

WWW.INSTANTESTORE.COM.MY
D: JASMINE HOR MYN-LI, **C:** CHARLES TANG
A: ESOLVED.COM SDN. BHD., **M:** JASZY76@YAHOO.COM

WWW.OCULART.COM
D: GEOFF LILLEMON
M: GEOFF@OCULART.COM

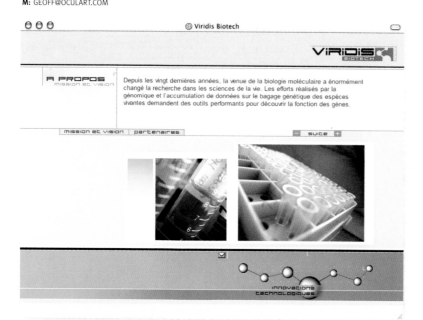

WWW.VIRIDISBIOTECH.COM
D: STEPHANE GROLEAU
A: BLASFEM INTERACTIF, **M:** SGROLEAU@BLASFEM.COM

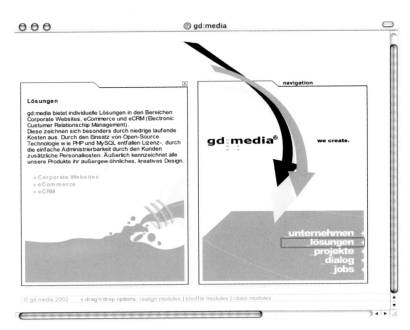

WWW.GDMEDIA.DE
D: MICHAEL GRAF, ANDREAS DIETERLE
A: GD:MEDIA GRAF & DIETERLE GBRW, **M:** INFO@GDMEDIA.DE

WWW.CYNTHIA@MALARAN.COM
D: CYNTHIA MALARAN
M: ONYXWATERS@HOTMAIL.COM

WWW.DEWEL.DE
D: JOCHEN KUCKUCK
M: KUCKY@DEWEL.DE

@ | hydro.seven.four | welcome. digital design ...

menu.
ABOUT
PORTFOLIO
PRINT
 BRANDING
 SHIRTS
GUEST BOOK
DOWNLOAD
CONTACT

WWW.HYDRO74.COM
D: JOSHUA SMITH
M: JOSHUA@HYDRO74.COM

@ Willkommen bei Q

WWW.Q-HOME.DE
D: THILO VON DEBSCHITZ
A: Q, **M:** TVD@Q-HOME.DE

@ Stucch'Italia – Products and services for int...

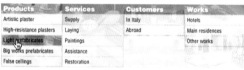

Products and services for interior decoration and building

Stucch'Italia produces, sells, sets up and restores stucco decorations, artistic plasters and prefabricated modules. Its customers and works recognize it as an ideal partner in developing projects and material production.

WWW.STUCCHITALIA.COM
D: STEFANO DOMINICI, **C:** FRANCESCA CRISAFI
A: TR-ASSOCIATI, **M:** S.DOMINICI@TR-ASSOCIATI.IT

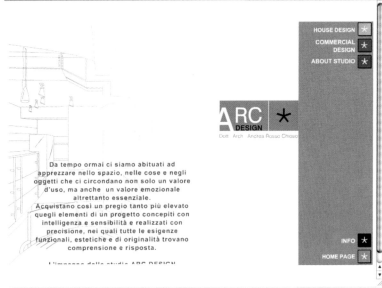

WWW.ARCDESIGN.INFO
D: DANIELE PODDA
A: LINEACURVA, **M:** INFO@LINEACURVA.IT

WWW.MAS-DES-SOURCES.COM
D: SEGURA STÈPHANE
A: ACTIVELAB, **M:** CONTACT@ACTIVELAB.NET

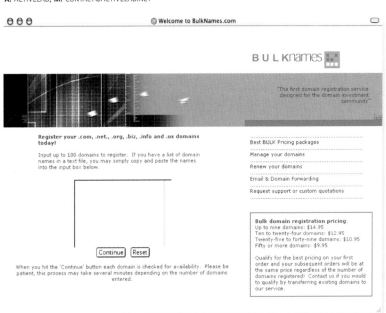

WWW.BULKNAMES.COM
D: LAWRENCE DOMELLO, **C:** JASON MURRAY, **P:** ELISABETH RIZZI
A: MELBOURNE IT, **M:** LAWRENCE@MELBOURNEIT.COM.AU

WWW.HOMEPAGE.NTLWORLD.IE/DAVEJACKO
D: DAVID JACKSON
M: DAVEJACKO@NTLWORLD.IE

WWW.YOUR-MISSING-LINK.COM
D: JOERN TOELLNER
M: JOERN_TOELLNER@WEB.DE

WWW.BERGENGROUP.COM
D: HELGE WINDISCH, **C:** WOLFGANG LEHMANN, **P:** BERGEN GROUP
A: FLANEUR DESIGN, **M:** INFO@FLANEUR.DE

A multidisciplinary solutions

Company

azienda / servizi internet / soluzioni cad-cam / partners / clienti   www.achelon.it

supporto / lavora con noi / mappa del sito

News

Martedì 21/05/2002
3DView rinominato in Spinfire Professional!

Lunedì 29/04/2002
Achelon e Actify presentano Spinfire Enterprise, una soluzione client-server che permette di eliminare innumerevoli dispersioni di risorse

Eventi

Giovedì 02/05/2002
La Achelon parteciperà alla 5 edizione del Mek (Mostra della Meccanica e Servizi innovativi) ...

Mercoledì 20/02/2002
La Achelon parteciperà alla 5ª edizione di Eurostampi (European Dies & Molds, Presses & Injection

Case Study

Carlisle's Automotive Components Group
Carlisle Engineered Products, settore Automotive Components della Carlisle Companies Incorporated, ha acquistato 50 postazioni collegate con Spinfire Enterprise per realizzare la

contact / legal / privacy

WWW.ACHELON.IT
D: FABRIZIO PASQUERO, **C:** ROBERTO BRONDOLO
A: ACHELON WEB DESIGN S.N.C., **M:** INFO@ACHELON.IT

@ ASSORTED MATERIAL, Johnny Ryan

start   curriculum vitae   writing   design   3D   sketches   links

DESIGN

Publications
Magazine\ LHM: Journal Edition
Magazine\ LHM (2001)
Magazine\ COGITO MAGAZINE
Tabloid\ The College Tribune 8 page 'Insert' supplement
Magazine\ LHM (2000)
Magazine\ PHILSOC Magazine

Poster & Logo design
Logo Gallery\ Gallery
Poster Gallery\ Gallery

Web site design
Recent\ The Magazine
Recent\ LiteraryAndHistorical.com and read review
Old\ UCD Philosophy Department
Old\ Miscellany online
Old\ Dublin Business Innovation Centre
Old\ 1998 Spin a Web finalist (from this site)
Old\ tdp corporate site (from this site)

WWW.GEOCITIES.COM/X4401
D: JOHNNY RYAN
M: X4401@YAHOO.COM

@ WELCOME TO mPAYMENT

Home | Company | Technology | News&Events | Partners | Download

HOME

mPayment is a specialist mobile payment solutions provider, m-commerce enabler and m-marketing solutions company. It holds 4 patent-pending technologies - mPurse™, mDebit™, mCredit™ and mF2P™. mPurse™ is a world-first end-to-end mobile stored-value micro-payment solution fully deployed on an extensive, secure and reliable multi-bank multi-merchant payment infrastructure.

Our Target Vertical Markets
■ Public service & government agencies
■ Financial services industry (FSI)
■ Travel, hospitality & entertainment
■ Education & healthcare

CONTACT | SITEMAP

Privacy Policy   For Simple Chinese Translation, Click Here.

WWW.2MPAYMENT.COM
D: JOANNE ANG
M: JOANNE@2MPAYMENT.COM

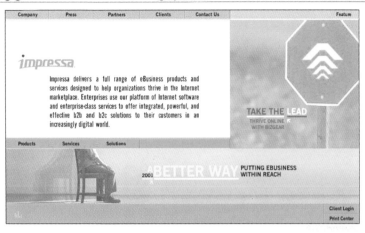

WWW.IMPRESSA.COM
D: CARLO VEGA, **C:** KEN BREEDEN, **P:** DEAN SCHUSTER
A: IMPRESSA, **M:** CARLO.VEGA@IMPRESSA.COM

WWW.NIMMERGRUEN.CH
D: RETO SANTSCHI, MICHAEL BAEHN
A: UPART, **M:** BAEHNI@APPROX.CH

WWW.PLANCHAEXPRESS.COM
D: PEDRO REY SANCHIZ
A: LUMIA ESTUDIO, **M:** PEDROREY@USC.ES

Familie

» Doppeleinfamilienhaus
» Reihenhaus
» Chalet
» Einfamilienhaus
» Bauland
» Einfamilienhaus
» Eigentumswohnungen
» Eigentumswohnungen
» Terrassenhaus
» Bauland

Seite: 1 2

Bauland Aussicht garantiert...

...von den Alpen bis zum Jura! Die eigenen vier Wände in Schwarzenburg planen und konzipieren oder sich für ein Niederigstenergiehaus entscheiden das als Projekt «Sonnenhaus» entstanden ist?

- Parzelle 598 m2
- Richtpreis Fr. 275000.-

weitere Infos...

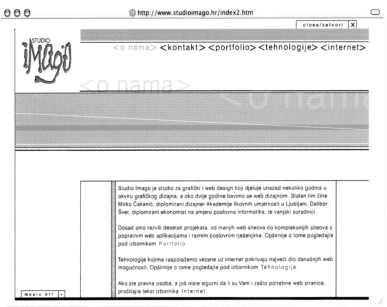

WWW.ZIMMERMANN-IMMOBILIEN.CH
D: SANDRA BAUMANN, MICHAEL BAEHNI
A: UPART, **M:** BAEHNI@APPROX.CH

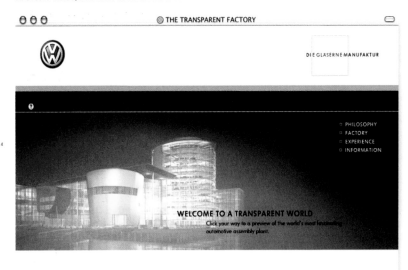

WWW.STUDIOIMAGO.HR
D: MIRKO CAKANIC, **C:** DALIBOR SVER
A: STUDIO IMAGO, **M:** STUDIO@STUDIOIMAGO.HR

WWW.GLAESERNEMANUFAKTUR.DE
D: RALPH SONNTAG
M: INFOSERVICE@GLAESERNEMANUFAKTUR.DE

bfp

BUNDESVERBAND FREISCHAFFENDER PIANISTEN E.V.

- Home
- Aktuelles
- PianoDepesche
- Wir über uns
- Ziele
- Leistungen
- Mitglieder
- VisitenKarte
- Linkliste
- Kontakt
- Umfrage
- Suche
- Login
- Disclaimer
- Impressum

--> Herzlich willkommen auf unserer WebSeite

Warum brauchen Pianisten eine Lobby?

Pianisten (Pianistinnen sind selbstredend stets mitzudenken) verbringen die meiste Zeit ihres künstlerischen Lebens in »Einzelhaft am Klavier«*. Das Üben und überwiegend solistische Musizieren führt daher automatisch zur Ausprägung von Individualismus, Einzelgängertum, ja Isolation.

Das hat den Vorteil, daß Pianisten oft ausgeprägte Persönlichkeiten werden, aber auch den Nachteil, daß dadurch viel zu wenig Gemeinschaftssinn ausgeprägt wird, der zu Problemen in der Realität des künstlerischen Berufsalltags (vor allem Kommunikation) führen kann.

Da viele Pianisten jedoch häufig mit denselben Fragen und Schwierigkeiten konfrontiert sind, ist es nur folgerichtig, wenn sie sich gemeinsam für ihre Sache stark machen, also eine Lobby bilden. Daher haben einige Pianisten mit Pioniergeist 1994 in Hamburg im Hotel Atlantic den »B.F.P. Bundesverband Freischaffender Pianisten e.V. (Deutscher Pianistenverband)« gegründet.

* Grete Wehmeyer: Carl Czerny und die Einzelhaft am Klavier, oder: Die Kunst der Fingerfertigkeit und die industrielle Arbeitsideologie, Kassel 1983

Was bringt eine Lobby für Pianisten?

MedienNews
»Der Pianist« von...
Roman Polanski (68) dürfte die Vorfreude gepackt haben. Sein Film »Der Pianist« gilt als heißer...
mehr...

Namen & News
Argerich mit Pletnev
Der russische Klavier-Großmeister Mikhail Pletnev, wird seine neu arrangierte Konzert-Suite für...
mehr...

KurzPorträt
Christoph Spendel (B.F.P.)
Wer sich mit der künstlerischen Biographie des Pianisten Christoph Spendel (B.F.P.) befaßt, wird...
mehr...

Neue Noten
Henle Verlag
Zimmermann
Schott
Bärenreiter
mehr...

Neue Klaviere
Die patente Rolle
Wer bisher vielleicht dachte, daß im Klavierbau im Grunde keine (r)evolutionären Entwicklungen mehr...

WWW.BFP-EV.ORG
D: ULI PAHLKE
M: MAIL@ULIPAHLKE.DE

B3 Elementos de escaparate

01 **B3, LA EMPRESA**
Conozcanos mas a fondo. Breve recorrido por nuestra empresa
02 **ELEMENTOS DE ESCAPARATE**
Ya disponible: Moda Infantil 2001
Proximamente: Moda Adulto 2001
03 **CONTACTENOS**

the best look for your shop-window

WWW.B3ESCAPARATE.COM
D: EMILIO GARCIA VAZ
A: EDISSENY.COM*NOVESCOMUNICACIONS, **M:** INFO@EDISSENY.COM

Qa
business improvement

welcome
venture matrix
what we do
our work
the team
news and links
contact

introduction
purpose
people
processes

what we do
introduction

Today we live in an environment in which turbulence seems 'the norm' and change is the only constant. Many factors are forcing organisations to look for new ways to meet market demands quickly, efficiently and effectively. Such factors include the need for speed, to respond to vast technological change, the trend towards globalisation, increased market pressures, and the need to perform more efficiently.

To succeed in this high-pressure, ever-changing environment the knowledge, skills, experience and perspectives of a wide range of **people** must be brought together. Only in this way can organisations solve problems, make effective decisions and deliver optimal solutions to their customers.

◄ 1 of 3 ►

WWW.QABI.CO.UK
D: JUSTIN COCKBURN, **C:** PHELIM CAVLAN
A: ONEBESTWAY, **M:** MIKE@ONEBESTWAY.COM

WWW.SEBASTIANDEYLE.DE
D: INGO WIEDERODER
A: TELEMEDIA GMBH, **M:** INGO.WIEDERODER@TELEMEDIA-GMBH.DE

WWW.AWEZOOM.COM
D: VICTOR VERGARA
A: AWEZOOM, **M:** AWEZOOM@AWEZOOM.COM

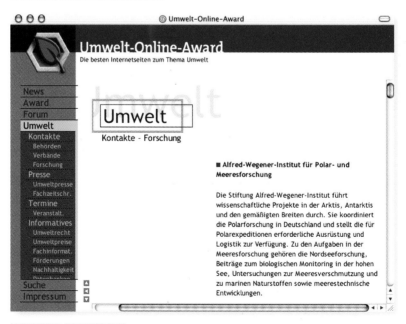

WWW.UMWELT-ONLINE-AWARD.DE
D: GUSTAVO PEDROZA, ALFIE GARCIA, **P:** HERIBERTO GUEVARA
A: PAUDAN, **M:** ALFIE@SATELITEZONAAZUL.COM

Net Maxis is a Pakistani web development company with new ideas and a new approach. We don't struggle to invent new technologies; we build on what's proven and readily available. And we revel in openness, providing visibility into the end-to-end development process. This is our opportunity. We value long-term relationships, so we're straightforward and honest. Our success is driven by client interaction. Engage our services. You'll be impressed by our commitment to customer satisfaction, and your results. Net Maxis is a custom web development company. We believe that information technology can unleash incredible productivity and market advantages. And that strategic planning and strong project management are imperative prerequisites in harnessing that power. Our projects are driven by strategy, and managed by communication.

Net Maxis services help clients plan, develop and manage information technology. We are a web solution provider company with business management capabilities. Our experienced teams combine planning, programming and organizational skills to deliver individual solutions tied to overall business value. Net Maxis projects produce results. We charge reasonable rates for our services. And our commitment to customer satisfaction is second-to-none.

Currently we are working together with Soft System and we provide them all of the their web solutions with one team.

WWW.NETMAXIS.COM.PK
D: KAMRAN ASLAM
A: NET MAXIS, **M:** CEO@NETMAXIS.COM.PK

WWW.ALLCONNECTIONS.NET
D: MIKEL.LOPEZ, STEN.SVENSSON
A: WWW IBERCOM, **M:** STEN.SVENSSON@IBERCOM.ES

WWW.YESKARTA.SK/AKTIVACIA.HTM
D: MARTIN KALIS, **C:** ROMAN BALAZ, **P:** DAGMAR TONKOVICOVA
A: EASTERN | WEBMEDIA, **M:** KALIS@NEXTRA.SK

Fernando**Travieso**   designfolio**'01**

WWW.INTOTUM.COM/FERNANDO
D: FERNANDO TRAVIESO
A: TOUCHECOMUNICACION VISUAL, **M:** TRAVIESO@INTERNET.COM.UY

WWW.CREATIVESENSES.DE
D: CHRISTOPHER JONES
A: CREATIVESENSES, **M:** CHRIS@CREATIVESENSES.DE

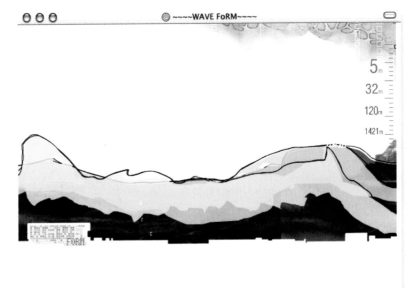

WAVEFORM001.FREE.FR
D: FREDERIC BONTEMPS
M: FRED_BONTEMPS@HOTMAIL.COM

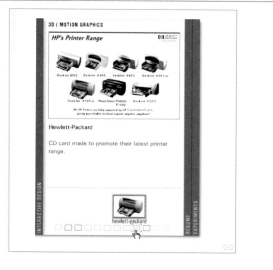

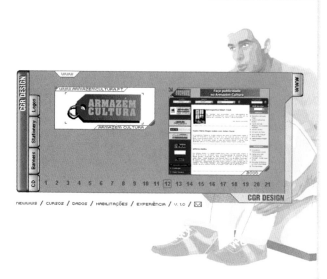

WWW.SOERIANTO.NET
D: HENDRI SOERIANTO
M: HENDRI@SOERIANTO.NET

WWW.OLOGRAFIX.ORG
D: NICOLA D'AGOSTINO
A: NEZMAR, **M:** NEZMAR@OLOGRAFIX.ORG

WWW.CGRDESIGN.COM
D: GUSTAVO ROSCITO
A: CGR DESIGN, **M:** CGR@CGRDESIGN.COM

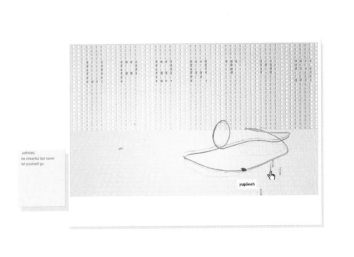

WWW.SUPERTM.COM
D: LARS WOEHNING
A: V2A**NETFORCE**RUHR, **M:** LW@V2A.NET

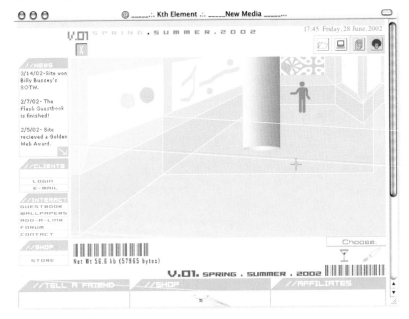

WWW.KTHELEMENT.COM
D: KHANH VU
A: KTH ELEMENT, **M:** KVU@KTHELEMENT.COM

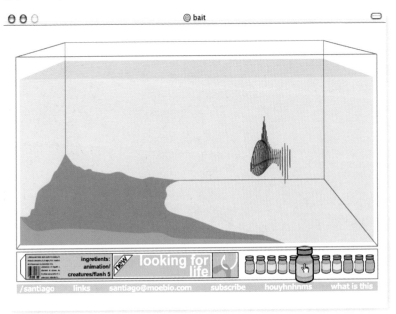

WWW.MOEBIO.COM/SANTIAGO
D: SANTIAGO ORTIZ
A: MOEBIO, **M:** SANTIAGO@MOEBIO.COM

cubemen.com⁺⁺

what's new
profile
portfolio
visual
wallpaper
link
guestbook
contact us

what's new ++

20.07.2001
cubemen officially launched now, enjoy it !!!
[version5]
special thanx -- taka chan

news archive ++

wallpaper ++

submit your work ++
more ++

link ++

d i s t a n c e m a g a z i n e {:^]]

Few years ago, "distance" is a copied black and white
magazine, tiny and lively. Every author had to copy her/
his own part and they put them together and bind them up.
this web site is designed by my friend - del .Her design is
very creative , and warm.

WWW.CUBEMEN.COM
D: TOBY YEUNG, **C:** TAKA CHAN
A: CUBEMEN STUDIO, **M:** TOBY@DG21.COM

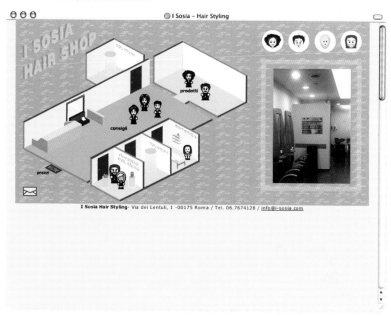

WWW.I-SOSIA.COM
D: ROMINA RAFFAELLI, **C:** STEFANO MARINI
A: WINKLER & NOAH, **M:** INFO@WINKLER-NOAH.IT

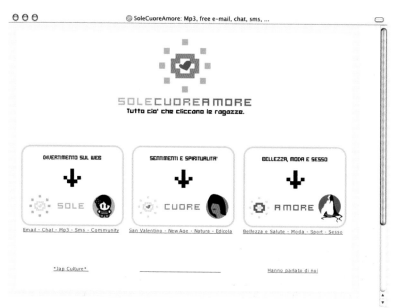

WWW.SOLECUOREAMORE.IT
D: ROMINA RAFFAELLI, **C:** STEFANO MARINI
A: WINKLER & NOAH, **M:** INFO@WINKLER-NOAH.IT

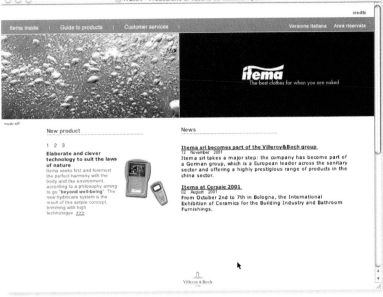

WWW.ITEMA.IT
D: ANGELO BANDINU
A: RE-LOAD.IT, **M:** ANGELO@DROP.IT

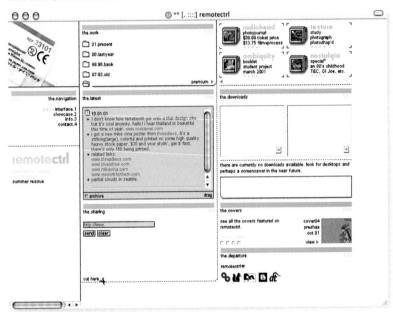

WWW.REMOTECTRL.ORG
D: JOSEPH KING
M: MAIL@REMOTECTRL.ORG

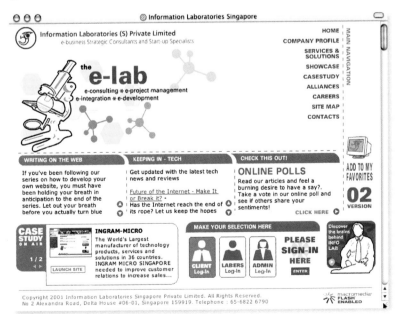

WWW.INFO-LAB.COM
D: WAYNE_MIN OOI
A: INFO-LAB, **M:** WAYMIN@INFO-LAB.COM

WWW.ORGALAB.DE
D: KARL SERWOTKA, **C:** ALEX SCHWINDT, **P:** VOLKER LIEBIG
A: PROMEDIA, **M:** INFO@ART-OF-VISION.DE

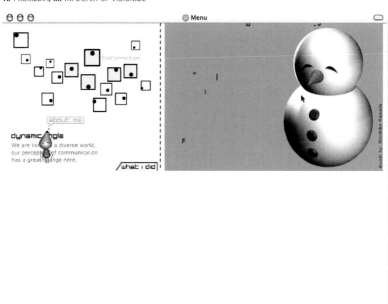

WWW.DYNAMICANGLE.COM
D: TERRY LAI
M: DESH001@DYNAMICANGLE.COM

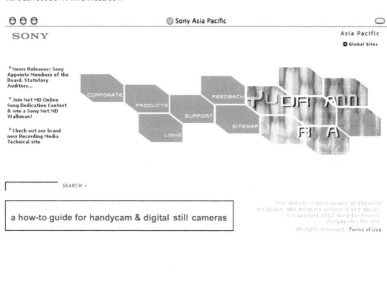

WWW.SONY-ASIA.COM
D: IVAN MP TAN, **C:** LYNDON OH, **P:** PAUL KAN
M: IVAN.TAN@ACLAIM.COM.SG

WWW.FIGOO.NET
D: DIDIER LAMMENS
A: GOOFI, **M:** DIDZ@FIGOO.NET

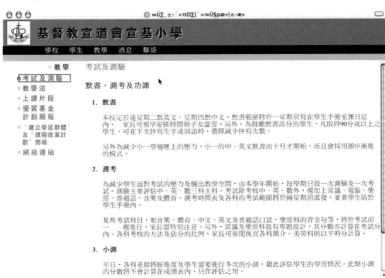

WWW.SUNKEI.EDU.HK
D: GORDON CHAN
A: VIVIDTONE CORPORATE LIMITED, **M:** GORDON@GORDONCHAN.CA

WWW.ILLOGICZ.COM
D: STUART SCHONEVELD
M: STUART@ILLOGICZ.COM

WWW.SAT-STORE.COM
D: RICCARDO TOCCACIELO
A: SAT-STORE.IT, M: INFO@SAT-STORE.IT

WWW.QUIKSILVER.BE
D: DIDIER LAMMENS
A: GOOFI, M: INFO@GOOFI.BE

WWW.TMS.DE
D: DIETMAR SCHMIDT, C: FRANK MÜLLER, P: TMS AG
A: KINGMEDIA GMBH, M: SCHMIDT@UNIT-MEDIENHAUS.DE

WWW.MOOREMEDICAL.COM
D: MIKHAIL PESCHAN
M: MISHA@FORMSCIENCE.COM

WWW.MARBLE-CO.NET/T-SHIRT.HTML
D: HIROAKI OHTA
A: MARBLE.CO, **M:** MAIL@MARBLE-CO.NET

WWW.IBIRAPUERA.COM.BR
D: MARCIO TAKETOMI, **P:** VITOR MARADEI
A: VAD, **M:** ZILLION@IG.COM.B

WWW.VAICAGLIARI.IT
D: CARLO GALLINO
A: UNIONESARDA, **M:** GALLINO@UNIONESARDA.IT

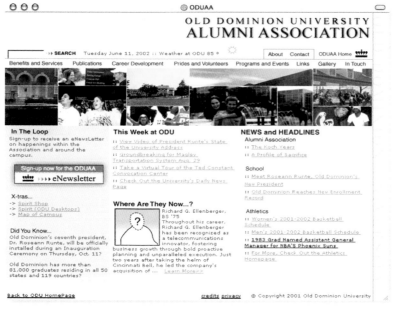

ALUMNI.ODU.EDU
D: RONNIE THOMPSON, **C:** RICK WILLIAMS, **P:** CHRIS DALLAVILLA
A: DALLAVILLA DESIGN, **M:** RON@DVDSGN.COM

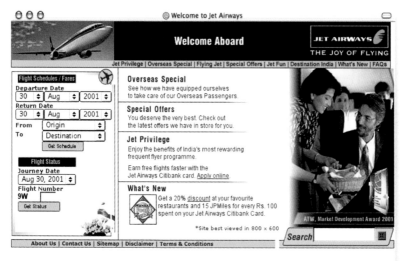

WWW.JETAIRWAYS.COM
D: KUNAL SHAH, **C:** SUDEEP NAMBIHAR
A: OGILVY INTERACTIVE WORLDWIDE, **M:** KUNAL.SHAH@OGILVY.COM

WWW.TIERRAVIRTUAL.NET
D: OSCAR PEREZ
A: TIERRA VIRTUAL, **M:** INFO@TIERRAVIRTUAL.NET

WWW.SITEUP.COM/FIDO
D: MARTIN KALIS, **P:** BOB GIBBONS
A: EASTERN | WEBMEDIA, **M:** KALIS@NEXTRA.SK

WWW.NEWAGECREATIONS.COM
D: MIKE EWING
A: NEW AGE CREATIONS, **M:** DOMINIC@FOUNDATION7.COM

WWW.STEVEROWELL.COM
A: STEVEROWELL DESIGN, **M:** STV@STEVEROWELL.COM

WWW.POSTMAN.IT
D: JOHNNIE MANEIRO
A: GRAFF.NET, **M:** JOHNNIEMANEIRO@MAC.COM

WWW.UCUNCUGOZ.GEN.TR
D: ERCAN CALISKAN
A: NEXUM, **M:** E.CALISKAN@NEXUMTR.COM

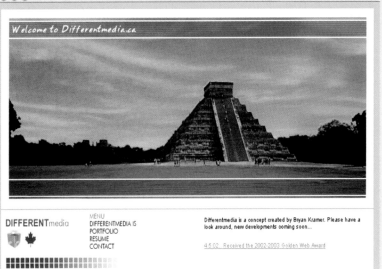

WWW.BECOMINGHUMAN.ORG
D: BRYAN KRAMER
M: BRYANKRAMER@SHAW.CA

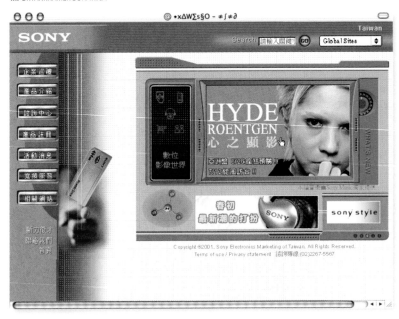

WWW.SONY.COM.TW
D: ELLIE YANG, **C:** JASON YANG, **P:** SETTHA LEE
A: TYA STUDIO LTD., **M:** SETTHA@TYA.COM.TW

WWW.LEONTIENVANMOORSEL.NL
D: JEROEN HERMES
A: KWATTA, **M:** JEROEN@HERMES.NU

WWW.UBQ.IT/MANES
D: DOMENICO MANES
A: UBQ, **M:** MANES@LIBERO.IT

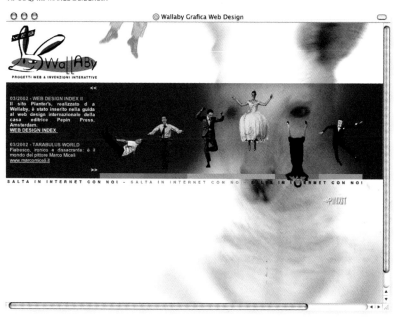

WWW.WALLABY.IT
D: GAIA DE PAOLI
A: WALLABY WEB, **M:** GAIA@WALLABY.IT

WWW.ARDANACOMM.COM
D: ECO ILUSIKU, **C:** BARTLEY, **P:** MIRZA
M: TO_OL@ARDANACOMM.COM

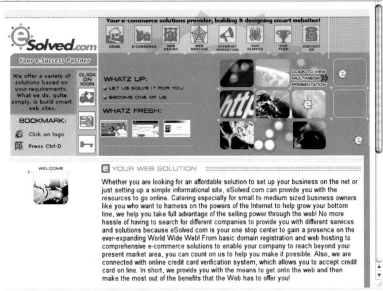

WWW.ESOLVED.COM
D: JASMINE HOR MYN-LI, **C:** CHARLES TANG
A: ESOLVED.COM SDN. BHD., **M:** JASZY76@YAHOO.COM

WWW.PLANETSER.IT
D: ANGELO FOGGETTA
A: PLANET SERVICE SRL, **M:** ANGELO@PLANETSER.IT

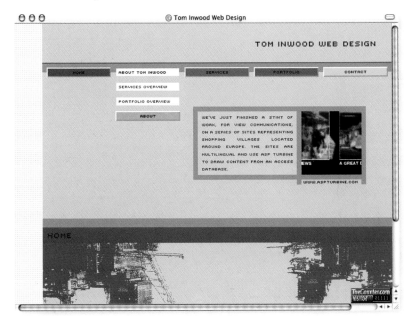

WWW.MAREEN.CO.UK
D: TOM INWOOD
A: TOM INWOOD WEB DESIGN, **M:** CONTACT@MAREEN.CO.UK

WWW.TANIA-ZAMPARO.IT
D: STEFANO PEDRETTI
A: PULP, **M:** INFO@PULPIT.IT

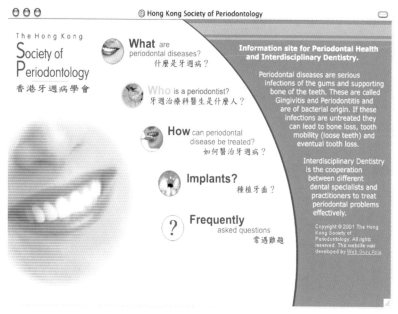

WWW.HKPERIO.ORG
D: KATHY LO
A: WEB GURU ASIA, **M:** KATHY@WEBGURUASIA.COM

WWW.GLOBALSTUDENT.CO.NZ
D: RONALD STALLMACH
A: TEXTUS DESIGN, **M:** INFO@TEXTUSDESIGN.CO.NZ

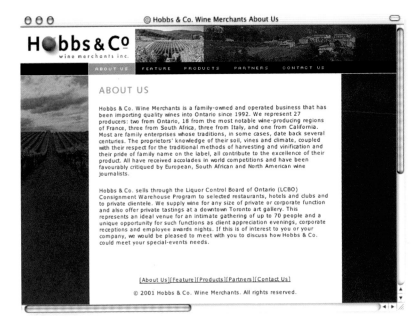

WWW.HOBBSWINES.COM
D: STEVE GAUDER, **C:** MICHELLE SMITH
A: GAUDER DESIGN, **M:** STEVIEG@SYMPATICO.CA

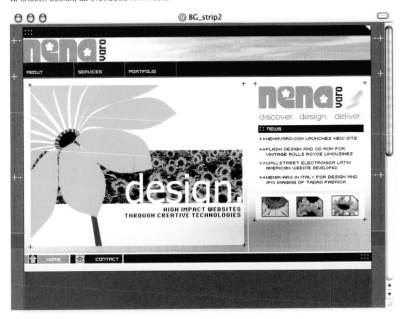

WWW.NENAVARO.COM
D: NENA OTALVARO
A: NENAVARO.COM, **M:** NENAVARO@AOL.COM

WWW.DIDACTICA.IT
D: NICOLA SCOTTO DI CARLO, **C:** GIANLUCA LOMUTO
A: QBO, **M:** STAFF@QBO.IT

WWW.1-TO-MANAGE.DE
D: DIETMAR SCHMIDT, **C:** FRANK MÜLLER, **P:** TAW, WUPPERTAL
A: KINGMEDIA GMBH, **M:** SCHMIDT@UNIT-MEDIENHAUS.DE

WWW.M1-THECLUB.COM
D: JOE LANDEN, **C:** MARCUS SCHUSTER
A: TWINPIX MEDIA LAB, **M:** LANDEN@TWINPIX.DE

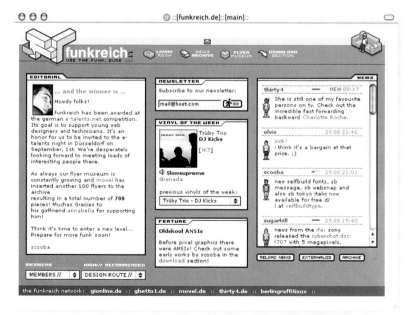

WWW.FUNKREICH.DE
D: TOBIAS KREMER, STEFAN ULRICH
A: URBIA.COM AG, **M:** STEFAN.ULRICH@URBIA.COM

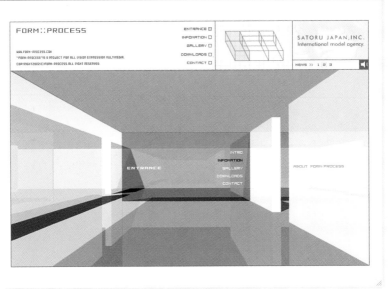

WWW.FORM-PROCESS.COM
D: TAKAAKI YAGI
A: FORM::PROCESS, **M:** INFO@FORM-PROCESS.COM

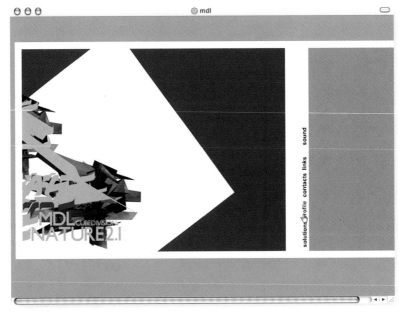

WWW.MAXDESIGNLAB.COM
D: MASSIMO ARALDI
A: MAXDESIGNLAB, **M:** M.ARALDI@LIBERO.IT

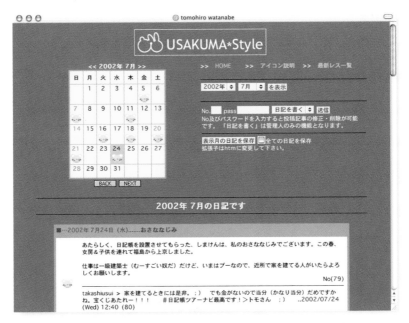

WWW.ARTISANSTREAM.COM
D: TOMOHIRO_WATANABE
A: USAKUMASTYLE, **M:** TOMO@USAKUMA.COM

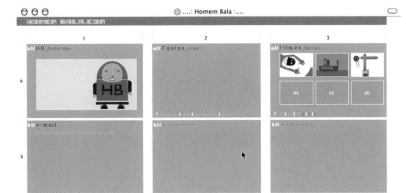

WWW.HOMEMBALA.COM
D: BRUNO OLIVEIRA
A: HOMEM BALA, **M:** BRUNO.JULIO@IPT.PT

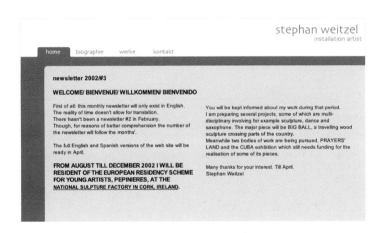

WWW.STEPHANWEITZEL.COM
D: THOMAS WEITZEL
A: WEITZELDESIGN, **M:** INFO@STEPHANWEITZEL.COM

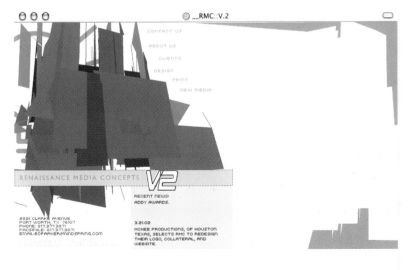

WWW.AREYOUENLIGHTENED.COM
D: BO PARKER
A: RENAISSANCE MEDIA CONCPETS, **M:** BOPARKER@MINDSPRING.COM

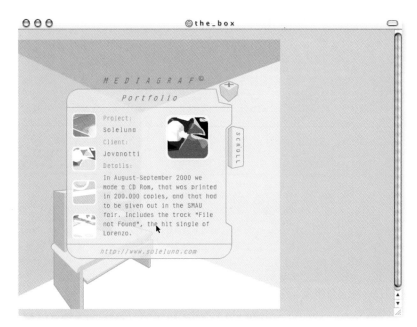

WWW.MEDIAGRAF.IT
D: LUCA SANTOLAMAZZA
A: LSDESIGN, **M:** ELLESSE_D@LIBERO.IT

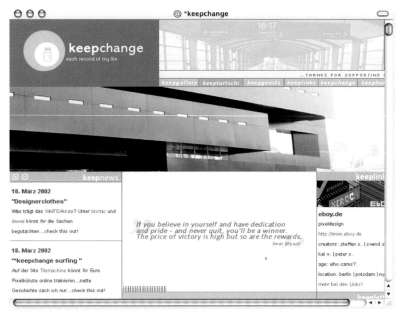

WWW.KEEPCHANGE.DE/INDEX2.HTM
D: CHRISTIAN.HARTMANN
M: FOURNINTY@KEEPCHANGE.DE

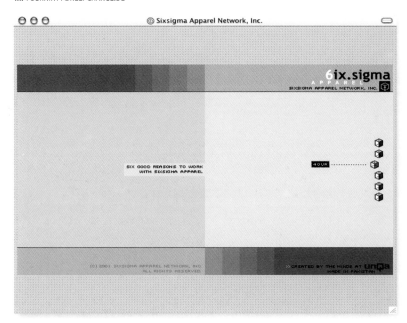

WWW.SIXSIGMA-APPAREL.COM
D: TANYA ELAHI
A: UNQA, **M:** AIYAZ@HOTMAIL.COM

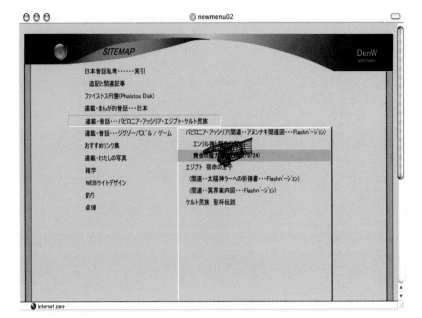

WWW.BD.WAKWAK.COM/~P-PLAZA
D: YAMASHIRO MASUMI, **C:** P-PLAZA
A: DENW, **M:** P-PLAZA@BD.WAKWAK.COM

WWW.HOTELEC.DE
D: OLIVER OERTEL, **C:** FRITZ KRAUfl
A: ANALOG MULTIMEDIA, **M:** ANALOG@ANALOG.DE

WWW.OSCARCABALLERO.NET
D: OSCAR CABALLERO
M: OSCAR@OSCARCABALLERO.NET

WWW.NASONLINE.NL
D: PETER HUT
A: BRATPACK, **M:** P.HUT@BRATPACK.NL

WWW.INSTANTESTORE.COM
D: JASMINE HOR MYN-LI, **C:** CHARLES TANG
A: ESOLVED.COM SDN. BHD., **M:** JASZY76@YAHOO.COM

WWW.SCOREGOLF.COM
D: STEVE GAUDER, **C:** CRAIG WELLER, **P:** RICK BROWN
A: DESIGN 2.0, **M:** STEVIEG@SYMPATICO.CA

WWW.THENEWSPAPERTODAY.COM
D: KUSHAL GROVER
A: TNT ART DEPTT., **M:** KGROVER@INDIA-TODAY.COM

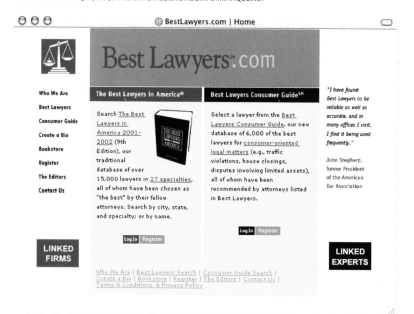

WWW.PHOTO12.COM
D: JEAN-LUC CHEVALLIER
A: MDB INFORMATIQUE, **M:** JEANLUC.CHEVALLIER@MDBINFORMATIQUE.NET

WWW.BESTLAWYERS.COM
D: MARK BARKLEY, **C:** JASON WIDENER,
A: LEVINE & ASSOCIATES, INC., **M:** MBARKLEY@BESTLAWYERS.COM

WWW.PAKBEAT.COM
D: GHAZALI BEHZAD, **C:** AHSAN & SHOUKAT, **P:** UMBER IBAD
A: YESTONET, **M:** VICKYUMER@HOTMAIL.COM

WWW.EICMF.DK
D: JESPER STEVNHOVED
A: JSPR, **M:** JESPER@JSPR.DK

WWW.USERS.SKYNET.BE/RAMDAM
D: VALÈRIE DEBATISSE
A: RAMDAM DESIGN, **M:** RAMDAM_DESIGN@HOTMAIL.COM

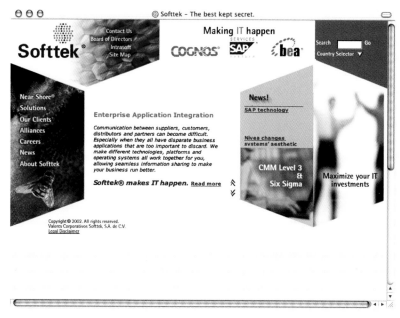

WWW.SOFTTEK.COM
D: HECTOR VELASCO, **P:** FERNADA TREVINO
A: SOFTTEK SOFTWARE FACTORY, **M:** HECTOR.VELASCO@SOFTTEK.COM

WWW.MATERIO.COM
D: AMY KILLOREN CLARK, **C:** KOHEI NAGANUMA, **P:** PHILIP CLARK
M: CLARK@MONDORONDO.COM

WWW.NEWDEALWEB.COM
D: HIROSY YOKOI
A: R.S.COCOON, **M:** HIROSYYY@MAC.COM

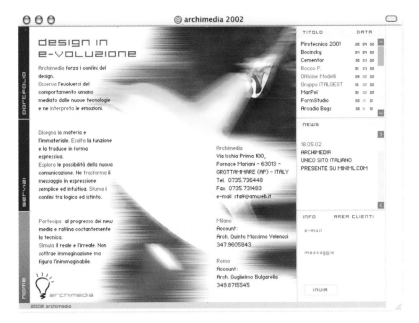

WWW.AMWEB.IT
D: MARCO BOLLETTINI, **C:** AMERICO TRAINI
A: ARCHIMEDIA SNC, **M:** STAFF@AMWEB.IT

WWW.SUMMITLAW.COM
D: ERICH SCHRECK, **C:** STEPHANIE KRIMMEL,
A: GIRVIN INC., **M:** SCHRECK@GIRVIN.COM

WWW.NOISE.FM
D: ANNINA ANTINRANTA
A: NOITATIETO OY, **M:** ANNINA@NOITATIETO.FI

At Media Labs Innovation, we provide mission-critical hosting for a variety of our clients. We offer powerful & affordable Web servers, reliable network connections to make sure that once you're online you stay there!

Media Labs Innovation offers the coverage you can depend on.

As part of our consultancy plan, we encourage you to take up our design consultancy and development services to bring up the professional look and feel to your corporate website.

If you are looking for a complete solution under one roof, Media Labs Innovation has the right formula for you.

Media Labs Innovation Solution Plan
This plan is basically to provide companies with a whole solution package. We will analyze and work closely with you to implement viable business solutions, providing you with a proposal to reach out to your target audience in the Internet. Click here now, and allow Media Labs to propose an economical solution for you.

Media Labs Innovation Design Plan
This plan is suitable for companies that have an existing infrastructure but would like to integrate creative design concept to their website. Being a creative firm with technological know-how, we plan, design & execute user-centric design based on your company's infrastructure & technologies. Click here now, and allow Media Labs to propose an economical solution for you.

Media Labs Innovation Hosting Plan
We offer many economical prices for our hosting plan. Below are the hosting plans available.

Unix Packages

WWW.MEDIALABS.COM.SG
D: VINCENT HO
A: MEDIA LABS INNOVATION, **M:** ZOLAo@SINGNET.COM.SG

WWW.DESIGNERSLIFE.COM
D: KIKE BESADA
A: DESIGNERSLIFE*, **M:** KIKE@DESIGNERSLIFE.COM

WWW.SOULMANLAPELI.COM
D: JUAN CARLOS CORDERO, **P:** SOUL MAN
A: RAVALNET, **M:** JUANCARLOS@RAVALNET.ORG

WWW.MITRICH.DF.RU
D: MITRICH, **C:** NATALY
A: MITRICH&NATALY DESIGN, **M:** MITRICH@FLASHMASTER.RU

WWW.TAMBOURIN.BE
D: LAC NHAN PHAN MAI
A: GCITY, **M:** ACNHAN@PEMPLUM.BE

ROMIGLIA.P1X.ORG
D: KALI ROMIGLIA
M: KALI@ROMIGLIA.COM

WWW.RBA.ES
D: JORDI GRANELL
A: PUKKAS WEB'S DESIGN, **M:** INFO@PUKKAS.COM

WWW.WEBMASTER-REPUBLIC.COM
D: ROMINA RAFFAELLI, **C:** STEFANO MARINI
A: WINKLER & NOAH, **M:** INFO@WINKLER-NOAH.IT

WWW.IT-GATEWAY.COM
D: KIMMO KUUSISTO, MISA KANNOS
A: AC-MAINOS, **M:** KIMMO@ACMAINOS.FI

127

We add
3D perspective
to
Corporate
Communications.

CROSSMEDIA
communications

click viewer's knob to find topics or....
| english| update | vision | expertise | solution | contact us |
Copyright© 2002 Crossmedia Communications, Inc

WWW.CROSSMEDIA.CO.JP
D: KAZ AMEMIYA
A: CROSSMEDIA COMMUNICATIONS, INC., **M:** AMEMIYA@CROSSMEDIA.CO.JP

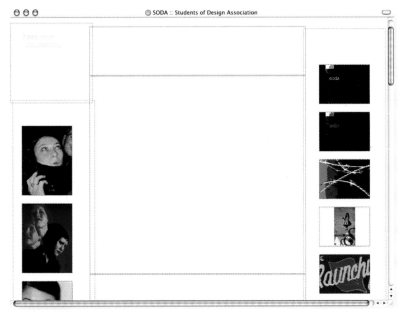

INTERNET.DESIGN.CURTIN.EDU.AU
D: MICHAEL EFFORD
M: EFFORD@IINET.NET.AU

Ad Arezzo,
libreria d'arte,
volumi prestigiosi
e ultime novità.

Libreria Pellegrini
dal 1895

Libreria Pellegrini s.a.s.
di Ennio Gori & C.
Piazza S. Francesco, 7 - Arezzo

chi siamo
catalogo
servizi
Arezzo
info

Una realizzazione StoriediWeb

WWW.LIBRERIAPELLEGRINI.IT
D: FRANCESCA MORBIDELLI
M: FRENS@LIBERO.IT

```
5mal gewartet…
14mal telefoniert…
mehrmals geschwitzt…
nochmal drübergeschwitzt…
16mal auf'm klo…
…weisst du überhaupt wie waldmeister schmeckt?
```

WWW.SODA.CH
D: PETA KOBROW
A: WEBLOTION, **M:** P.KOBROW@KMS-TEAM.DE

ON THE MOVE

DESPERATELY SEEKING A STUDIO !!!!

THE FIRE DEPARTMENT CLOSED DOWN THE PLACE I USED TO
WORK. IF YOU KNOW A PLACE I CAN RENT IN ROTTERDAM
PLEASE LET ME KNOW (EXCLUSIVE, SIGNED AND NUMBERED
MODERN LIVING SILKSCREEN PRINT AS A REWARD)

MANY THANKS IN ADVANCE.

H.HOOGERBRUGGE

han@hoogerbrugge.com

WWW.HOOGERBRUGGE.COM
D: HAN HOOGERBRUGGE
M: HAN@HOOGERBRUGGE.COM

WWW.WORKINGVENTURES.CA
D: SHAWN SQUIRES
A: MARCH NETWORKS, **M:** SSQUIRES@MARCHNETWORKS.COM

WWW.DCONTINUUM.COM
D: ED MILANO
A: CONTINUUM, **M:** INFO@DCONTINUUM.COM

WWW.FASHCAT.COM
D: BORILLO & CESPEDES, **C:** SALVADOR CATAL
A: FASHCAT, **M:** ESTUDIO@FASHCAT.COM

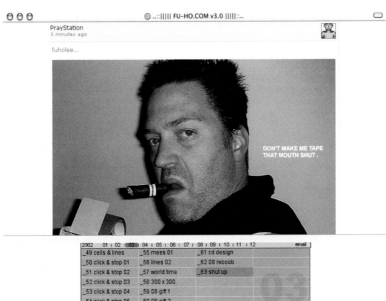

WWW.FU-HO.COM
D: FUHO FUHOLEE
M: FU_HO_LEE@HOTMAIL.COM

WWW.GAILCHEN.COM
D: GERARD TAN
M: GAILATWORK@HOTMAIL.COM

WWW.WITH-M.COM
D: MASAKI
M: MASAKI@WITH-M.COM

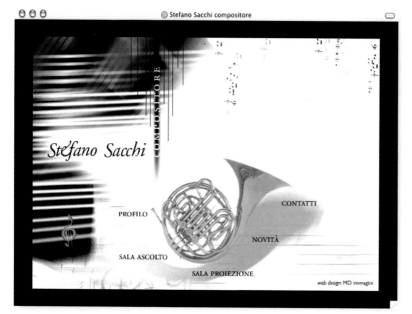

WWW.STEFANOSACCHI.COM
D: MARIO DONADONI
A: MD IMMAGINI, **M:** MD@MDIMMAGINI.COM

augustus 2001   juli 1999   augustus 1999

© www.oplijn.nl

WWW.VLERK.NL
D: GREA VAN VLERKEN
A: OPLIJN, **M:** VLERK@CHELLO.NL

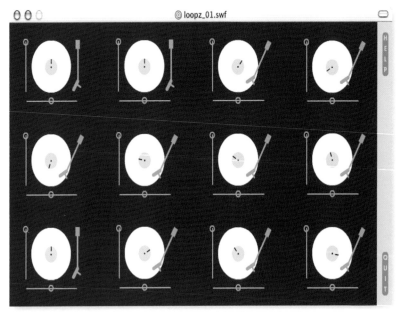

@ loopz_01.swf

WWW.LOOPZ.CH
D: BATCHAS
A: SP-MULTIMEDIA, **M:** INFO@SP-MULTIMEDIA.CH

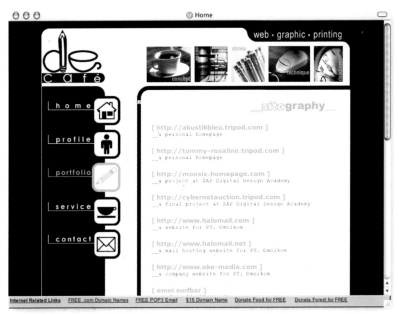

@ Home

web · graphic · printing

sitography

[http://akustikbleu.tripod.com]
__a personal homepage

[http://tommy-rosaline.tripod.com]
__a personal homepage

[http://moosix.homepage.com]
__a project at ZAP Digital Design Academy

[http://cybernetauction.tripod.com]
__a final project at ZAP Digital Design Academy

[http://www.halomail.com]
__a website for PT. Omnikom

[http://www.halomail.net]
__a mail hosting website for PT. Omnikom

[http://www.oke-media.com]
__a company website for PT. Omnikom

[omni surfbar]

Internet Related Links   FREE .com Domain Names   FREE POP3 Email $15 Domain Name   Donate Food for FREE   Donate Forest for FREE

WWW.DECAFE.COM-1.NET
D: ROSALINE DJAYASUKMANA
A: DE-CAFE WEB & GRAPHIC DESIGN, **M:** D_ROSALINE@MAIL.COM

WWW.SERPENTINITY.COM
D: JESSICA BERGLUND
M: DIEHARDCHIC@HOTMAIL.COM

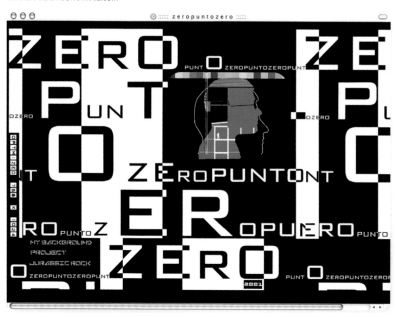

SPAZIOWEB.INWIND.IT/ZEROPUNTOZERO
D: LUIGI PANTUSA
A: KIXART'S, **M:** LUIGIPANTUSA@INWIND.IT

WWW.EVLAB.CJB.NET
D: STEFANO GATTI
M: EFOG@VIRGILIO.IT

MP3.SAMSUNG.RU
D: OLEG TISCHENKOV, **C:** IGOR SHERGIN, **P:** ANDREY VORONKOV
A: ART LEBEDEV STUDIO, **M:** OLEG@DESIGN.RU

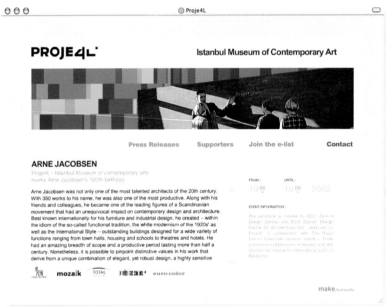

WWW.PROJE4L.ORG
D: OYGAR ERDAL
A: MAKE FRESH MEDIA, **M:** GULG@MAKEFRESHMEDIA.COM

WWW.ZAHNOW.NET
D: JÖRG ZAHNOW
M: JOERG@ZAHNOW.NET

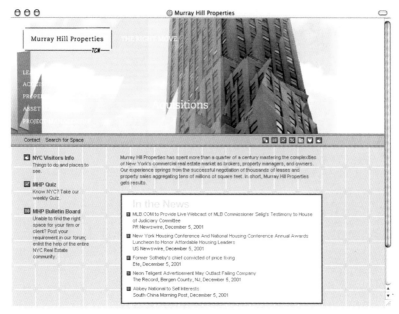

WWW.MURRAYHILL.COM
D: CURTIS MCCLAIN, **C:** KEN MARX
M: AMARGOLIN@MURRAYHILL.COM

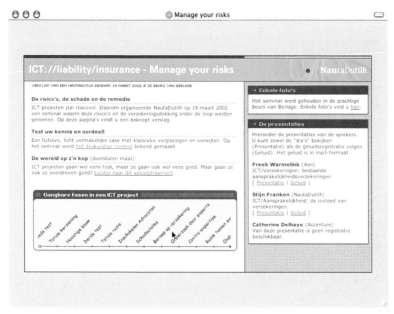

WWW.MANAGEYOURRISKS.NL
D: YACCO VIJN, **P:** HANS VAN DIJK
A: SKIPINTRO, **M:** YACCO@SKIPINTRO.NL

WWW.OLIVECREATE.COM
D: CHIALIANG LIN, **P:** OLIVE GROUP
A: OILVE DESIGN, **M:** CHIALIANG@OLIVECREATE.COM

WWW.01-LA.COM
D: TONY NOVAK
M: INFO@2ADVANCED.COM

WWW.EPISODE12.COM
D: WONG YU HSIANG, **P:** PHYLLIS POH
A: EPISODE 12, **M:** YUHSIANG@EPISODE12.COM

WWW.ZAKI.IT
D: STEFANO PAMPALONI
M: ZAKI@ZAKI.IT

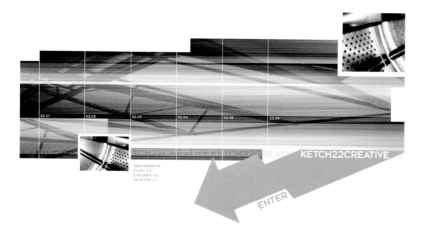

WWW.KETCH22.COM
D: SCOTT KETCHUM
A: KETCH 22 CREATIVE, **M:** SCOTT@KETCH22.COM

WWW.BETWEENDESIGN.COM
D: STANLEY LEUNG
A: -BETWEEN-, **M:** STANLEY@BETWEENDESIGN.COM

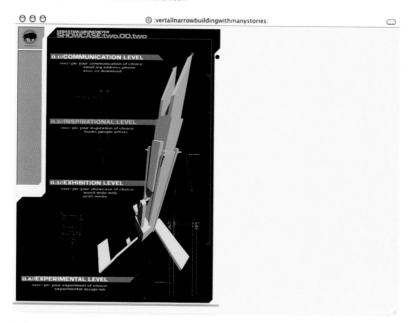

WWW.INDEPENDENTBLUE.COM
D: SEBASTIAN GRONEMEYER
A: INDEPENDENT.BLUE, **M:** SEBASTIAN@INDEPENDENTBLUE.COM

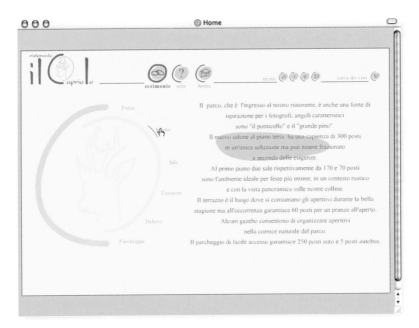

WWW.ILCAPRIOLO.IT
D: DANIELE PODDA
A: LINEACURVA, **M:** INFO@LINEACURVA.IT

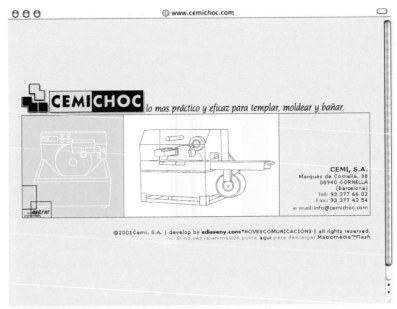

WWW.CEMICHOC.COM
D: EMILIO GARCIA VAZ
A: EDISSENY.COM*NOVESCOMUNICACIONS, **M:** INFO@EDISSENY.COM

WWW.DSPKOMM.DE
D: LUTZ ESSERS
A: DER SPRINGENDE PUNKT KOMMUNIKATION GMBH, **M:** ESSERS@DSPKOMM.DE

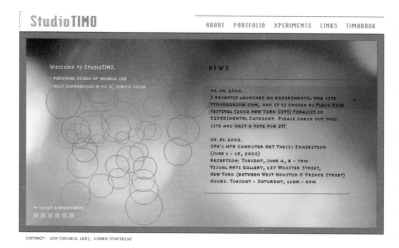

WWW.STUDIOTIMO.COM
D: GICHEOL LEE
M: CAMEO@STUDIOTIMO.COM

WWW.ANNEGRET.DE
D: FRUITCAKE
M: ANNE_FRUITCAKE@HOTMAIL.COM

WWW.D5IVE.COM
D: PAUL B. DROHAN
A: D5IVE, **M:** PAULDROHAN@HOTMAIL.COM

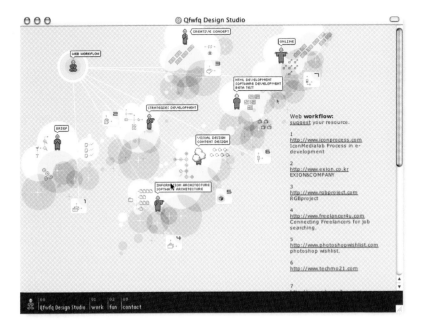

WWW.QFWFQ.COM
D: FRANCESCO MISERERE
A: QFWFQ DESIGN STUDIO, **M:** CICCIO@QFWFQ.COM

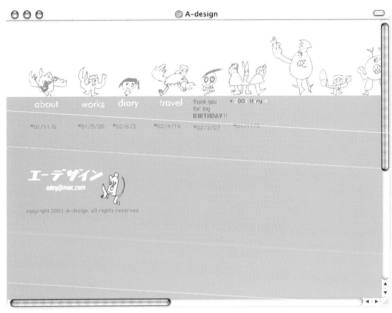

WWW.H3.DION.NE.JP
D: AYA ISHIDA
A: A-DESIGN, **M:** ADEG@MAC.COM

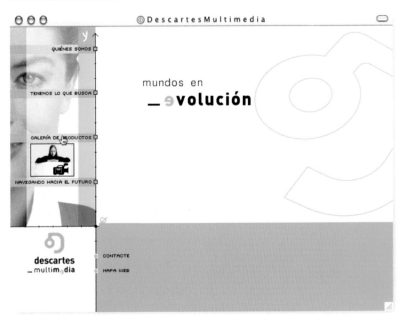

WWW.DESCARTESMULTIMEDIA.ES
D: ESTEBAN-MANCEBO-RIBELLES, **C:** MONTEAGUDO, **P:** USTARAN
A: DESCARTES MULTIMEDIA, **M:** CRIBELLES@DESCARTESMULTIMEDIA.ES

140

⟶ Bgn ⬍	⟶ Dj Pagano ⬍	⟶ Lab01 Dsgn Stmls Dgst ⬍

BGN

Location. Bologna, Italy

Medium. Website: It's a little zine hosting events, shows and culture in pixels. It already counts up some contributions, such as the Frank 151 and Eve 01 illustrations. Print: busisness cards for the Bgn Staff.

DJ PAGANO

Location. Milan, Italy

Medium. Logo. Website: djpagano.it, showcasing all the dj's tour dates, sounds, links, the entire italian tech-house clubscene. The whole project will be online since the summer 2002.

LAB01

Location. Bologna, Italy

Medium. Logo. Website: Lab01 Dsgn Stmls Dgst is an online design zine and it showcases lots of links, interviews with the best designers and some contributions, such as the one with Obinna Izeogu from The Memphis Notebook. It is a personal project.

WWW.KRGHETTOJUICE.COM
D: GIOVANNI PALETTA
M: ME@KRGHETTOJUICE.COM

WWW.FOTOSINTESE.COM
D: FABRICIO S-MENDONCA
A: FOTOSINTESE, **M:** FABRICIO@FOTOSINTESE.COM

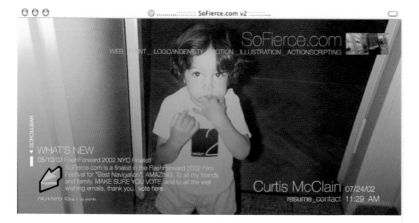

WWW.SOFIERCE.COM
D: CURTIS MCCLAIN
M: CURTIS@SOFIERCE.COM

issue **09**

spring 2002 V. 9

_summary_news_services_mail_chat_versión española

WWW.MUNDOFLY.COM
D: JOSÈ ALFONSO SANZ CLARAMONTE, **C:** ROBERTO RUIZ GUERRERO
A: 3MELLEVO!, **M:** VOLAR@MUNDOFLY.COM

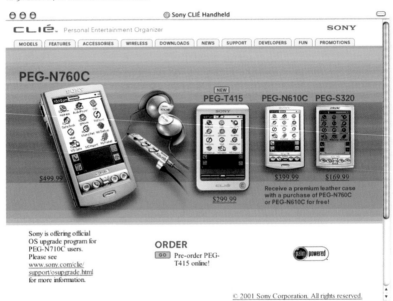

WWW.SONY.COM/CLIE
D: GUNNAR LOCKWOOD, **C:** MATT KARDOS, **P:** RYAN O'LEARY
A: DIGITARIA INTERACTIVE, INC., **M:** DAIGA@DIGITARIA.COM

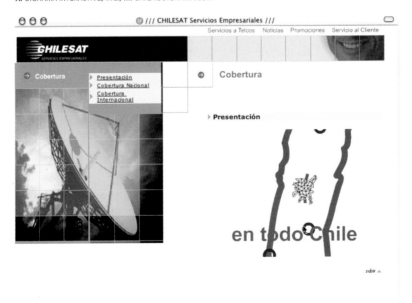

WWW.CHILESATEMPRESAS.CL
D: MAURICIO OLGUIN, MARCOS CORREA
A: EAGENCY.CL, **M:** CONTACTO@MAURICIOOLGUIN.COM

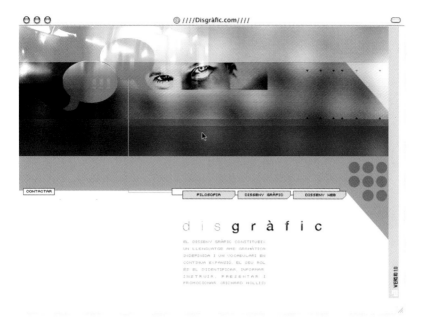

WWW.DISGRAFIC.COM
D: EMMA REIXACH COLL, **P:** ALBERT BATCHELLÌ BAHÌ
A: DISGRAFIC.COM, **M:** INFO@DISGRAFIC.COM

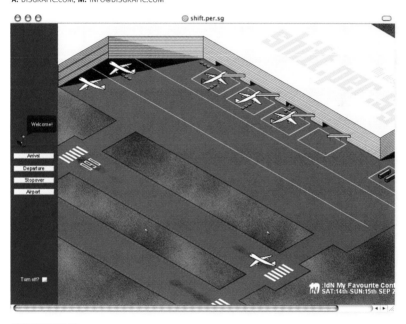

WWW.SHIFT.PER.SG
D: KELVIN TAN
M: LEFT@SHIFT.PER.SG

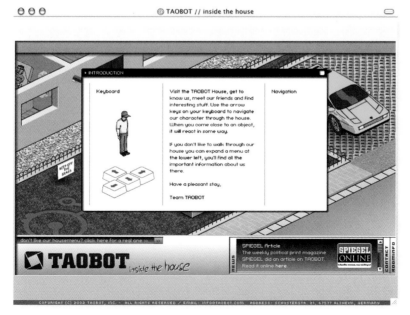

WWW.TAOBOT.COM
D: DANNY FRANZREB
M: DANNY@FRANZREB.COM

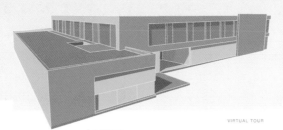

HEALTH CLUB   BEAUTY SALON   RESTAURANT   HOTEL   CONFERENCE FACILITIES   RESERVATIONS   FAQ   CONTACT

VIRTUAL TOUR

Welcome to the website of CLASSFIT.

The company was founded in 2000 with the aim of creating a network of health clubs based on a philosophy of "health, beauty and welfare".
We are looking forward to receiving you as soon as early next year on the new modern premises of the first such club in Let ň any in Prague. You will find there a sports club (squash court and fitness, relaxation and aerobic studios), restaurant, beauty salon, hotel and conference facilities. We believe that the wide choice, along with professional services, will satisfy even the most demanding clients.
On this website, we are going to keep you up to date on the progress of the construction and bring more details about the specific services to be offered.

ãesky   ✉ CLASSFIT

WWW.CLASSFIT.COM
D: MICHAEL CERVENKA, **C:** VACLAV KARGER
M: VACLAV.KARGER@NE.CZ

WWW.DIN.OR.JP/~NEURON
D: MIHO OBINATA
M: NEURON@DIN.OR.JP

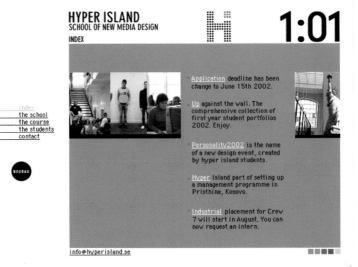

WWW.HYPERISLAND.SE
D: HYPER ISLAND STUDENTS, **P:** ROGER SJÖGREN
M: INFO@HYPERISLAND.SE

144

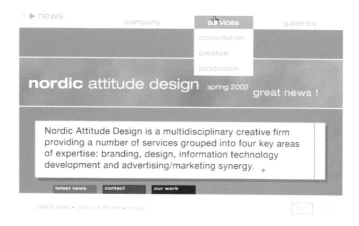

WWW.NORDICATTITUDE.COM
D: RONALD FILION MALLETTE, **P:** NELU WOLFENSOHN
A: NORDIC ATTITUDE DESIGN, **M:** RON@NORDICATTITUDE.COM

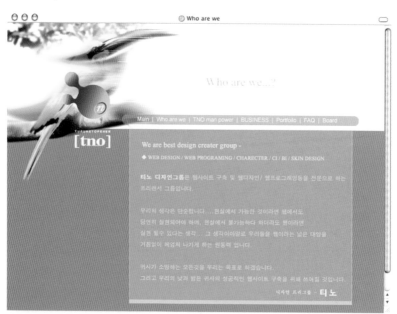

WWW.ORANGEBABIES.COM
D: YACCO VIJN, **P:** HANS VAN DIJK
A: SKIPINTRO, **M:** YACCO@SKIPINTRO.NL

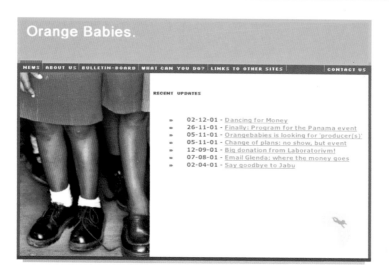

WWW.TNO.CO.KR
D: YOON MYUNG SUK
A: TNO, **M:** WEBMASTER@TNO.CO.KR

WWW.PORENTIEF100.DE
D: ELKE SCHIEMANN, KATRIN LAHR
M: ELKE@HUNGA.DE

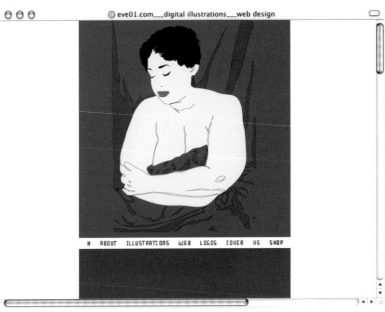

WWW.EVE01.COM
D: ROMINA RAFFAELLI, **C:** STEFANO MARINI
A: WINKLER & NOAH, **M:** INFO@WINKLER-NOAH.IT

WWW.FABRIZIOSILVETTI.COM
D: FABRIZIO SILVETTI
A: NEXUS DIGITAL SOLUTIONS, **M:** FABRIZIOSILVETTI@NEXUS-DS.COM

WWW.CHOPPAL.COM
D: NAOKI OHARA, HIROAKI OHTA
A: MARBLE.CO, **M:** OHTA@CHOPPAL.COM

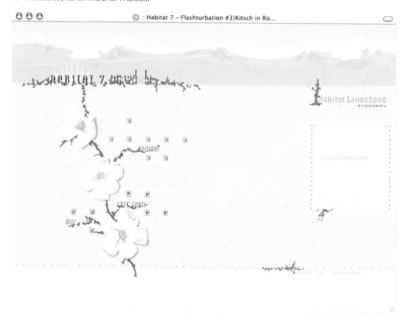

WWW.HABITAT7.DE
D: STEFFEN SCHAEFER
M: FOUNDER@HABITAT7.DE

WWW.GREYMETALDESK.NET
D: MAT POPROCKI
M: MAT@GREYMETALDESK.NET

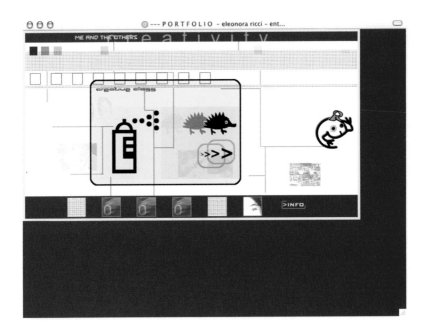

WWW.ELEOLOLA.COM
D: ELEONORA RICCI
M: E.RICCI@CALTANET.IT

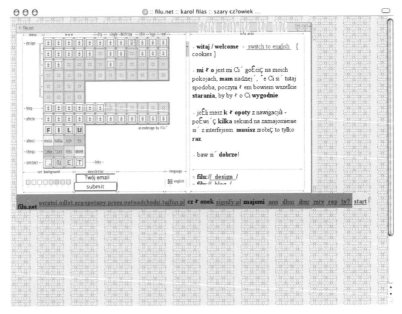

WWW.FILU.NET
D: KAROL FILAS
M: FILU@FILU.NET

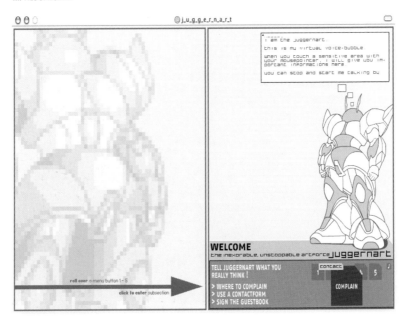

WWW.JUGGERNART.COM
D: MARKUS EICHLER
M: JUGGERNART@JUGGERNART.COM

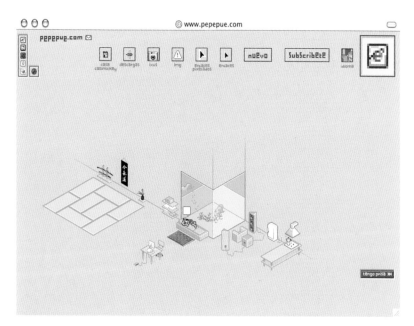

WWW.PEPEPUE.COM
D: PEPEPUE
M: PEPEPUE@PEPEPUE.COM

WWW.GUIAVISUALMADRID.CJB.NET
D: MARCOS GAMELLA
A: GUÌA VISUAL MADRID, **M:** MARCOSGAMELLA@HOTMAIL.COM

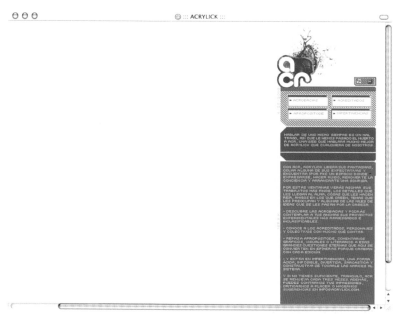

WWW.ACRYLICK.COM
D: NATALIA R.-NOVAL
A: ACRYLICK CO, **M:** INFO@ACRYLICK.COM

WWW.DUASPACE.COM.MY
D: HENRY KHOR
A: DUA SPACE DANCE THEATRE, **M:** HENRYKHOR@LYCOS.COM

WWW.HEKTIK.COM.AU
D: LUCA IONESCU
M: ACUL@OPTUSHOME.COM.AU

WWW.19760203.COM
D: KUMIKO TANAKA
M: TANAKA@19760203.COM

WWW.MARIALBISTUR.COM.AR
D: MAGALI PITERMAN
A: MAGA WEB & GRAFICA, **M:** MARIALBISTUR@HOTMAIL.COM

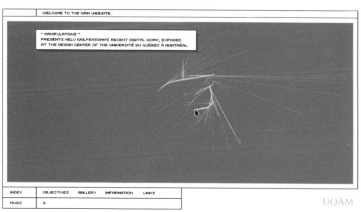

WWW.UQAM.CA/CRIN
D: RONALD FILION MALLETTE, **P:** NELU WOLFENSOHN
A: NORDIC ATTITUDE DESIGN, **M:** RON@NORDICATTITUDE.COM

WWW.HALFPROJECT.COM
D: DREW EUROPEO
A: TEAM HALFPROJECT, **M:** SHOUT@HALFPROJECT.COM

Kommunikation im Internet hat Seltenheitswert:
Sicher, Sie sehen häufiger animierte Bilder, kleine Filmchen, wahre Ebenenfluten.
Aber ist das Kommunikation? Multimedial.

kulturschock versteht sich als Multiplikator der Zukunft. Schockwirkungen als
Energieschub.

DAS KREATIVOGRAMM

WWW.KULTUR-SCHOCK.NET
D: BORIS HAHN, **C:** KATJA BÖHM
A: KULTUR-SCHOCK, **M:** BOEHM@KULTUR-SCHOCK.NET

WELCOME TO SPLENDID.
On this site we will keep you
informed about our activities
throughout the country. Splendid is
the main organisation for UK, US,
2step, underground garage -parties.
Our parties are from an exclusive
nature. The finest people and the
finest sounds are our main target. We
hope you'll enjoy our site and catch
the vibe we stand for.

Yours sincerely,

Selection Splendid Crew

NEW SITE ONLINE.
DIGITAL TRAFFIC has delivered once
again... prepare and get inspired by
their vision!!!

SPLENDID SUMMER SPECIAL
THE ULTIMATE GARAGE MAYHEM...
Prepare for the best. Prepare 4
SPLENDID!

info@splendid-crew.com

WWW.SPLENDID-CREW.COM
D: GLENN LEMING, **C:** JEROME DE KONING, **P:** STEVE TIRBENI
A: DIGITAL TRAFFIC, **M:** S.R.TIRBENI@CHELLO.NL

WWW.HERWORLD.COM
D: HAIKAL LIM
A: SPH ASIAONE LTD., **M:** HAIKAL.LIM@ASIAONE.COM.SG

'Little Red Riding Hood'

e-store | shirts | caps | video | cut

E-STORE | TALES | LABEL | SHOPS | LINKS

WWW.LITTLEREDRIDINGHOOD.DE
D: SUSANNE FUNK
A: STUDIO ORANGE, **M:** DIRK@STUDIOORANGE.DE

WWW.BILDSTATT.DE
D: CHRISTIAN BÜTTNER, MARKUS TEBBERT
A: TEMA MEDIEN GMBH, **M:** CB@TEMA-MEDIEN.DE

WWW.DOLLCOLL.COM.AU
D: JOSH MURRAY
A: JOSH MURRAY DESIGN, **M:** HELLO@JOSHMURRAY.COM.AU

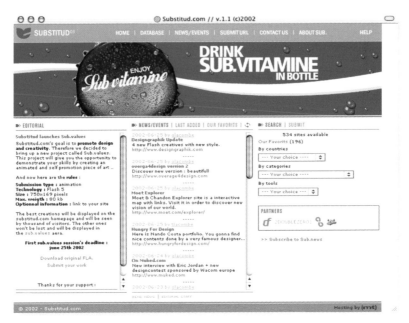

WWW.SUBSTITUD.COM
D: OLIVIER LACOMBE
M: OLACOMBE@SUBSTITUD.COM

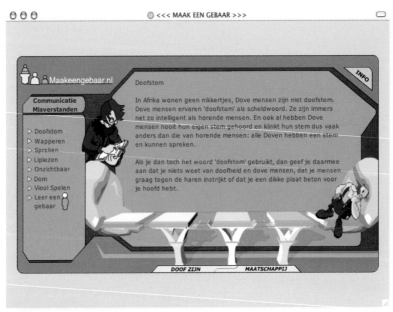

WWW.MAAKEENGEBAAR.NL
D: EMMA HKU, **C:** SANDER VERHOF
A: HKU, **M:** S.VERHOF@CHELLO.NL

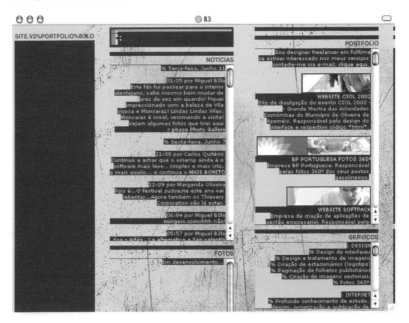

WWW.B3LO.COM
D: MIGUEL BELO
A: MIGUEL@B3LO.COM

A Broad-based Technology Services Integrator

INTIQUA International is a global broad-based technology services integrator that helps companies leverage, develop, and deploy intelligent solutions. Our unique range of offerings are designed to provide the flexibility to clients that require a combination of owning, building, and outsourcing their technology needs.

Services | **Solutions**

News & Events

Business Consulting | Software Engineering | Application Implementation | Outsourcing

February 19, 2002
INTIQUA and Navision Sign Strategic Reseller and Solution Implementation Partnership...
More»

January 24, 2002
Merck Singapore Partners with INTIQUA for Online Branding and Content Management Solution.
More»

Company | Solutions | Services | Partners | Clients | News & Events | Knowledge Center | Careers | Contact us
© Copyright 2002 INTIQUA International Pte Ltd. All rights reserved.

WWW.INTIQUA.COM
D: SELWYN TAN, **C:** FREDERIC LIOW
A: INTIQUA, **M:** SELWYN.TAN@INTIQUA.COM

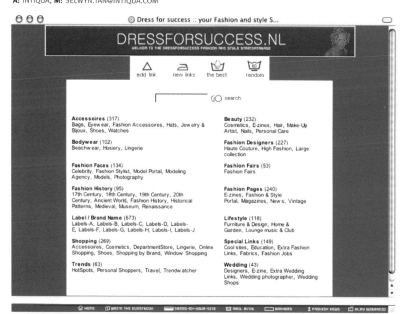

WWW.DRESSFORSUCCESS.NL
D: BIRGIT VAN DEN BEEMT, **C:** DUTCHWEB
A: BLAASJE, **M:** PETER@DRESSFORSUCCESS.NL

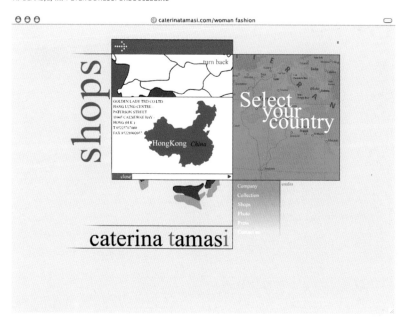

WWW.CATERINATAMASI.COM
D: ANNACHIARA FIGLIA, **P:** TREVI TRADE
A: PAPER DESIGN SNC, **M:** INFO@PAPERDESIGN.NET

WWW.CAROLIN-WREDE.DE
D: CAROLIN WREDE
A: JOURENALISTEN-ZENTRUM HAUS BUSCH, **M:** WREDE@HAUSBUSCH.DE

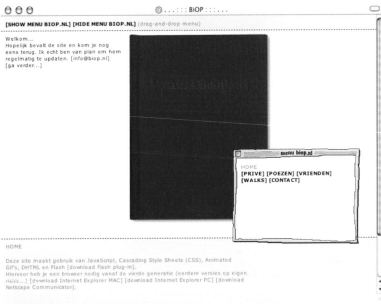

WWW.BIOP.NL
D: JOOST KUIJPERS
M: INFO@BIOP.NL

WWW.DOMESTIKA.ORG
D: WENCESLAO SANZ
M: EQUIPO@DOMESTIKA.ORG

WWW.73553.COM
D: JESSE BRAUN
M: INFO@73553.COM

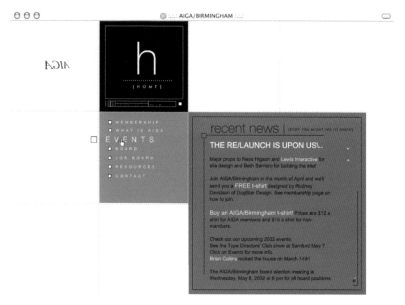

MY OWN
GRAVITY

diseño
b-design

BIOGRAFIA MUSICA NOTICIAS LETRAS CONTACT

REVERSE

WWW.QUEPUNTO.NET
D: MARTIN GARCES
A: B-DESIGN, **M:** MOMIOSTROSKA@ERESMAS.NET

AIGA

h
[HOME]

MEMBERSHIP
WHAT IS AIGA
EVENTS
BOARD
JOB BOARD
RESOURCES
CONTACT

recent news | (STUFF YOU MIGHT YES TO KNOW)

THE RE/LAUNCH IS UPON US!..

Major props to Ness Higson and Lewis Interactive for
site design and Beth Santoro for building the site!

Join AIGA/Birmingham in the month of April and we'll
send you a FREE t-shirt designed by Rodney
Davidson of DogStar Design. See membership page on
how to join.

Buy an AIGA/Birmingham t-shirt! Prices are $12 a
shirt for AIGA members and $16 a shirt for non-
members.

Check out our upcoming 2002 events.
See the Type Directors' Club show at Samford May 7
Click on Events for more info.
Brian Collins rocked the house on March 14th!

The AIGA/Birmingham board election meeting is
Wednesday, May 8, 2002 at 6 pm for all board positions.

WWW.AIGABHAM.COM
D: NESSIM HIGSON, **P:** BETH SANTORO
A: LEWIS COMMUNICATIONS, **M:** NESS@LEWISCOMMUNICATIONS.COM

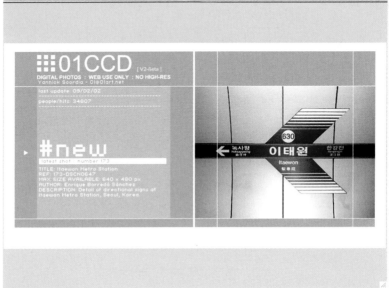

WWW.01CCD.COM
D: YANNICK SCORDIA
M: SUPPORT@01CCD.COM

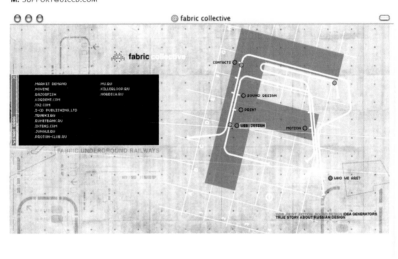

WWW.FABRICCOLLECTIVE.COM
D: ANDREY PELENKOV
A: FABRICCOLLECTIVE, **M:** ONDRIK@NOVENE.COM

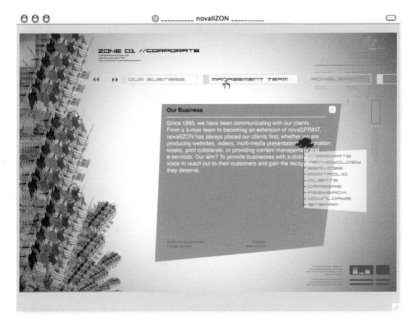

WWW.IIZON.COM
D: GERARD TAN, **C:** ADRIAN NG
M: ROGER.TAN@NOVASPRINT.COM

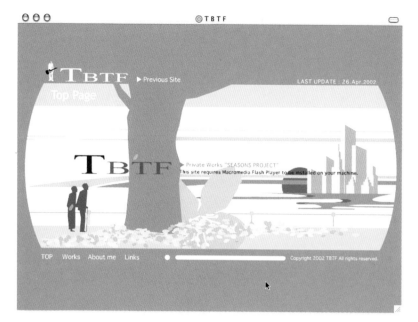

WWW1.TTCN.NE.JP/~TOSHIFUMI
D: TOSHIFUMI TANABU
M: T_TANABU@YBB.NE.JP

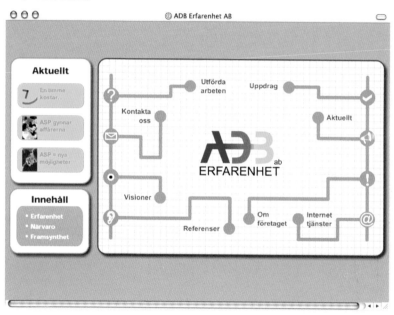

WWW.ADBERFARENHET.SE
D: MAGNUS AGARD / FÈLIX GARCÌA
A: ARKIPO, **M:** FELIX@ARKIPO.COM

WWW.BILLABONG-USA.COM/STORE
D: TODD PURGASON, **C:** PHIL SCOTT
A: JUXT INTERACTIVE, **M:** TODDHEAD@JUXTINTERACTIVE.COM

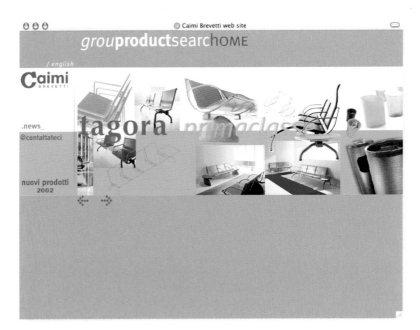

WWW.CAIMI.IT
D: CHIARA MUSSINI, **C:** PAOLO CHIESA
M: INFO@FACTORYGROUP.IT

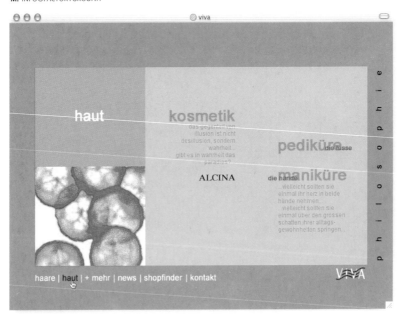

WWW.VIVA-IHR-FRISEUR.DE
D: ANTJE WEBER
A: DIE QUERDENKER, **M:** ANTJEWEBER2000@GMX.DE

WWW.OBJECTS-IN-MOTION.COM
D: TOBIAS IMMEL
A: OBJECTS IN MOTION, **M:** MAILBOX@OBJECTS-IN-MOTION.COM

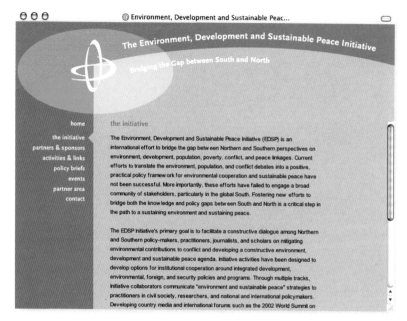

WWW.SUSTAINABLE-PEACE.ORG
D: HELGE WINDISCH, **C:** NIELS MUELLER, **P:** ADELPHI-RESEARCH GMBH
A: FLANEUR DESIGN, **M:** INFO@FLANEUR.DE

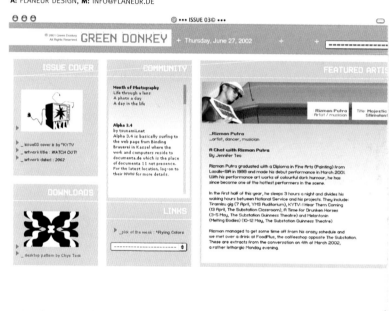

WWW.GREENDONKEY.INFO
D: GERARD TAN
M: PLAYBEN@HOTMAIL.COM

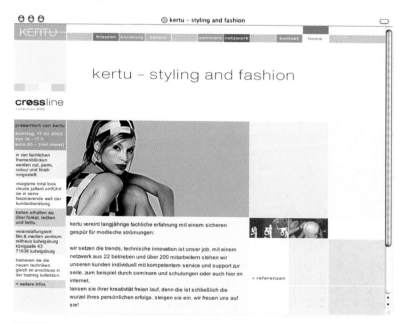

WWW.KERTU.DE
D: MARION BURBULLA, **C:** STEFAN HAACK
M: SCHWARZ.MALER@WEB.DE

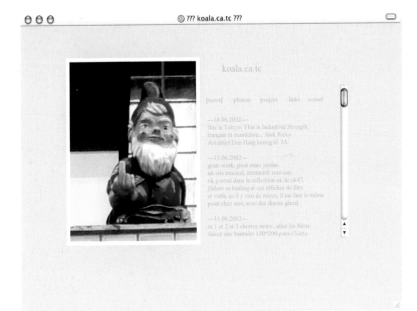

WWW.KOALA.CA.TC
D: PLOUVIER DJE
A: KOALA INC., **M:** KOALA@CA.TC

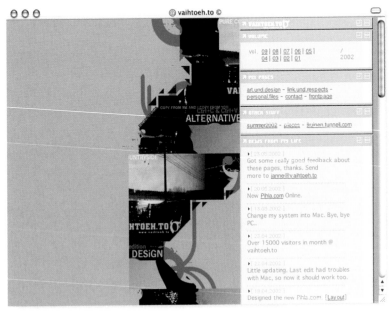

WWW.VAIHTOEH.TO
D: JANNE GYLLING
M: JANNE.GYLLING@VAIHTOEH.TO

WWW.DCTRL.COM
D: LORENZ ANDREAS, **C:** ROBERTO EBERHARD
A: DCTRL - INTERACTIVE MEDIA AND MOTION GRAPHICS, **M:** AL@DCTRL.COM

WWW.FORNARI.COM
D: ANGELO BANDINU
A: RE-LOAD.IT, **M:** ANGELO@DROP.IT

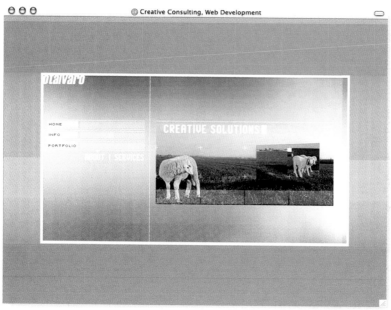

WWW.OTALVARO.COM
D: ANTONIO OTALVARO
M: TONYOTA@HOTMAIL.COM

WWW.NICOLASALAMI.COM
D: MAX BOSCHINI, **P:** NICOLA SALAMI
A: GELATINA, **M:** IO@MAXBOSCHINI.COM

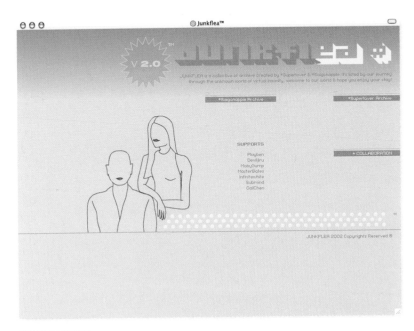

WWW.JUNKFLEA.COM
D: GERARD TAN
M: PLAYBEN@HOTMAIL.COM

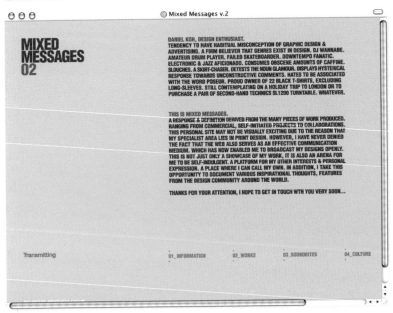

WWW.AMATEURPROVOKATEUR.COM
D: DANIEL KOH
M: DANIEL@AMATEURPROVOKATEUR.COM

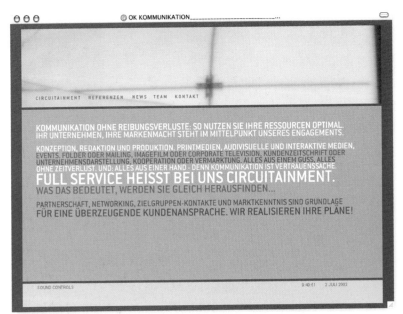

WWW.OK-KOM.DE
D: LARS WOEHNING
A: V2A**NETFORCE**RUHR, **M:** LW@V2A.NET

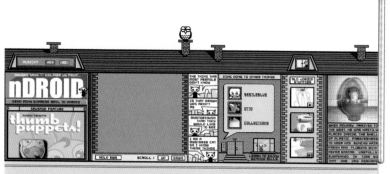

11/15/01
GO TO OT-TO NOW!!!!!!! IT'S HERE, GO GO GO GO (need I explain why nDroid hasn't been updated in months?)

Other nDroid news: some of my illustrations can be found in the second issue of Rojo (the printed magazine).

If you're in the Boston area, please check out

SHOWCASE04 :: UNDERGROUND ANIMATED
Location, Directions :: Berwick Research Institute
When :: Nov 17th, 5:30pm - 11:00pm

Apparently I have a couple pieces showing.

WWW.NDROID.COM
D: VICKI WONG
M: VWONG@MEOMI.COM

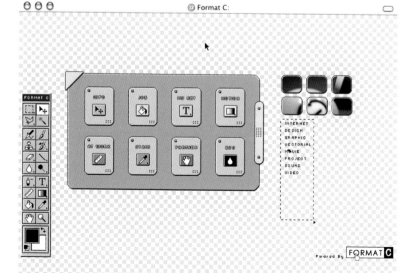

WWW.DABAUS.IT
D: VALERIO LOCATELLI
M: VALERIO.LOCATELLI@DABAUS.IT

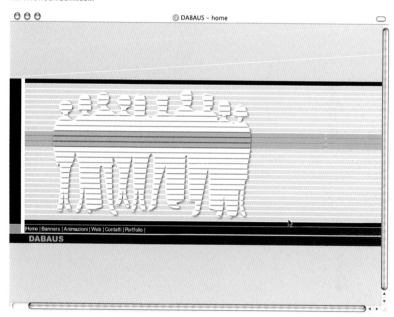

WWW.FORMATC.IT
D: RICCARDO IANNARELLI, **C:** VALERIA RIPPA
A: FORMAT C, **M:** RICCARDO@FORMATC.IT

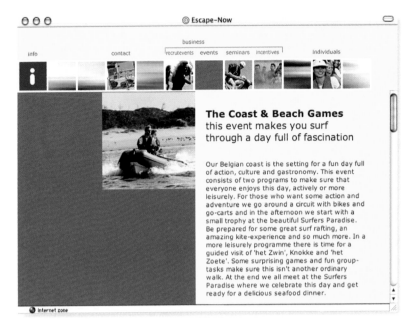

WWW.ESCAPE-NOW.BE
D: BART LEUCKX
A: MAC-A-LEUCKX, **M:** BART@MAC-A-LEUCKX.BE

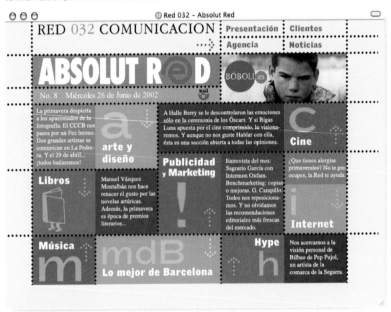

WWW.ABSOLUTRED.COM
D: FERRAN PIQUER, MIRIAM PIQUER, **C:** RAUL MINCHINELA
A: RED 032 COMUNICACION, **M:** ELLAKURIA@RED032.COM

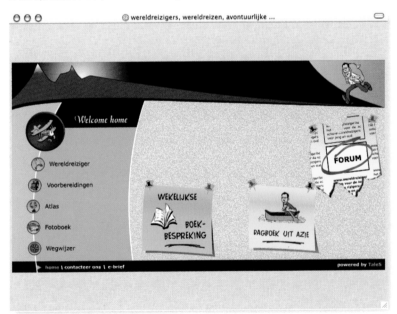

WWW.WERELDREIZIGER.BE
D: BART KENNES
M: BART.KENNES@PANDORA.BE

WWW.MF.DK
D: JON VIBE, **C:** MIKAEL KLANTE
A: SCANAD UDVIKLINGBUREAU, **M:** JV@SCANAD.DK

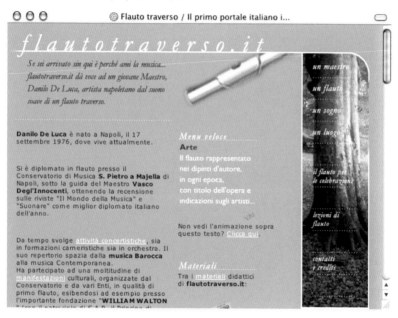

WWW.FLAUTOTRAVERSO.IT
D: ANNACHIARA FIGLIA
A: PAPER DESIGN SNC, **M:** INFO@PAPERDESIGN.NET

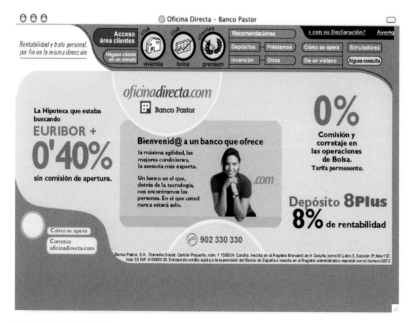

WWW.OFICINADIRECTA.COM
D: LEIRE MAZIZIOR, **C:** ENTREWEBS
A: DIMENSION_INTERACTIVA, **M:** INFO@DIMENSIONINTERACTIVA.COM

WWW.STICKERS.CH
D: CONRAD DEMIAN
A: POINTPIXEL | COMMUNICATION DESIGN, **M:** INFO@POINTPIXEL.COM

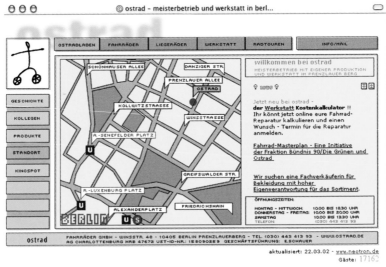

WWW.OSTRAD.DE
D: MICHAEL ZALEWSKI , MAHLKE
A: NEOTRON, **M:** INFO@NEOTRON.DE

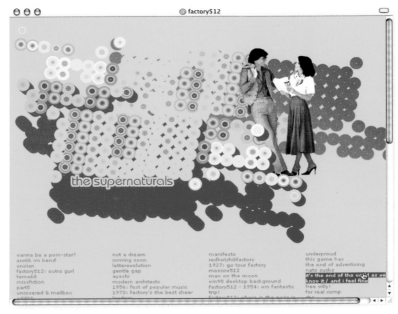

WWW.FACTORY512.COM
D: DMITRY UTKIN
M: DU@FACTORY512.COM

WWW.TCFACTORY.COM
D: OLGA BELYAKOVA
M: INFO@TCFACTORY.COM

WWW.AGFA.COM/AYCC/2001/
D: KOENRAAD CANT
A: GD, **M:** KOEN_CANT@PI.BE

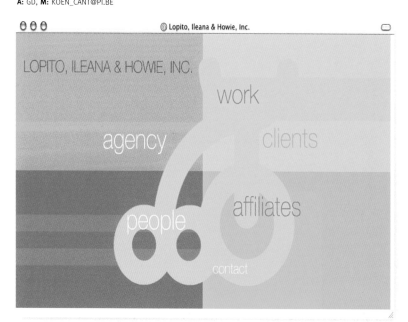

WWW.LIH.COM
D: MARGIE CANTO, **C:** DAVID PARCERISA
A: POPULICOM, **M:** MCANTO@POPULICOM.COM

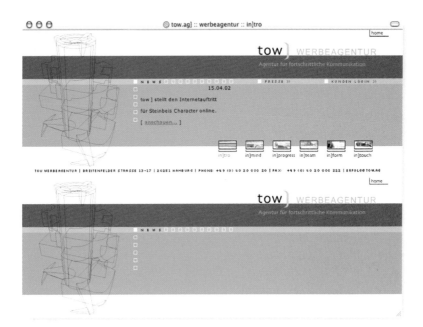

WWW.TOW.DE
D: MAIKE KNOBLAUCH, **C:** BERNHARD PFEIFFER, **P:** TIM TEICHERT
A: TOW] WERBEAGENTUR, **M:** TEICHERT@TOW.DE

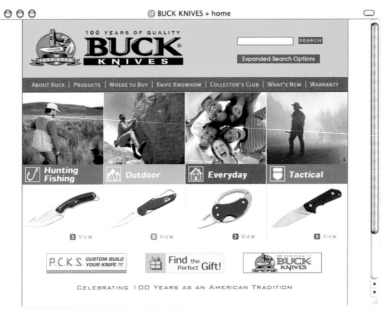

WWW.BUCKKNIVES.COM
D: DAIGA ATVARA, **C:** MATT KARDOS, **P:** RYAN O'LEARY
A: DIGITARIA INTERACTIVE INC., **M:** DAIGA@DIGITARIA.COM

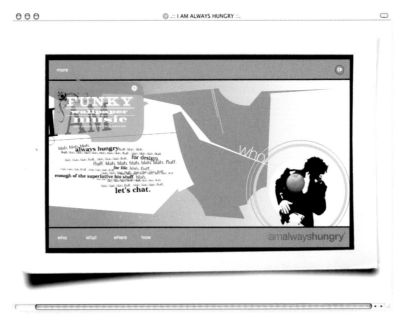

WWW.IAMALWAYSHUNGRY.COM
D: NESSIM HIGSON
M: NESS@IAMALWAYSHUNGRY.COM

WWW.BOSS-SOUNDS.ORG
D: GIORGIO BOSS
A: BOSS-SOUNDS.ORG, **M:** GIORGIO@BOSS-SOUNDS.ORG

WWW.DRUGSTER.ORG
D: BEN HIBON,
A: UNIT9, **M:** UNIT9@UNIT9.COM

WWW.EVIL-MACHINE.COM
D: KEN LEUNG
A: EVIL-MACHINE, **M:** KEN@EVIL-MACHINE.COM

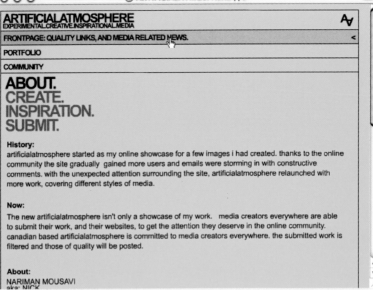

WWW.ARTIFICIALATMOSPHERE.COM
D: NARIMAN MOUSAVI
A: ARTIFICIALATMOSPHERE, **M:** NARIMANM@SHAW.CA

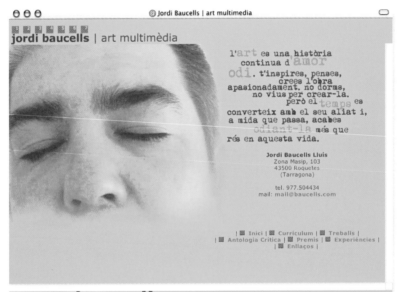

WWW.BAUCELLS.COM
D: JORDI BAUCELLS LLUÌS, **C:** XAVIER CUGAT
A: BAUCELLS.COM, **M:** MAIL@BAUCELLS.COM

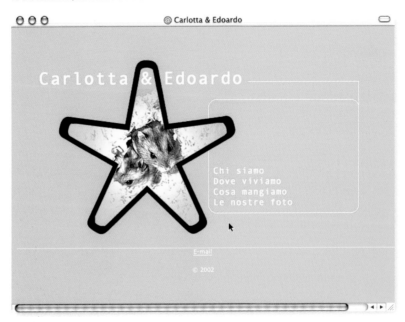

WWW.QUICKDESIGN.IT/CRICETI
D: SVETLANA LEVACHOVA
M: INFO@QUICKDESIGN.IT

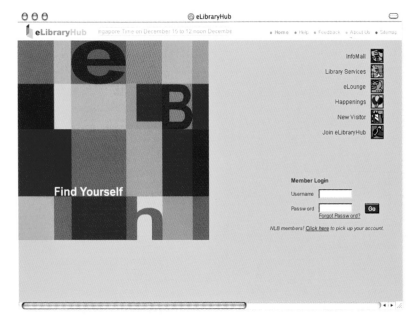

WWW.ELIBRARYHUB.COM
D: LEONG TZI PING, IVAN MP TAN
A: ARETAE LTD., **M:** IVAN.TAN@ARETAE.COM

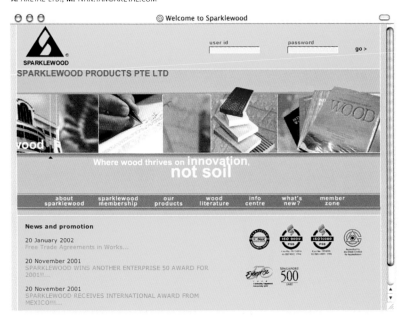

WWW.SPARKLEWOOD.COM
D: HENDRI, **C:** RAGHU, **P:** TAN MANN CHUAN
A: VOXMEDIA, **M:** JOE@VOXMEDIA.COM.SG

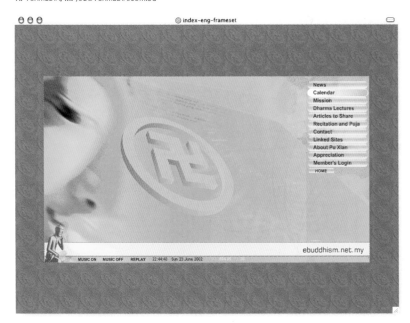

WWW.EBUDDHISM.NET.MY
D: HENRY YAP SWEE CHENG
A: CARDOS MULTIMEDIA SDN. BHD., **M:** SC.YAP@CARDOS.COM.MY

WWW.BESTCHOCOLATEINTOWN.COM
D: JOHN WALKER
A: FLIPSIDE GRAPHICS, **M:** PRINGLE32@AOL.COM

WWW.NOMADRSI.ORG
D: FRANCOIS MORIN
A: FRANKOY DESIGN, **M:** FRANKOY@SYMPATICO.CA

WWW.BIBBIAEDU.IT
D: GIAMPIERO NERI
A: SEED EDIZIONI INFORMATICHE, **M:** G.NERI@GLAUCO.IT

WWW.EOSMEXICO.COM
D: LUIS FERNANDO CASTRO KARG
A: LUFT DESIGN, **M:** LIFER@LUFT.COM.MX

WWW.WAHYUDESIGN.COM
D: WAHYU DEWANTO, **C:** DENYS
A: WAHYUDESIGN, **M:** WAHYU@WAHYUDESIGN.COM

WWW.FAVOURITEWEBSITEAWARDS.COM
D: ROBERT FORD
A: FAVOURITE WEBSITE AWARDS, **M:** WEBMASTER@FAVOURITEWEBSITEAWARDS.COM

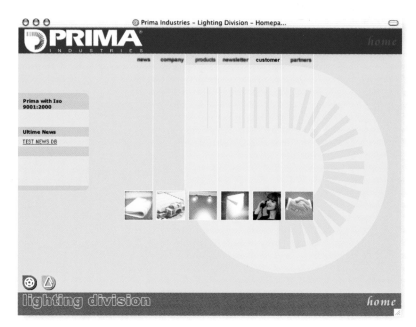

WWW.PRIMAINDUSTRIES.IT
D: ALBERTO ALBERTI
A: SOOLID DESIGN, **M:** INFO@SOOLID.IT

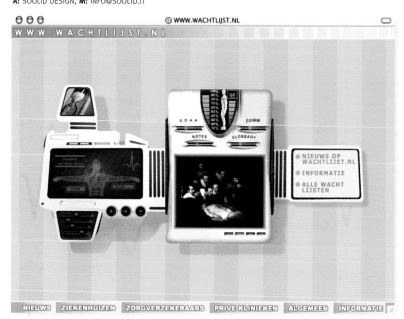

WWW.WACHTLIJSTEN.NL
D: SANDER VERHOF
M: S.VERHOF@CHELLO.NL

WWW.TRESDELINQUENTES.DE
D: THOMAS FIEDLER
A: TRESDELINQUENTES, **M:** THOMAS.FIEDLER@TRESDELINQUENTES.DE

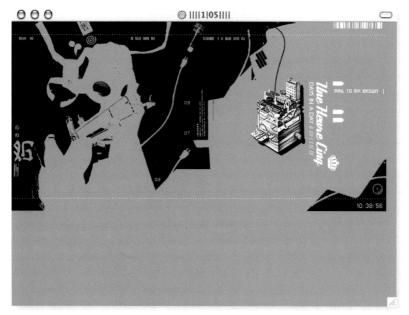

WWW.1H05.COM
D: PIERRICK CALVEZ
A: 1H05, **M:** PCALVEZ@1H05.COM

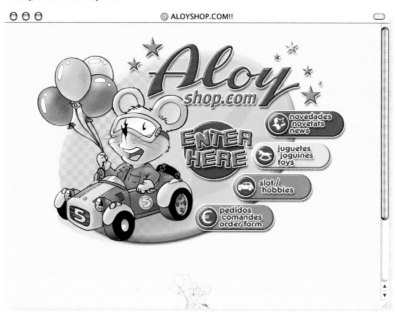

WWW.ALOYSHOP.COM
D: EMILIO GARCIA VAZ
A: EDISSENY.COM*NOVESCOMUNICACIONS, **M:** INFO@EDISSENY.COM

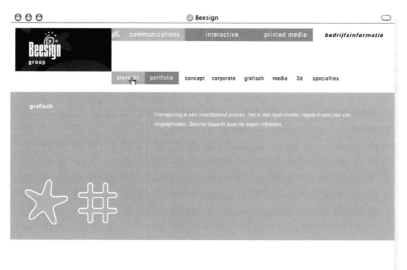

WWW.BEESIGN.NL
D: JEROEN VAN DER HAM, **C:** MARCEL BEEKMANS, **P:** HUGO RAAIJMAKERS
A: BEESIGN INTERACTIVE, **M:** JOEBOB@HETNET.NL

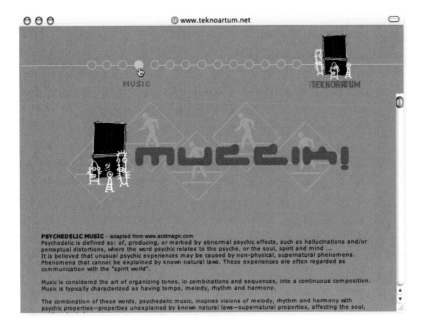

PSYCHEDELIC MUSIC - adapted from www.acidmagic.com
Psychedelic is defined as: of, producing, or marked by abnormal psychic effects, such as hallucinations and/or perceptual distortions, where the word psychic relates to the psyche, or the soul, spirit and mind ...
It is believed that unusual psychic experiences may be caused by non-physical, supernatural phenomena. Phenomena that cannot be explained by known natural laws. These experiences are often regarded as communication with the "spirit world".

Music is considered the art of organizing tones, in combinations and sequences, into a continuous composition. Music is typically characterized as having tempo, melody, rhythm and harmony.

The combination of these words, psychedelic music, inspires visions of melody, rhythm and harmony with psychic properties—properties unexplained by known natural laws—supernatural properties, affecting the soul,

WWW.AANONYMOUS.FREE.FR
D: PAUL JANSSEN
A: INTRASITES, **M:** PJANSSEN@INTRASITES.COM

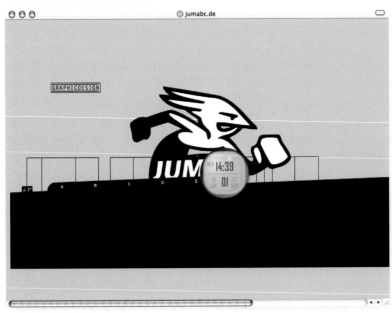

WWW.FORM-ONE.DE/JUM
D: JENS UWE, **C:** CARLO KRUEGER
A: FORM ONE - VISUELLE KOMMUNIKATION, **M:** KRUEGER@FORM-ONE.DE

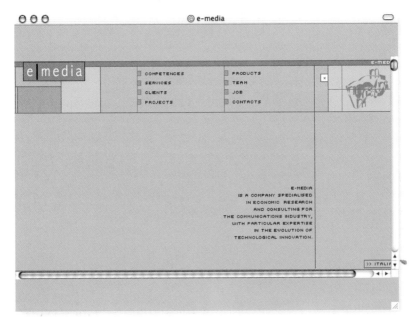

WWW.E-MEDIA.IT
D: CATERINA AGUECI
M: CATE@MARKINO.NET

WWW.INFONEGOCIO.COM
D: MONICA CALVO GIL
M: EENDAR@YAHOO.COM

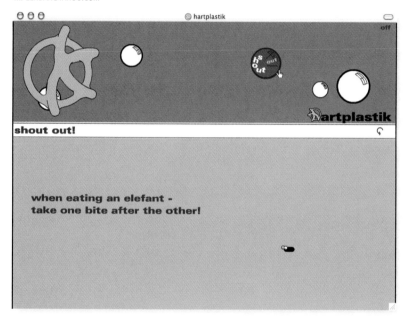

WWW.HARTPLASTIK.COM
D: THOMAS NUSSMÜLLER
A: HARTPLASTIK, **M:** HOME@HARTPLASTIK.COM

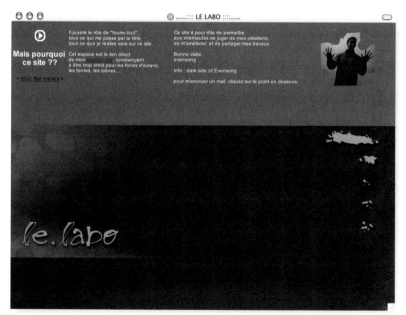

WWW.LABO.T2U.COM
D: LOUIS GAETAN
M: EVENSONG@CARAMAIL.COM

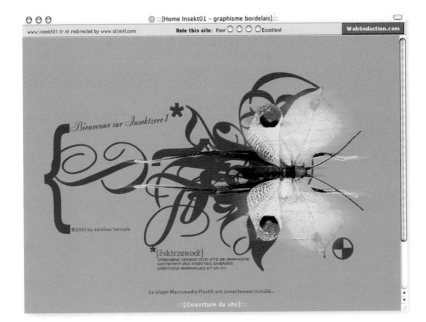

WWW.INSEKT01.FR.ST
D: AURÈLIEN TERRADE
M: INSEK01@FR.ST

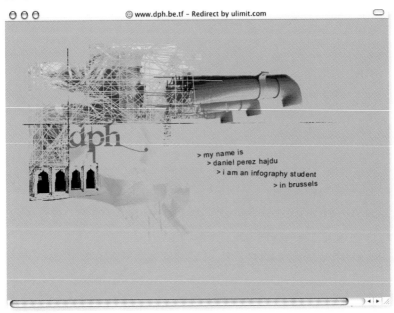

WWW.DPH.BE.TF
D: DANIEL PEREZ HAJDU
M: DANIEL.PEREZ@CHELLO.BE

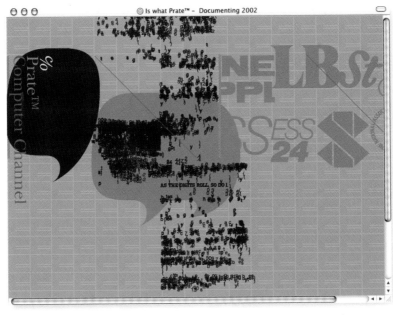

WWW.PRATE.COM
D: JEMMA GURA
M: LENTIL@PRATE.COM

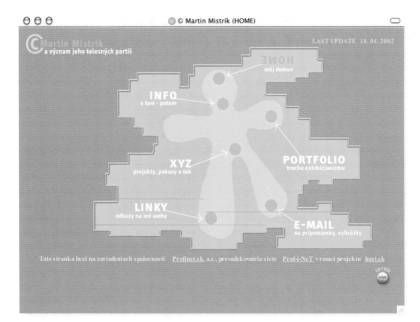

WWW.MISTRIK.HOST.SK
D: MARTIN MISTRIK
M: DVEEM@EMAIL.CZ

WWW.DALIAN-HOGAR.COM
D: ABRAHAM ROIG, **C:** DANI AGUILAR
M: ABRAHAM@ROIG.NET

WWW.MORJAC.DK
D: THOMAS BRIXEN
A: VISUELT DESIGNBUREAU, **M:** BRIXEN@VISUELT.DK

shan shui zeigt neue Wege Körperbewußtsein zu lernen und zu behalten. Es ist ein persönlicher Weg, unseren Organismus aufs neue zu entdecken. Zu verstehen was gut für ihn ist und was nicht.

WWW.SHANSHUI.DE
D: CLAUDIA STEIN
A: CLAUDIA STEIN | DESIGN, **M:** INFO@CLAUDIA-STEIN-DESIGN.COM

WWW.SATORUJAPAN.CO.JP
D: TAKAAKI YAGI
A: FORM::PROCESS, **M:** INFO@FORM-PROCESS.COM

WWW.LABORATORIODIGRAFICAEDESIGN.COM
D: ANNACHIARA FIGLIA, FRANCESCO ESPOSITO
M: PICCERELLA@FREEMAIL.IT

WWW.WEBMISTRESS.COM
D: STEVEN CHASTAIN, **P:** KAT VALENTINE
A: WEBMISTRESS.COM, **M:** NATHALIE@WEBMISTRESS.COM

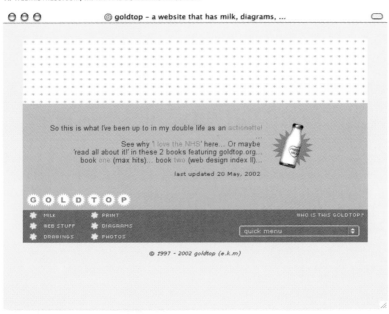

WWW.GOLDTOP.ORG
D: EMERALD MOSLEY
M: GOLDTOP@DIRCON.CO.UK

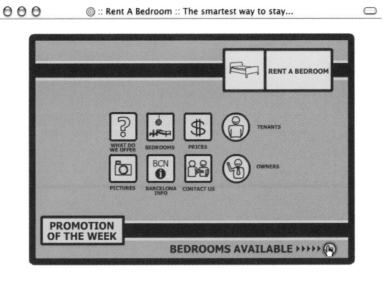

WWW.RENTABEDROOM.COM
D: EDGAR FERDEZ
M: INFO@RAGDE.NET

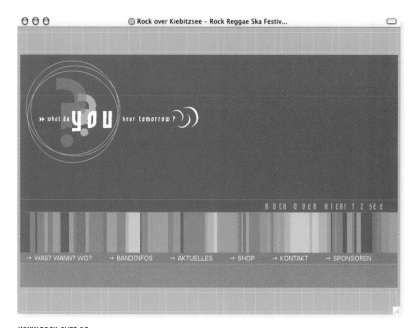

WWW.ROCK-OVER.DE
D: VERA HEIMANN, **C:** CHRISTOPH FRERICKS
A: ISION SALES + SERVICES GMBH & CO KG, **M:** VERA.HEIMANN@ENERGIS-ISION.COM

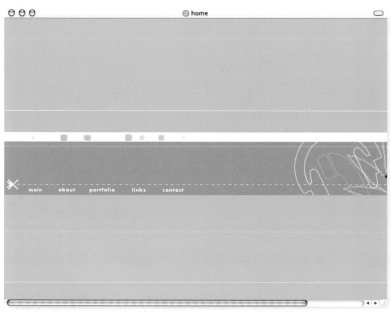

WWW.POPALOCUS.COM
D: YEN
M: YEN@POPALOCUS.COM

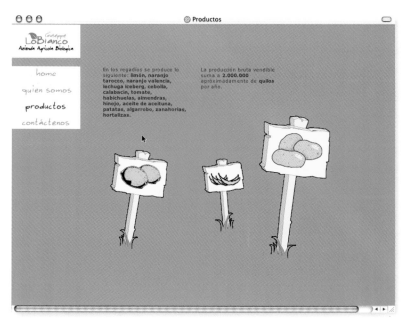

WWW.AGRIBIOLOBIANCO.IT
A: STAXOFT, **M:** D.STACI@STAXOFT.IT

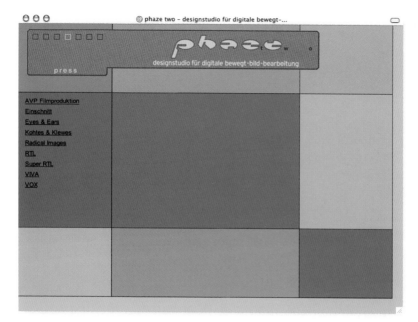

WWW.PHAZETWO.DE
D: UWE WIESEMANN
A: PHAZE TWO DESIGNSTUDIO, **M:** WEBMASTER@PHAZETWO.DE

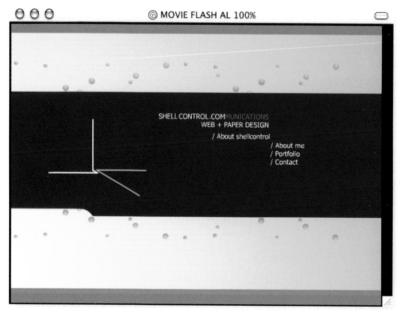

WWW.SHELLCONTROL.COM
D: LUCA ORLANDINI
A: SHELLCONTROL.COM, **M:** INFO@SHELLCONTROL.COM

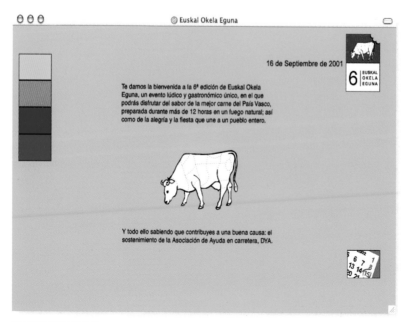

WWW.OKELAEGUNA.COM
D: I. BURGUI, **C:** ENTREWEBS
A: DIMENSION_INTERACTIVA, **M:** INFO@DIMENSIONINTERACTIVA.COM

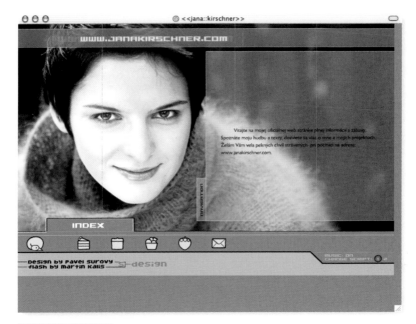

WWW.JANAKIRSCHNER.COM
D: PAVEL SUROVY, **C:** MARTIN KALIS, **P:** JOZKO SEBO
A: S-DESIGN, **M:** KALIS@NEXTRA.SK

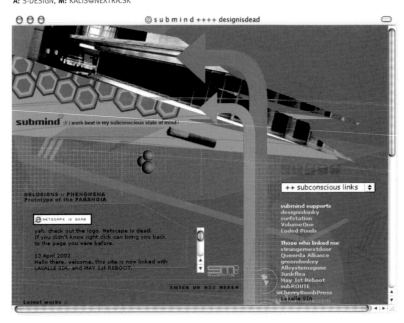

WWW.SUBMIND.I85.NET
D: RON HO
M: CYKOMANIAC@PACIFIC.NET.SG

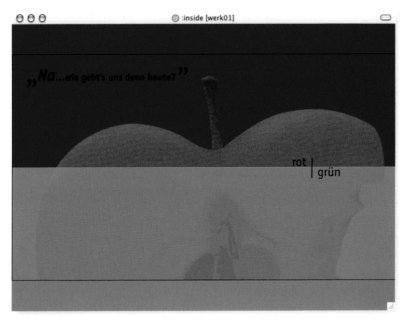

WWW.WERK01.DE
D: HANNO DENKER, **C:** OLIVER MICHALAK
M: HANNO@WERK01.DE

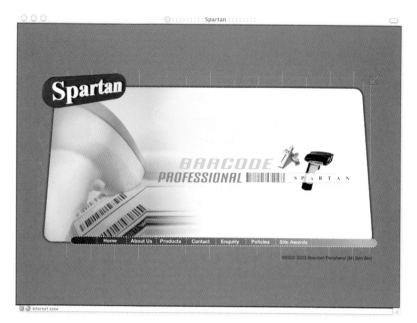

WWW.SPARTAN.COM.MY
D: YEVA CHOW LAI WAN
A: CARDOS MULTIMEDIA SDN. BHD., **M:** LW.CHOW@CARDOS.COM.MY

WWW.ARTEYPAISAJE.COM
D: BORJA BELLOD
A: IMAGEN CONSULTING, **M:** INFO@DARALANDALUS.COM

WWW.BLAASJE.COM
D: PETER BLAAS
A: BLAASJEDOTCOM, **M:** PETER@BLAASJE.COM

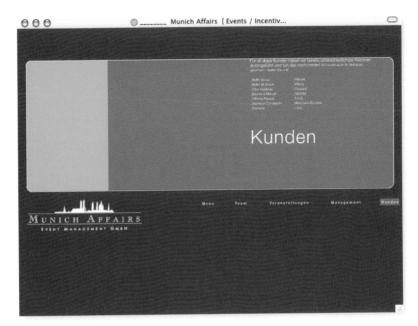

WWW.MUNICHAFFAIRS.DE
D: SEVERIN BRETTMEISTER
A: FA-RO MARKETING, **M:** SEVERIN@FA-RO.DE

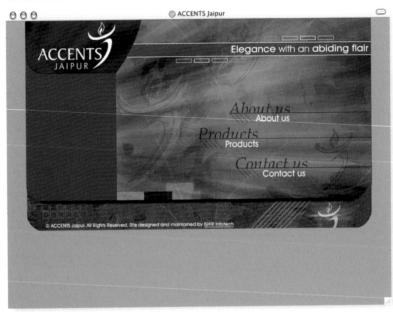

WWW.ACCENTSJAIPUR.COM
D: SUMIT RAMPAL
A: ISHIR INFOTECH, **M:** SRAMPAL@ISHIR.COM

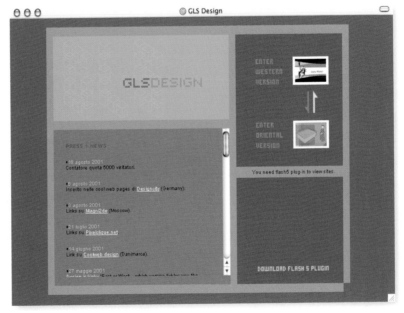

WWW.GLSDESIGN.IT
D: GIUSEPPE LA SPADA
A: GLS DESIGN, **M:** GLASPADA@LIBERO.IT

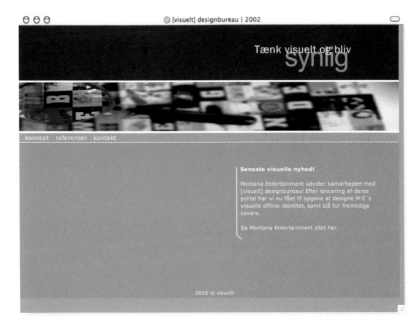

WWW.VISUELT.DK
D: THOMAS BRIXEN
A: VISUELT DESIGNBUREAU, **M:** BRIXEN@VISUELT.DK

WWW.KLEINGAERTNER.AT
D: MARTIN BUECHELE
M: BUECHELE@AON.AT

WWW.JULIANSANDEROBJEKTE.COM
D: JULIAN PHILLIP SANDER
M: JULIAN@JULIANSANDEROBJEKTE.COM

WWW.FUJIFILM.CA
D: SHAWN SQUIRES
A: MARCH NETWORKS, **M:** SSQUIRES@PATHCOM.COM

WWW.RICEBAY.COM
D: GARY CHUNG
A: PLUS ONE OFFICE, **M:** MYLC3@YAHOO.COM

WWW.MPDL.ORG
D: ELIAS MEGIDO
A: EMVISUAL, **M:** EMVISUAL@IMEDIA.ES

WWW.DEDECOM.DE
D: TINO DEGNER
A: DEDECOM :: DIGITAL SOLUTIONS, **M:** CONTACT@DEDECOM.DE

WWW.NOVALINEASCALE.IT
D: MASSIMO BAZZO, **C:** A. FACCHINI, **P:** DACOS NETWORK SOLUTIONS
M: MBAZO@MCLINK.IT

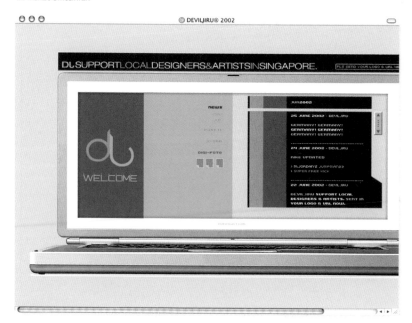

WWW.DEVILJIRU.COM
D: ROGER TAN
M: ROGER@DEVILJIRU.COM

WWW.BELGOBRIKO.IT
D: MADASCHI LUCA
M: LUCA@GRAFFITIVARESE.IT

WWW.HISPIC-CAFE.COM
D: HISASHI YUYA
A: HISPIC CAFE, **M:** BEACH@HISPIC-CAFE.COM

WWW.1844DESIGN.COM
D: DAN HUNTER
A: DGRAPHIKS.NET, **M:** DANHUNTERH@HOTMAIL.COM

WWW.INDEXNOW.COM
D: MARK MALONEY, **C:** DAVINCI EBUSINESS
A: NOIINX, **M:** MARK@NOINC.COM

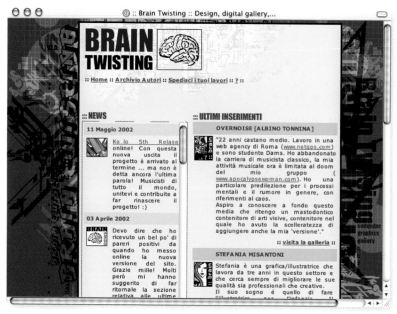

WWW.BRAINTWISTING.COM
D: DANIELE CASCONE
M: INFO@BRAINTWISTING.COM

WWW.KELGAN29.COM
D: KELVIN GAN KEN WEI
M: KELGAN29@KELGAN29.COM

WWW.MEDIUMRARE.NL
D: JAN GUICHELAAR
A: MEDIUMRARE ID, **M:** GUICH@MEDIUMRARE.NL

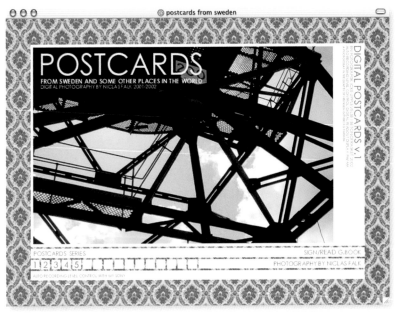

WWW.PLYSCH.CJB.NET
D: NICLAS FALK
A: ADAPTOR, **M:** NICLASFALK@SWIPNET.SE

WWW.ARTICHOKES.ORG
D: BRIAN GRATTAN
A: YNOT MEDIA, **M:** BRIAN@YNOTMEDIA.COM

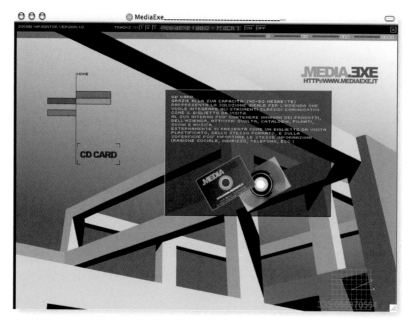

WWW.MEDIAEXE.IT
D: MARCO TESTONI
A: MEDIAEXE, **M:** INFO@MEDIAEXE.IT

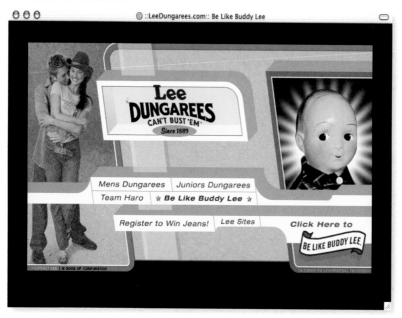

WWW.LEEDUNGAREES.COM
D: TRAVIS BECKHAM, LUKE KNOWLES
A: LOOKANDFEEL NEW MEDIA, **M:** COSHIELDS@LOOKANDFEEL.COM

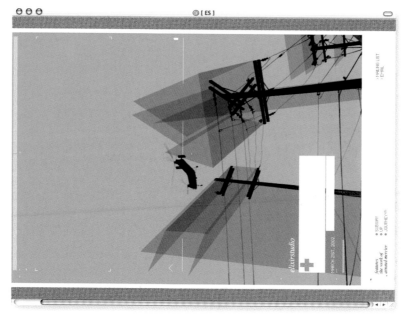

WWW.ELIXIRSTUDIO.COM
D: ARNAUD MERCIER
M: ARNAUD@ELIXIRSTUDIO.COM

WWW.BIODIVIETNAM.COM
D: DAVID NAVARRO GOMEZ, **P:** ENK3
M: NAVARRO@ENK3.COM

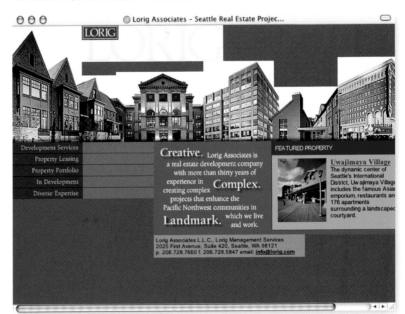

WWW.TEOTATO.COM
D: ALESSANDRA TAGLIABUE
A: PHASEZERO.DE, **M:** ALESSANDRA@PHASEZERO.DE

WWW.LORIG.COM
D: ERICH SCHRECK, **C:** STEPHANIE KRIMMEL
A: GIRVIN INC., **M:** SCHRECK@GIRVIN.COM

WWW.SOLIDAGO.QC.CA
D: FRANCOIS MORIN
A: FRANKOY DESIGN, **M:** FRANKOY@SYMPATICO.CA

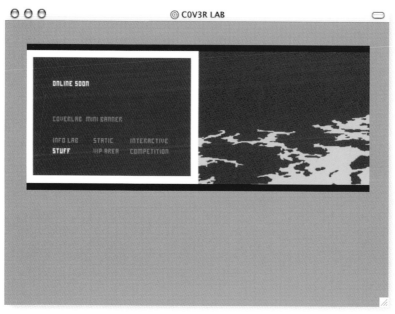

WWW.COVERLAB.COM
D: GIUSEPPE LA SPADA
A: GLS DESIGN, **M:** INFO@GLSDESIGN.IT

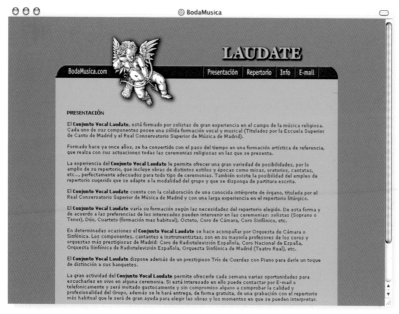

WWW.BODAMUSICA.COM
D: JORGE ZUBIRIA TOLOSA
A: ZUBIRIA DISENO, **M:** JORGE@ZUBIRIA.COM

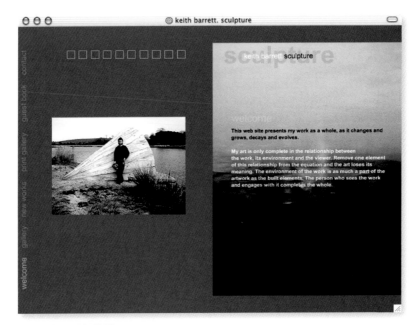

WWW.KEITHBARRETT.CO.UK
D: JUSTIN COCKBURN, **C:** PHELIM CAVLAN
A: ONEBESTWAY, **M:** MIKE@ONEBESTWAY.COM

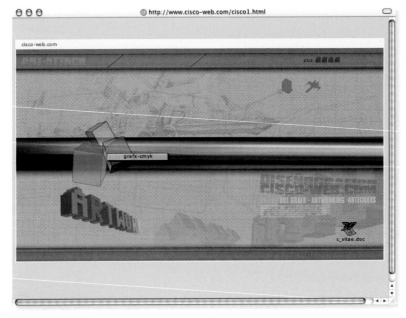

WWW.CISCO-WEB.COM
D: CISCO
M: CISCO@MENTA.NET

WWW.INFITEL.DE
D: CHRISTIAN BRACKMANN, **P:** INFITEL
A: ECC ONLINE RELATIONS, **M:** KA@OZ-ZONE.DE

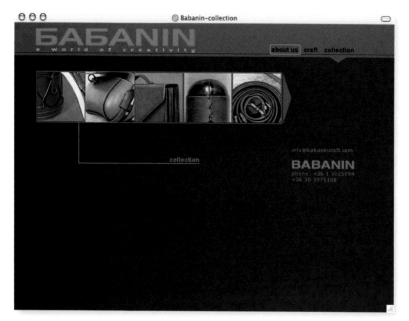

WWW.BABANINCRAFT.COM
D: NYIRY GEZA
A: NYK, **M:** MAIL@NYK.HU

WWW.TERMINMASCHINE.DE
D: ANDRÉ NITZE
A: NEW IMAGE, **M:** NITZE@N-IMAGE.COM

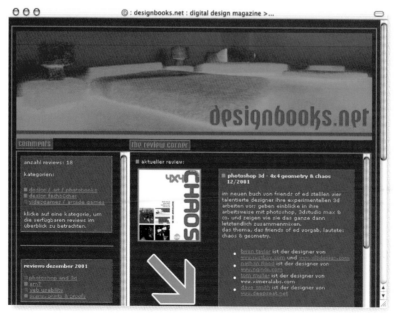

WWW.DESIGNBOOKS.NET
D: DIRK BEHLAU
A: PIXELEYE INTERACTIVE, **M:** DIRK@PIXELEYE.NET

WWW.PAPERDESIGN.NET
D: ANNACHIARA FIGLIA
A: PAPER DESIGN SNC, **M:** INFO@PAPERDESIGN.NET

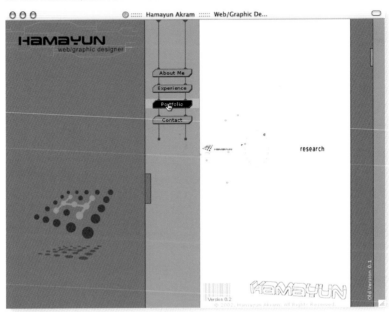

WWW9.BRINKSTER.COM/HAMAYUN
D: HAMAYUN AKRAM
M: AHAMAYUN@HOTMAIL.COM

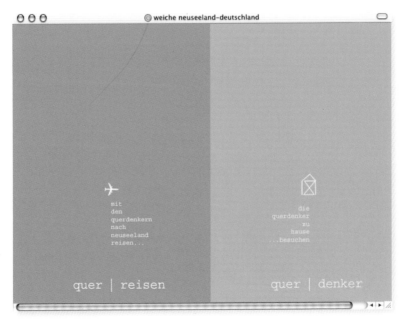

WWW.DIE-QUER-DENKER.DE
D: ANTJE WEBER, HANNO DENKER
M: QUERDENKER2000@GMX.DE

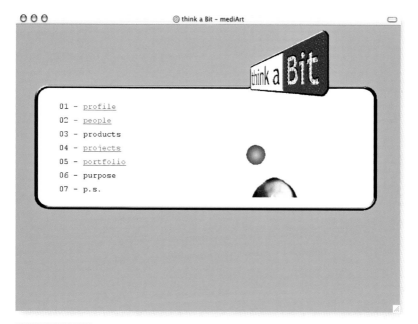

WWW.THINKABIT.NET
D: OLIVER HUNGER
A: THINK A BIT, **M:** OLIVER@THINKABIT.NET

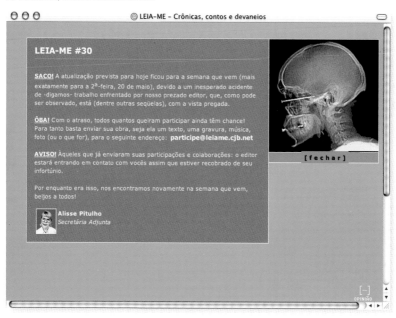

WWW.LEIA-ME.COM
D: JO SOARES
A: REDE GLOBO, **M:** JO@GLOBO.COM

WWW.ARTCOUP2.COM
D: BOOGIE
M: BOO@DEADBYDESIGN.COM

WWW.PHOTOSHOPWISHLIST.COM
D: SHANE PERRAN, **C:** ROBERT WHITE
A: STUDIO Z, **M:** SPERRAN@TELEPIX.COM

WWW.PEPPERMIND.DE
D: MARIA LUISA VALLEJO
M: ML.V@GMX.DE

WWW.GARAGEREGIUM.COM
D: PATRICIA FUENTES
A: BLUE PLANET, **M:** P.FUENTES@RETEMAIL.ES

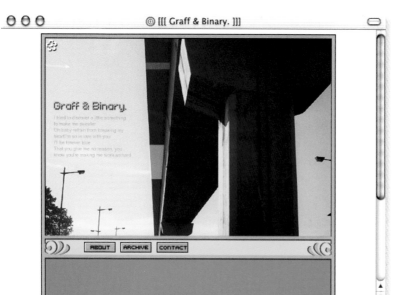

WWW.GRAFF-AND-BINARY.COM
D: HIROSHI YAMAGUCHI
A: GRAFF & BINARY, **M:** INFO@GRAFF-AND-BINARY.COM

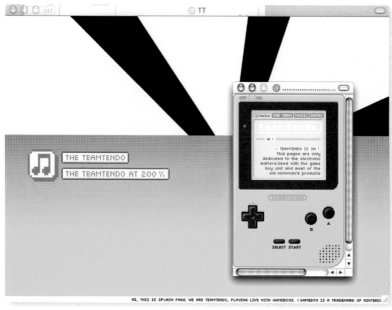

WWW.TEAMTENDO.NET
A: TEAMTENDO, **M:** TEAMTENDO@GO.COM

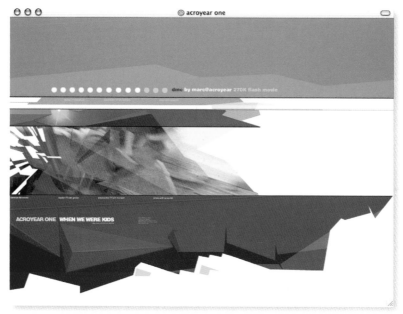

WWW.ACROYEAR.CO.UK
D: MARC GARFIELD, **C:** NICK LAND, **P:** JIM MORGAN
A: ACROYEAR DESIGN PROJECTS, **M:** INFO@ACROYEAR.NET

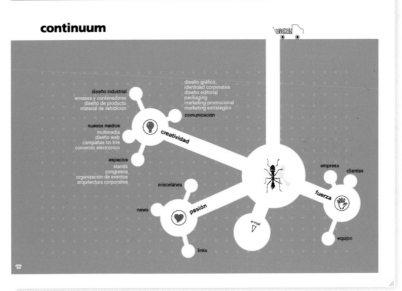

WWW.CONTINUUM.ES
D: SEBASTIAN PEREZ
A: CONTINUUM, **M:** CONTINUUM@CONTINUUM.ES

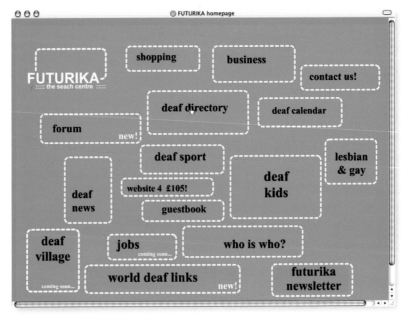

WWW.FUTURIKA.COM
D: BORA TUKENMEZ
A: FUTURIKA, **M:** FUTURIKA1@HOTMAIL.COM

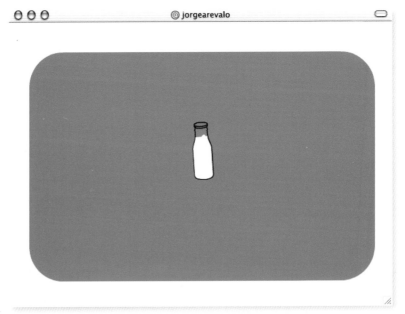

WWW.JORGEAREVALO.COM
D: MARTÌN ALVAREZ COMESAÑA, **P:** JORGE ARÈVALO
M: COMESANHA@TELELINE.ES

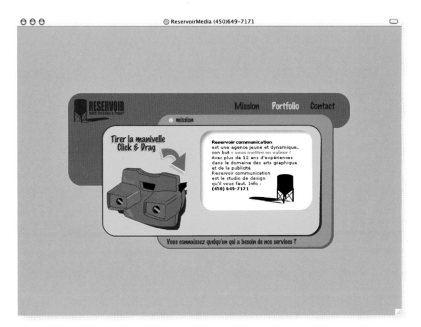

WWW.RESERVOIRMEDIA.COM
D: DARKCARD
M: MIKE@RESERVOIRMEDIA.COM

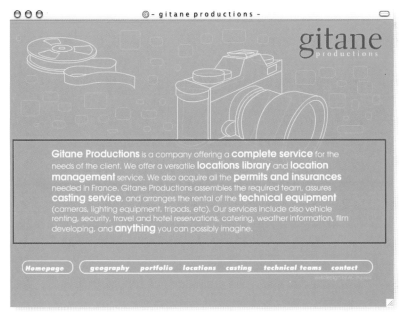

WWW.GITANEPRODUCTIONS.COM
D: KIMMO KUUSISTO, MISA KANNOS
A: AC-MAINOS, **M:** KIMMO@ACMAINOS.FI

WWW.CELTICONSULTING.COM
D: LUIS DIAZ CERVANTES, **P:** ALEX MENA
A: ESFERA - INTERACTIVA, **M:** LDIAZ@TINET.FUT.ES

WWW.LOOKANDCLICK.COM
D: NATALIA MOJICA, **C:** NETMARC, **P:** ALBERTO MARCH
A: GRAFMARC, **M:** NATALIAM@GRAFMARC.COM.VE

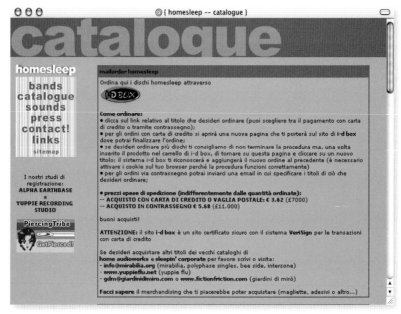

WWW.HOMESLEEP.IT
D: ALEX DI GANGI, **P:** HOMESLEEP RECORDS
M: ALEX@GAMMAWEB.IT

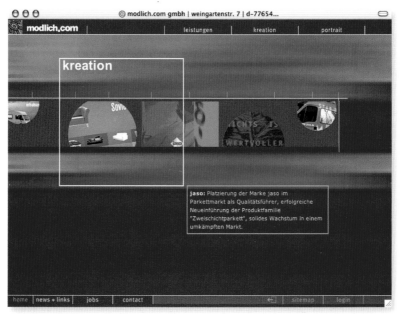

WWW.MODLICH.COM
D: GERD MODLICH, JEAN MIERECKE
A: MODLICH.COM GMBH, **M:** INFO@MODLICH.COM

206

WWW.DARKELEPHANT.COM
D: MELVIN DE LOS SANTOS
A: DARKELEPHANT, **M:** BABAR@DARKELEPHANT.COM

WWW.IDEALCARTA.IT
D: NICOLA DESTEFANO
A: GDG_MEDIA, **M:** EMPUSA@VIRGILIO.IT

WWW.DERUSH.COM
D: ANDERS SCHROEDER
M: ANDERS@DERUSH.NET

WWW.CHILILOUNGE.DE
D: FRANK SCHMIDT-ARNDT
A: ART.5 TEXTKONTOR INTERNET SUPPORT, **M:** FSA@ART5AGENTUR.DE

WWW.ESPACIA.NET
D: MIGUEL ARENCIBIA, **C:** ORLANDO PERDOMO, **P:** MILA GONZALEZ
A: ESPACIA NETWORKS, S.L.

WWW.VICCARBE.COM
D: HÈCTOR DIEGO
M: VICCARBE@VICCARBE.COM

NÖIGKEITE GIG'S D'BÄND DS ALBUM FÖTELI'S GÄSCHTEBUECH KONTAKT

WWW.PLUESCH.CH
D: NADIO LOOSLI
A: WEBLOTION, **M:** NADIA@NALOO.NET

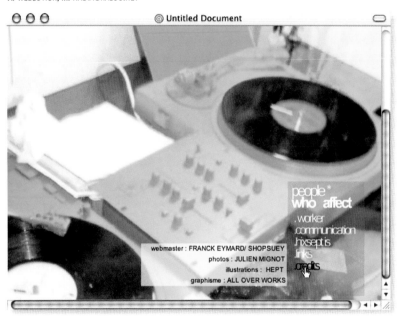

webmaster : FRANCK EYMARD/ SHOPSUEY
photos : JULIEN MIGNOT
illustrations : HEPT
graphisme : ALL OVER WORKS

people *
who affect
.worker
.communication
.hixsept.s
.links
.credits

WHIXSEPT.FREE.FR
D: FRANCK EYMARD
M: CONTACT@HIXSEPT.COM

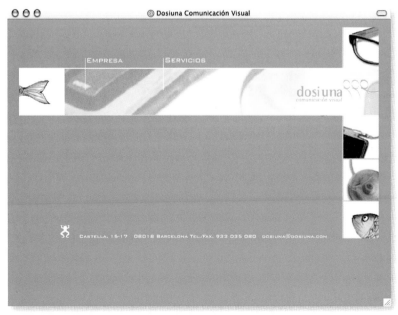

EMPRESA   SERVICIOS

dosi una
comunicación visual

CASTELLA, 15-17 08018 BARCELONA TEL./FAX. 932 035 080 DOSIUNA@DOSIUNA.COM

WWW.DOSIUNA.COM
D: ELISENDA VIVES PRATS
A: DOSIUNA, **M:** DOSIUNA@DOSIUNA.COM

WWW.PIACENZANIGHT.COM
D: NICOLA BELLOTTI, **C:** GHITA PASQUALI
A: BLACKLEMON S.R.L., **M:** E.PASQUALI@NUOVEMODELLE.COM

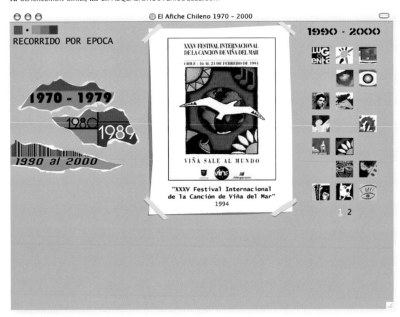

WWW.ELAFICHECHILENO.CL
D: JULIO GARCÌA, SUSANA BURGOS, **C:** CLAUDIO QUINTANA
A: CREA-DOS, **M:** AFICHE@MAIL.COM

WWW.PROGRIP.IT
D: BEPPE DIENA
A: LOGICAL NET, **M:** GIUSEPPE@LOGICAL.IT

WWW.HISTORISKA.SE/VITTOLJUD
D: SAM SOHLBERG
A: LONEGÅRD & CO, **M:** SAM@LONEGARD.SE

WWW.BLOTTY.COM
D: OTTY SOEMITRO
M: BLOTTY2@HOTMAIL.COM

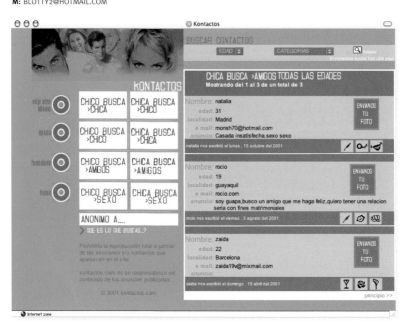

WWW.KONTACTOS.COM
D: CORI GRAU
A: WEBFACTORY INTERNET, S.L., **M:** WF@WEB-FACTORY.COM

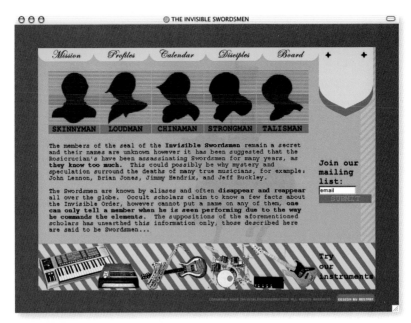

WWW.INVISIBLESWORDSMEN.COM
D: MARGARET PENNEY
M: MARGARET@RESTARTSTUDIO.COM

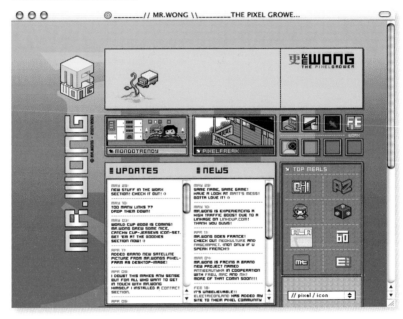

WWW.MRWONG.DE
D: MATHIAS TEMMEN
M: CHICKENSOUP@MRWONG.DE

WWW.EVAGARDE.IT
D: FEDERICO ROCCO, **C:** DAVIDE RUSSO
A: KETTYDO | BEAUTYFARM, **M:** FEDERICO@KETTYDO.COM

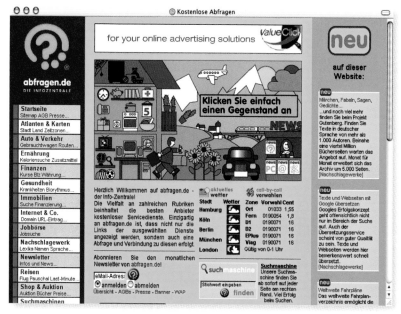

WWW.ABFRAGEN.DE
D: STEFAN BEHRINGER, **C:** JUERGEN WUNDERLE
A: D:\SIGN CREATIVECONCEPTS, **M:** BEHRINGER@DSIGN.DE

WWW.BODEGASOFOURNIER.COM
D: DAVID NAVARRO
A: ENK3, **M:** NAVARRO@ENK3.COM

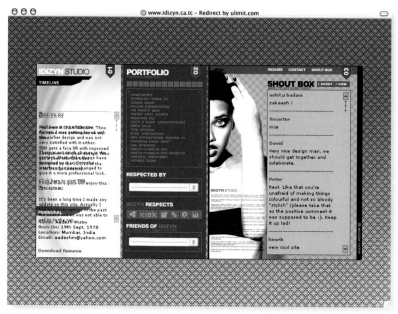

WWW.IDIZYN.CA.TC
D: AADESH MISTRY
A: IDIZYN STUDIO, **M:** AADESHM@YAHOO.COM

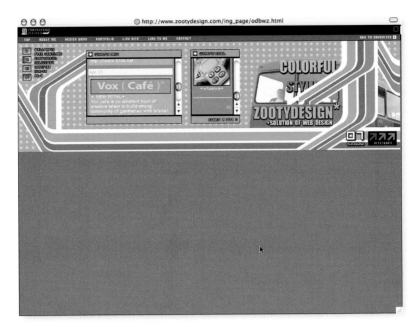

WWW.ZOOTYDESIGN.COM
D: SUNGSU-YOO
M: INFO@ZOOTYDESIGN.COM

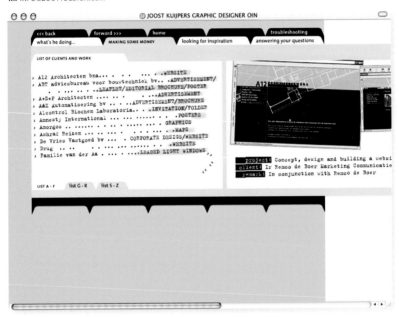

WWW.JOINK.NL
D: JOOST KUIJPERS
M: INFO@JOINK.NL

WWW.E-SHEEP.COM
D: PATRICK FARLEY
M: WEBMASTER@E-SHEEP.COM

sWISH* ist ein Ausstellungsprojekt an der Expo 02. sWISH* zeigt die Schweiz als eine Landschaft geheimer und ausgesprochener Wünsche. Flanieren Sie durch diese wachsende Wunschlandschaft und gestalten Sie sie mit: Was wünschen Sie sich?

WWW.SWISH.CH
D: VIOLA ZIMMERMANN, **C:** IBM & WEBLOTION
A: WWW.WEBLOTION.COM, **M:** V@VIOLA.CH

WWW.VERTIGE.ORG
A: VERTIGE, **M:** VERTIGE@MAIL.BE

WWW.FASHIONMAS.COM
D: ANNA MARIA LOPEZ
A: FASHIONMAS DESIGN SERVICES, **M:** ANNA@FASHIONMAS.COM

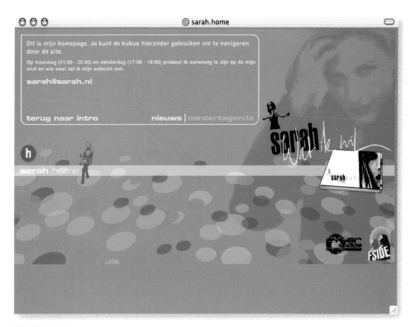

WWW.SARAH.NL
D: PASCAL DUVAL, **C:** RICHARD GROENENDIJK
A: BSUR, **M:** RICHARD@BSUR.COM

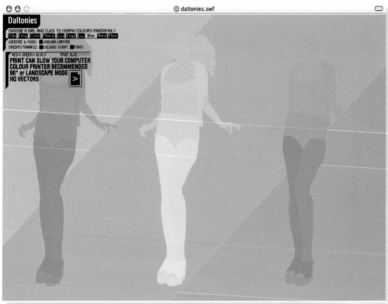

WWW.JLAPOTRE.FREE.FR
D: JOACHIM LAPOTRE
A: YOA, **M:** JLAPOTRE@NOOS.FR

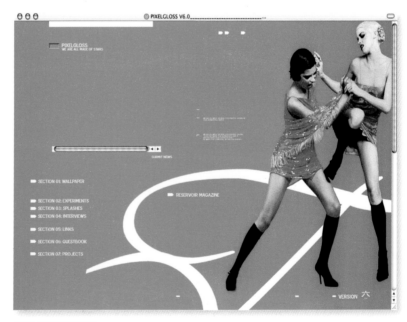

WWW.PIXELGLOSS.COM
D: JOERN STRATEN
M: JOERN@PIXELGLOSS.COM

WWW.ANYMO.COM
D: ADAM CHAN
A: MULTI.D, **M:** ADAM@MULTID.COM.HK

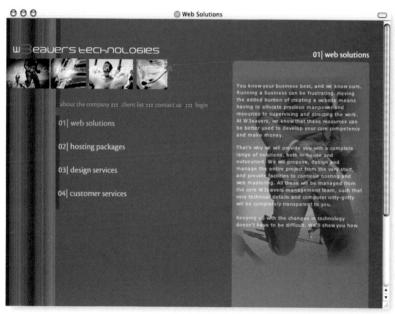

WWW.W3EAVERS.COM
D: YI FARN TAY
A: W3EAVERS TECHNOLOGIES, **M:** FARN@W3EAVERS.COM

WWW.ARYTHOGRAPHIX.COM
D: SHEIKH MOHAMAD AL-BAMADHAJ
A: ARYTHOGRAPHIX DESIGN SOLUTIONS, **M:** SHEIKH@ARYTHOGRAPHIX.COM

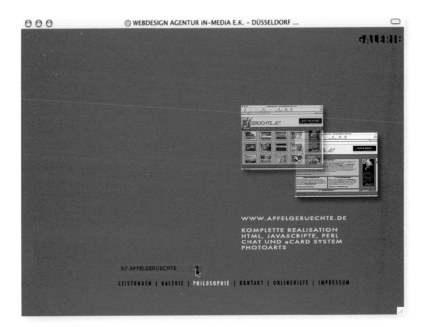

WWW.IN-MEDIA.DE
D: RALPH FREIBEUTER
M: INFO@IN-MEDIA.DE

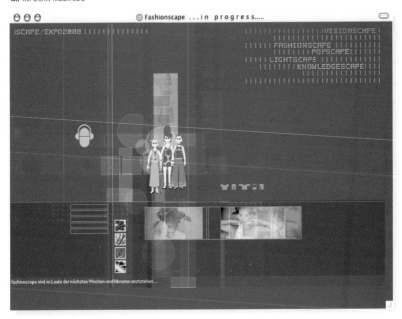

WWW.VISIONSCAPE.DE
D: NICOLETTA GERLACH, **C:** HOLGER HIRT
A: SCREENBOW, **M:** IDEFIX98@HOTMAIL.COM

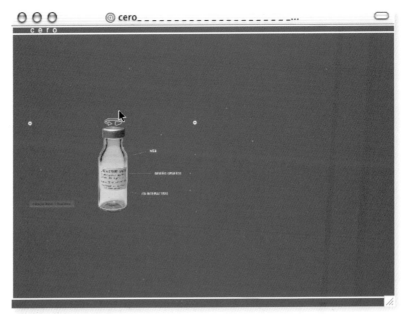

WWW.MENOSUNO.COM/CERO.HTML
D: MAITE CAMACHO PEREZ
A: MAMAS, **M:** MAITE00@OZU.ES

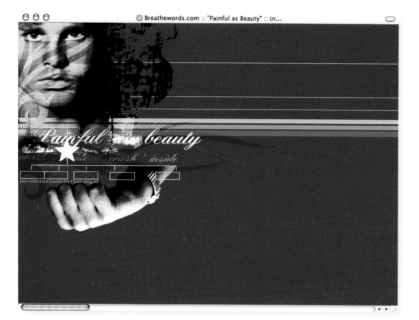

WWW.BREATHEWORDS.COM
D: ADRIANA DE BARROS
A: SCENE 360, **M:** CONTACT@SCENE360.COM

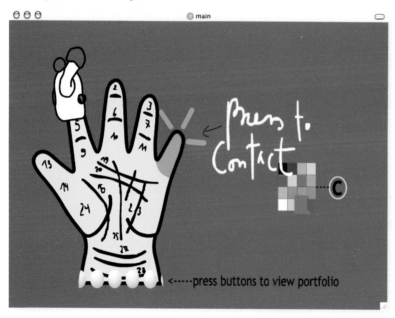

WWW.PINKER.BE
D: INES VAN BELLE
A: PINKER, **M:** INFO@PINKER.BE

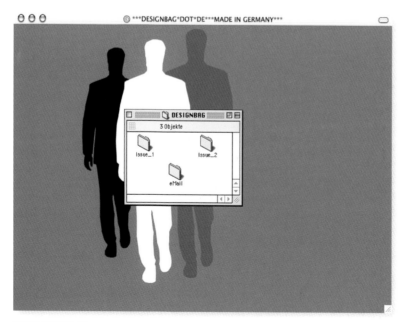

WWW.DESIGNBAG.DE
D: MARCEL SCHLER
M: MARCEL@DESIGNBAG.DE

WWW.ITCATMEDIA.COM
D: STEPHEN LO, **C:** PERIC SZE, **P:** NOVITA LEUNG
A: ITCAT MEDIA LIMITED, **M:** STEPHEN@ITCATMEDIA.COM

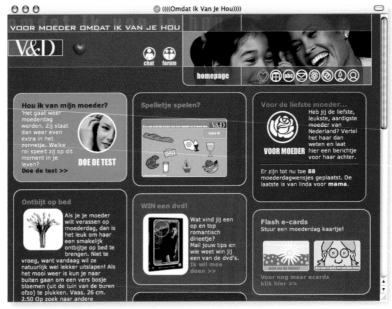

WWW.OMDATIKVANJEHOU.COM
D: NIENKE DIRKSE, **C:** MARCEL KLOMP, **P:** MARK MARTENS
M: NIENKE@IFTHEN.NL

WWW.RUGGERIPELLAMI.COM
D: GIANLUCA RECALCATI
A: MAGNETIKA, **M:** GREKA@MAGNETIKA.IT

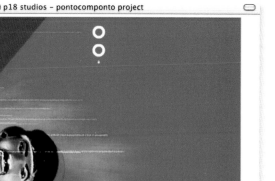

WWW.GSMBRASIL.COM.BR/P18STUDIOS
D: PAULO OLIVEIRA
A: P18 STUDIOS BRASIL, **M:** PA.OLIVEIRA@IG.COM.BR

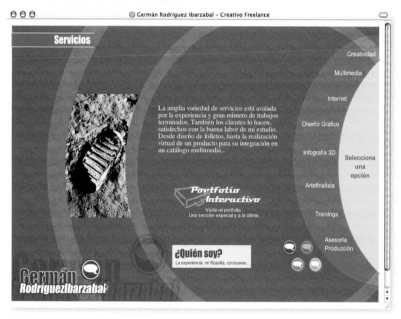

WWW.GERMAN-RODRIGUEZ.COM
D: GERMAIN RODRÌGUEZ
M: COMERCIAL@GERMAN-RODRIGUEZ.COM

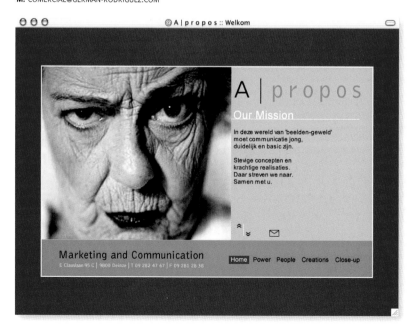

WWW.APROPOS.BE
D: DIDIER LAMMENS
A: GOOFI, **M:** INFO@GOOFI.BE

WWW.ULTRAFASHIONPORN.COM
D: FRANCESCO BERTELLI
A: TENSE, **M:** INFO@TENSE.IT

WWW.BNKIDS.NL
D: GIJS VAN DER SCHOOT, **C:** FORTUNATO GEELHOED, **P:** GERARD DE BOER
A: DBK OGILVY & MATHERS GRONINGEN, **M:** MARK@WEBINZICHT.COM

WWW.OPTION-SHIFT-HOME.COM
D: PHILIP FOECKLER
M: PHILIP@POCKETART.COM

WWW.PAXINAWEB.COM
D: MANUEL RODRIGUEZ
M: PAXINAWEB@MIXMAIL.COM

WWW.UNREALIDEAS.COM
D: WAYNE CHAN
M: INFO@UNREALIDEAS.COM

WWW.CONSTRUCCIONESDICAR.COM
D: JOSE MANUEL
A: TRISQUELMEDIA, **M:** JORGE@TRISQUELMEDIA.NET

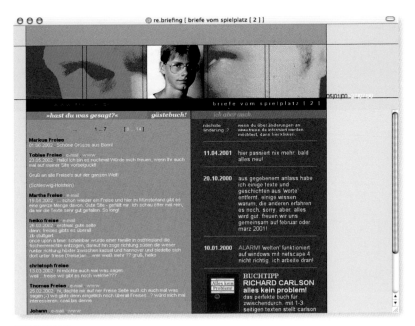

WWW.FREISE.DE
D: MARKUS FREISE
M: MARKUS@FREISE.DE

DEVRIES-VASTGOED.NL
D: JOOST KUIJPERS
M: INFO@DEVRIES-VASTGOED.NL

WWW.HAIKU-MEDIA.COM/TARRESSERRAT
D: MARTIN BETO
A: HAIKU TEAM, **M:** A@HAIKU-MEDIA.COM

WWW.MRENO.COM
D: MAXIME NEMOURS
A: IN EXTENSO MEDIA, **M:** ADMIN@IE-M.COM

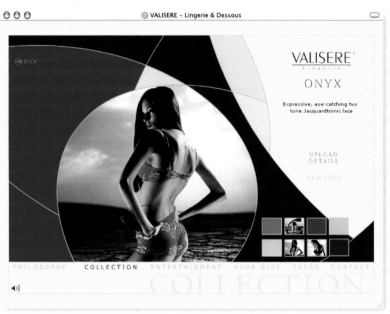

WWW.VALISERE.COM
D: MARINA SHTATLENDER, **C:** MARIO KLINGEMANN, **P:** COLLIN CROOME
A: COMA2, **M:** CONTACT@COMA2.COM

WWW.SCHMUCKBOERSE-HIDIR.DE
D: KAI GREIM
M: INFO@GRAFIKAI.DE

WWW.REDBEAN.COM
D: MELISSA CROWLEY
M: MELISSA@REDBEAN

WWW.DITTER.NET
D: THOMAS MALZKORN
A: MALZKORN - KOMMUNIKATION & GESTALTUNG GMBH, **M:** MALZKORN@MALZKORN.DE

WWW.AIRBAGCRAFTWORKS.COM
D: LARS WOEHNING
A: V2A**NETFORCE**RUHR, **M:** LW@V2A.NET

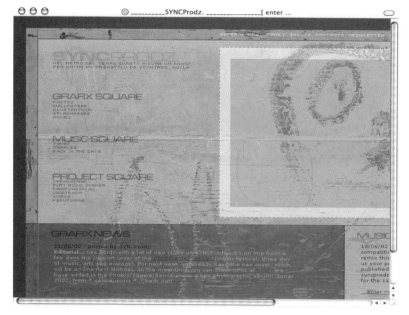

WWW.SYNCPRODZ.NET
D: JACK LAMOTTA
A: SYNCPRODZ. [MEZZI ESPRESSIVI], **M:** INFO@SYNCPRODZ.NET

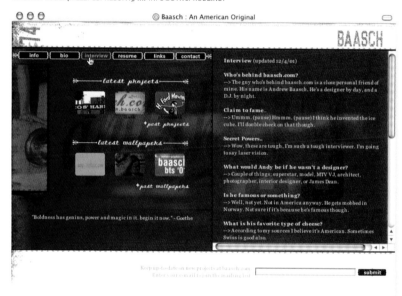

WWW.BAASCH.COM
D: ANDREW BAASCH
A: PREODE, **M:** ANDREW@BAASCH.COM

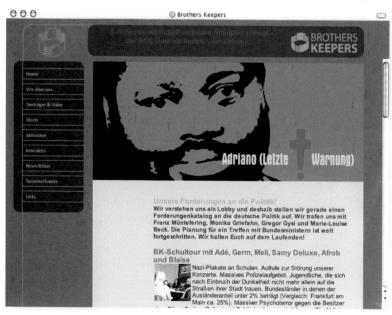

WWW.BROTHERS-KEEPERS.DE
D: ROLAND PECHER, **C:** NILS NOHNWALD, **P:** NITTY GRITTY MUSIC
A: KINGMEDIA GMBH, **M:** SCHMIDT@UNIT-MEDIENHAUS.DE

WWW.BETANCOR.DE
D: HERMANN KÖPF
A: NEOWELT MEDIA GMBH, **M:** HERMANN.KOEPF@NEOWELT.DE

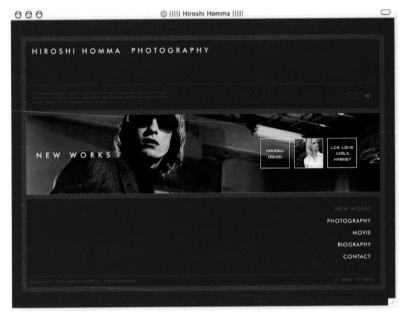

WWW.H-HOMMA.COM
D: TAKAAKI YAG
A: FORM::PROCESS, **M:** INFO@FORM-PROCESS.COM

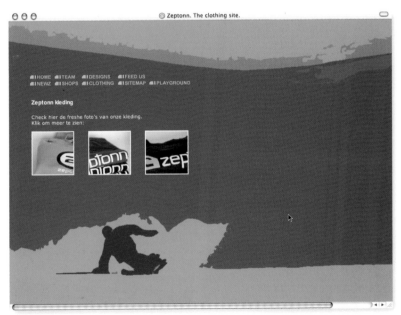

WWW.ZEPTONN.NL
D: JAN WILLEM WENNEKES
A: ANDRAWEBDESIGN, **M:** STINGER@ZEPTONN.NL

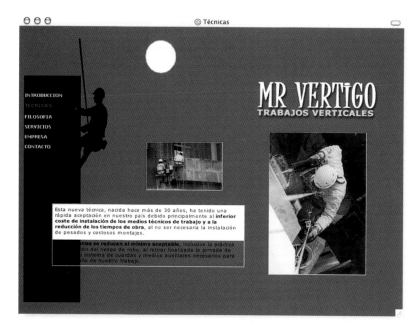

WWW.MISTER-VERTIGO.COM
D: JAVIER DONOSO
A: IMPRODEX S.L., **M:** JDONOSO@IMPRODEX.COM

WWW.FOCUS-MFG.COM
D: STEPHANE GROLEAU
A: BLASFEM INTERACTIF, **M:** SGROLEAU@BLASFEM.COM

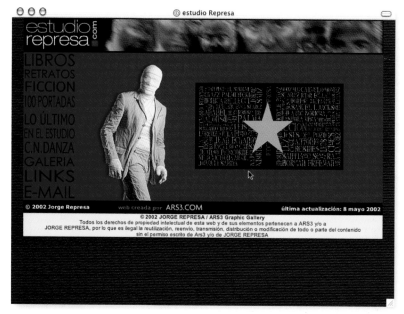

WWW.ESTUDIOREPRESA.COM
D: FERRAN SENDRA
A: ARS3, **M:** FERRANSENDRA@ARS3.COM

WWW.UNIT9.COM/VIDEOS/FULLMOONSAFARI
D: BEN HIBON,
A: UNIT9, **M:** UNIT9@UNIT9.COM

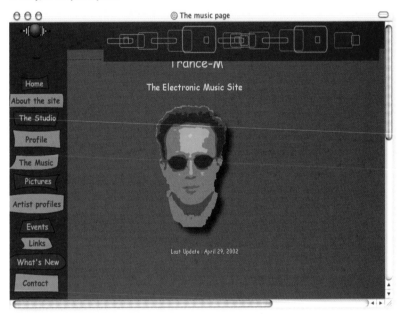

WWW.WELCOME.TO/TRANCE-M
D: TRANCE-M, **C:** MAURICE
M: TRANCE-M@WXS.NL

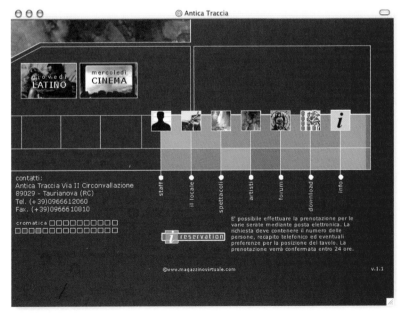

WWW.ANTICATRACCIA.COM
D: FRANCESCO VICARI, **P:** MARIA PAPA
A: MAGAZZINO VIRTUALE, **M:** INFO@MAGAZZINOVIRTUALE.COM

WWW.GOSSENRIJKEBOER.NL
D: GOSSEN RIJKEBOER
M: INFO@GOSSENRIJKEBOER.NL

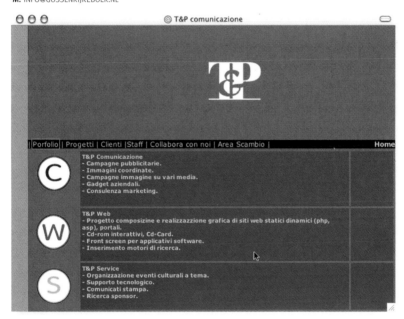

WWW.TPONLINE.IT
D: CELADIN TOMMY, **P:** MATTEO TORNIELLI
A: T&P, **M:** TOMMY@TPONLINE.IT

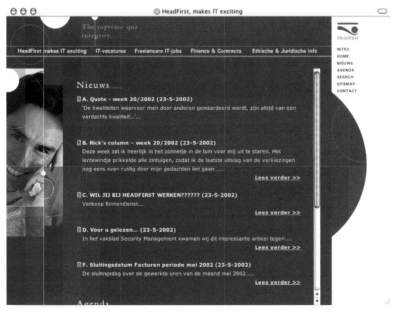

WWW.HEADFIRST.NL
D: JEROEN HERMES
A: BOOLEANPARK, **M:** JEROEN.HERMES@BOOLEANPARK.COM

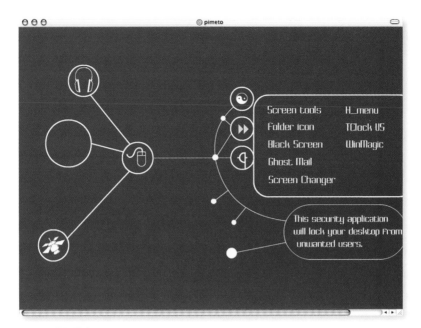

WWW.PIMETO.HIT.BG
D: MICHAL PAPADOPOLUS
A: PIMETO

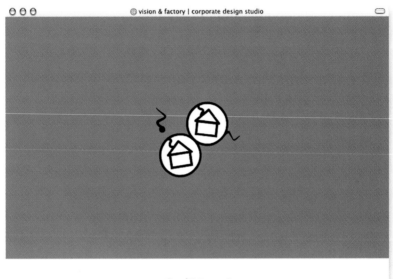

Brand (being raped)

WWW.VISIONANDFACTORY.COM
D: KIM MATTHÈ
A: THE KNOWLEDGE FACTORY , **M:** MARCEL@VISIONANDFACTORY.COM

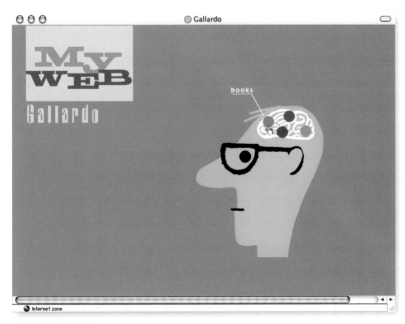

WWW.MULTISTUDIO.COM
D: TONI RICART
A: TONI RICART MULTISTUDIO SCP, **M:** TRICART@MULTISTUDIO.COM

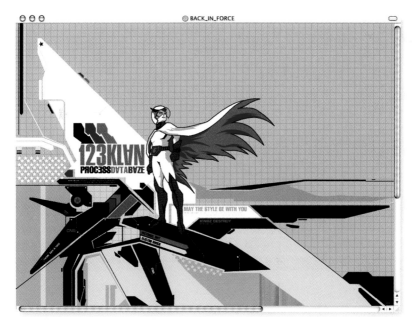

WWW.123KLAN.COM
D: SCIEN & KLOR
A: 123KLAN, **M:** SCIEN-KLOR@123KLAN.COM

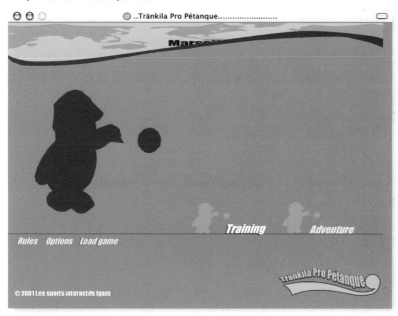

WWW.TRANKILA.COM
D: A-T-N, **C:** RNOZ, **P:** TRANKILA
M: TRANKILA@FREE.FR

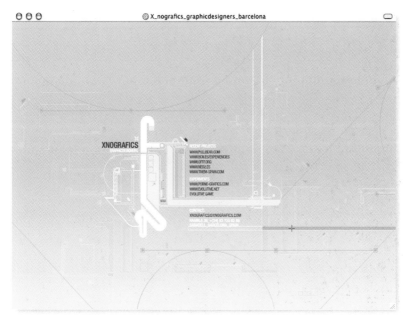

WWW.XNOGRAFICS.COM
A: XNOGRAFICS, **M:** LLUIS@XNOGRAFICS.COM

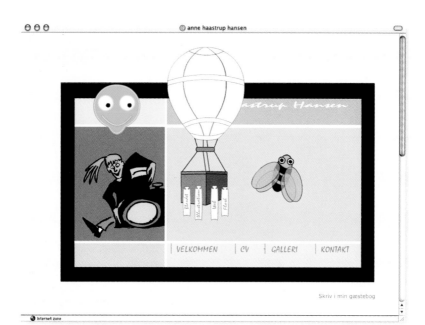

WWW.ODENSE.KOLLEGIENET.DK
D: ANNE HAASTRUP HANSEN
A: DOLPHIN_DESIGN, **M:** DOLPHIN@OFIR.DK

WWW.RASPADESIGN.IT/GLO.HTML
D: GIULIO RASPAGLIESI
A: BYRASPADESIGN, **M:** HAIR@RASPADESIGN.IT

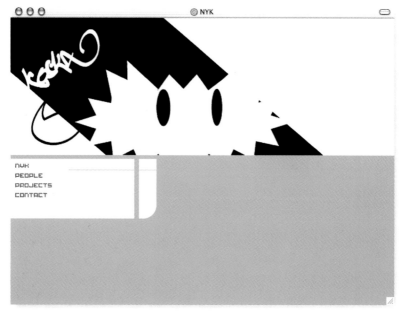

WWW.NYK.HU
D: NYIRY GEZA
A: NYK, **M:** MAIL@NYK.HU

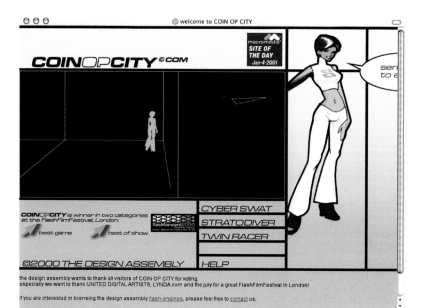

WWW.COIN-OP-CITY.COM
D: THOMAS WAGNER
A: THE DESIGN ASSEMBLY GMBH, **M:** INFO@DESIGNASSEMBLY.COM

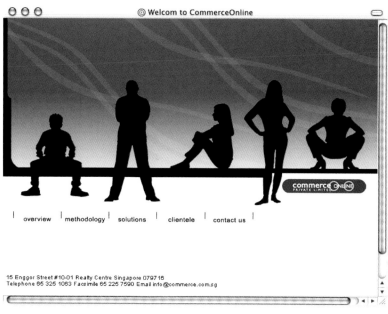

WWW.COMMERCE.COM.SG
D: MATTHEW TAN
A: COMMERCEONLINE PTE. LTD., **M:** ZENITH@PACIFIC.NET.SG

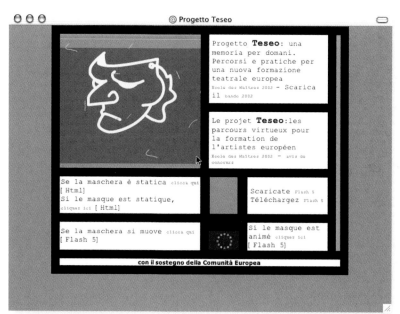

WWW.PROGETTO-TESEO.IT
D: SARA PACOR, **C:** BARBARA VATTA, **P:** CRISTINA ROGGI
A: INCIPIT SRL, **M:** INFO@INCIPITONLINE.IT

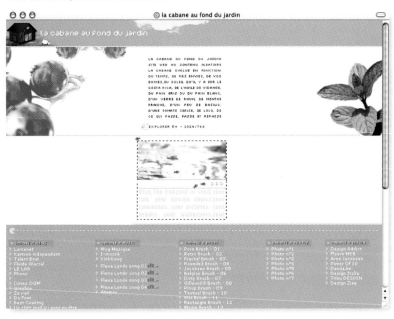

WWW.SHARKYDESIGN.NET
D: SHARKY, **C:** FRANÁOIS RENÈ
A: SHARKY DESIGN, **M:** SHARKYDESIGN@NOOS.FR

WWW.BAH.BE/GILLES/CABANE.ASP
D: GILLES BAZELAIRE
M: GBAZELAIRE@SKYNET.BE

WWW.LINKDUP.COM
D: ROB CORRADI
A: PRELOADED, **M:** REMOTE@PRELOADED.COM

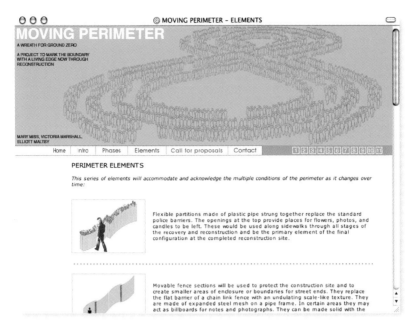

WWW.MARYMISS.COM
D: NYIRY GEZA
A: NYK, **M:** MAIL@NYK.HU

WWW.TALKOMAT.DE
D: ELKE SCHIEMANN
M: ELKE@HUNGA.DE

WWW.FUNBIKERS.NET
D: ERICK MARTINUZZI
A: EMAKINA, **M:** NUZZIFUMI@HOTMAIL.COM

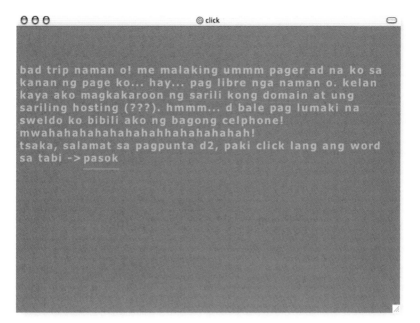

bad trip naman o! me malaking ummm pager ad na ko sa
kanan ng page ko... hay... pag libre nga naman o. kelan
kaya ako magkakaroon ng sarili kong domain at ung
sariling hosting (???). hmmm... d bale pag lumaki na
sweldo ko bibili ako ng bagong celphone!
mwahahahahahahahahhahahahahah!
tsaka, salamat sa pagpunta d2, paki click lang ang word
sa tabi -> pasok

WWW.GEOCITIES.COM/ARTOFBLUB
D: KRIST MENINA
M: PALE_BLUE@LINUXMAIL.ORG

WWW.BEAGOODGIRL.COM
D: BARBARA JAUMANN, **C:** CHRISTIAN BEZDEKA
M: B.@VIENNA.AT

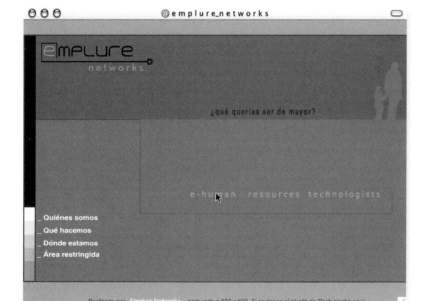

WWW.EMPLURE.COM
D: MARIO GUTIERREZ
A: MAMAS, **M:** MARIOGCRU@HOTMAIL.COM

238

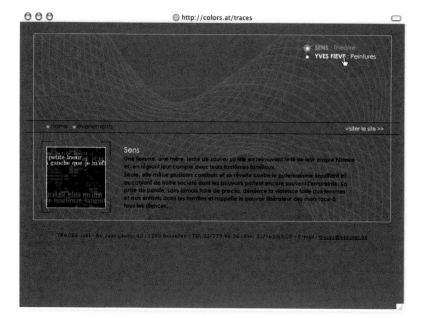

WWW.COLORS.AT/TRACES
D: OLIVIER DE MARTINO
M: DEMARTINO@EASYNET.BE

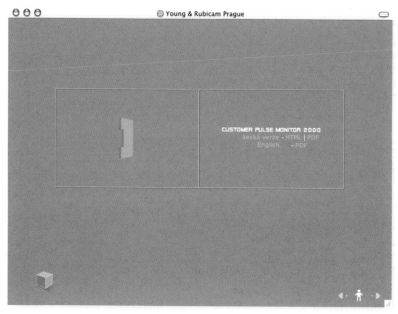

WWW.YOUNG-RUBICAM.CZ
D: MICHAEL CERVENKA, **C:** VACLAV KARGER
M: VACLAV.KARGER@NE.CZ

WWW.TOPIMATGE.COM
D: RAMON LLIBRE, **C:** LAMPROSSMEDIA, **P:** TOP IMATGE
M: TOP@TOPIMATGE.COM

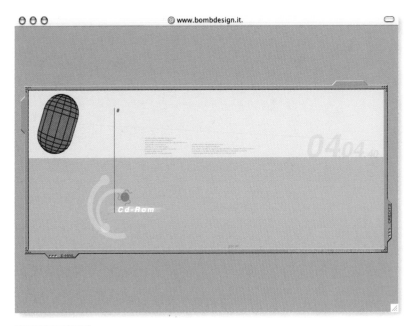

WWW.BOMBDESIGN.IT
D: LUCIANO LIMOLI
M: INFO@BOMBDESIGN.IT

WWW.GRAFFODISIAK.COM
D: CARLO VEGA
M: DIGITALPIMP@GRAFFODISIAK.COM

WWW.ELLESOUND.DE
D: SEVERIN BRETTMEISTER
A: FA-RO MARKETING, **M:** SEVERIN@FA-RO.DE

WWW.OKTOBER.DE
D: RENE WYNANDS
A: OKTOBER GMBH, **M:** POST@OKTOBER.DE

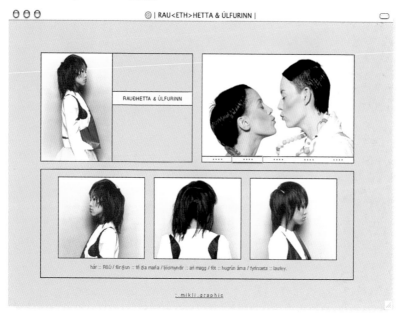

WWW.RAUDHETTA.IS
D: MUMMI
A: MIKLI, **M:** MIKLI@KAGSAA.DK

WWW.G56.8M.COM
D: FABIO COLLET
M: ASTUTIX@YAHOO.COM

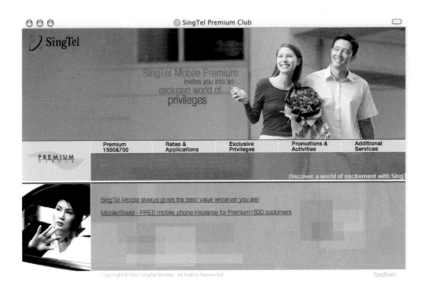

HOME.SINGTEL.COM/PREMIUM
D: IVAN MP TAN
A: ARETAE LTD., **M:** IVAN.TAN@ARETAE.COM

WWW.INKO.CJB.NET
D: DAN NANASI
M: DAN@INKO.CJB.NET

WWW.ICHOOSERADIO.COM
D: ADAM GRAHAM
A: WWW.GO3W.CO.UK, **M:** MAIL@ICHOOSERADIO.COM

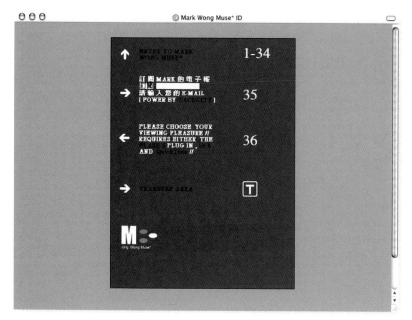

091280ARK.24CC.COM
D: MARK WONG
M: HIBIKI20@COCOA.FREEMAIL.NE.JP

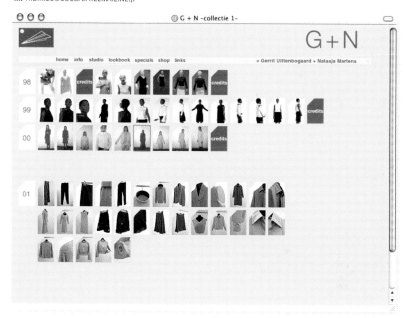

WWW.FASHIONFUGITIVE.NL
D: FABRICE KOOPMAN, SANDER PLUG
A: MEDIUMRARE ID, **M:** FABRICE@MEDIUMRARE.NL

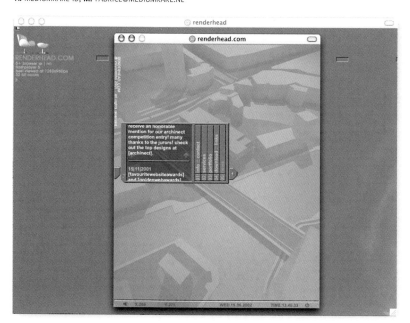

WWW.RENDERHEAD.COM
D: RONALD WISSE
A: VISUALDATA, **M:** VISUALDATA@CHELLO.NL

WWW.EVALOTTA-PRODUKTE.DE
D: LIDA PERIN
M: LIDA@ERROR65.NET

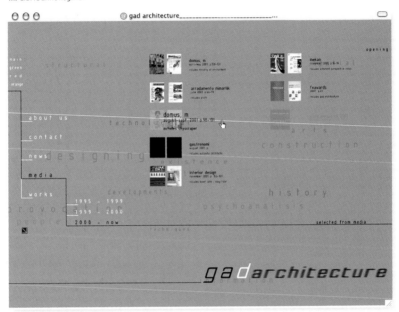

WWW.GADARCHITECTURE.COM
D: CAN BURAK BIZER
A: BIZER WEB SOLUTIONS, **M:** CANBURAK@BIZER.WS

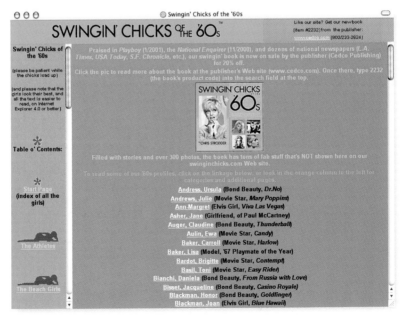

WWW.SWINGINCHICKS.COM
D: CHRIS STRODDER
M: SWINGINCHICKS@HOTMAIL.COM

WWW.SINTETICA.IT
D: MASSIMO RISCA, **C:** ANGELO LAZZARI
A: SINTETICA SRL, **M:** RISCA@SINTETICA.IT

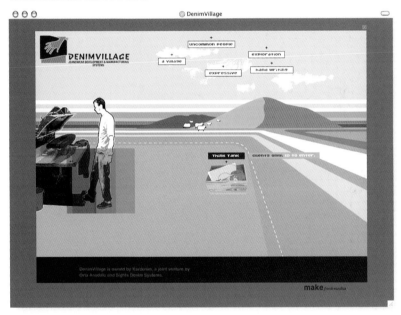

WWW.DENIMVILLAGE.COM
D: OYGAR ERDAL
A: MAKE FRESH MEDIA, **M:** GULG@MAKEFRESHMEDIA.COM

WWW.NICOLASTEPHANE.FREE.FR
D: NICOLAS STEPHANE
M: NICOLASTEPHANE@FREE.FR

WWW.I2ICN.COM
D: GERALD LOH, **C:** RAGHU, **P:** JOE CHUA
M: GERALD@VOXMEDIA.COM.SG

WWW.33KAPPA.IT
D: RICCARDO IANNARELLI, **C:** VALERIA RIPPA, **P:** ANTONELLO CASTELLI
A: FORMAT C, **M:** CONIGLIETTA2000@HOTMAIL.COM

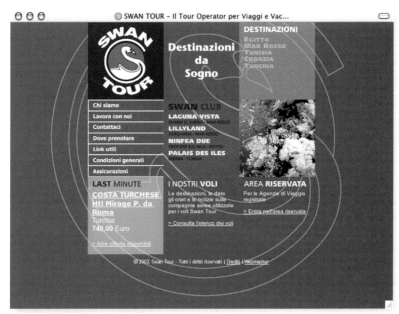

WWW.SWANTOUR.IT
D: STEFANO DOMINICI, **C:** FRANCESCO CRISAFI
A: TR E ASSOCIATI, **M:** S.DOMINICI@TR-ASSOCIATI.IT

WWW.SANTILLANA.ES
D: PATRICIA FUENTES
A: BLUE PLANET, **M:** P.FUENTES@RETEMAIL.ES

WWW.UNIDESAGAMING.COM
D: CARINA STINGA, **C:** BAS HORSTING
A: INTERWEB RESEARCH, **M:** CARINA@INTERWEB-RESEARCH.NET

WWW.CERESBEER.COM
D: DANILO ROLLE, **C:** PAOLO CASTELLI
A: DARTWAY, **M:** DROLLE@DARTWAY.COM

WWW.SALANASA.COM
D: RAUL MARINHO
A: DINAWEB NETWORKS S.L., **M:** RMARINHO@DINAWEB.COM

WWW.NOLOVEDESIGN.CJB.NET
D: RICARDO MARTÌN
A: RMI SOFTWARE, **M:** RMARTINHERRERO@TERRA.ES

WWW.JIMBOOM.COM
D: JIM BOOM
M: JIMBOOM@JIMBOOM.COM

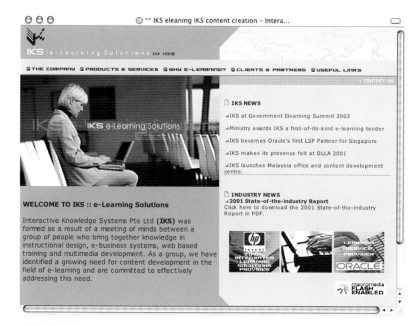

WWW.IKSONLINE.COM
D: KIM SENG
A: INTERACTIVE KNOWLEDGE SYSTEMS PTE LTD., **M:** KIMSENG@IKSONLINE.COM

WWW.MILLENNIUMSIM.IT
D: MARCO MARELLI, **C:** GIORGIO ANDREOLETTI, **P:** MARCO CASTAGNA
M: MMARELLI@ANTEAONLINE.COM

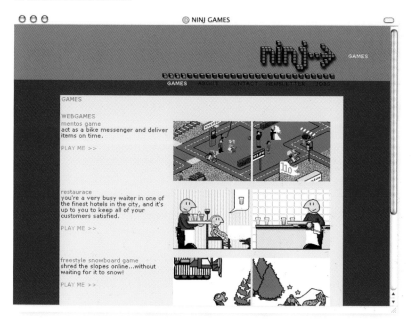

WWW.NINJ.COM
D: NADIA LOOSLI
A: WEBLOTION, **M:** NADIA@NALOO.NET

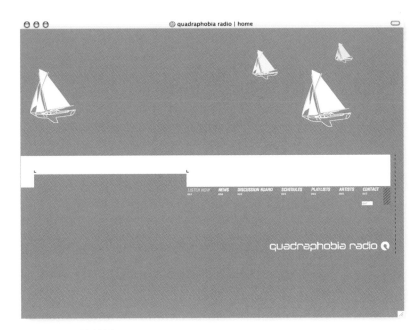

WWW.QUADRAPHOBIA.COM
D: MIKHAIL PESCHAN
M: MISHA@FORMSCIENCE.COM

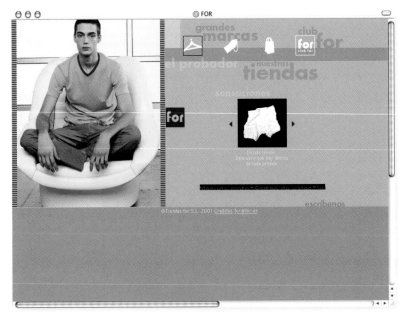

WWW.FOR.ES
D: BETO MARTÌN
A: HAIKU MEDIA, **M:** A@HAIKU-MEDIA.COM

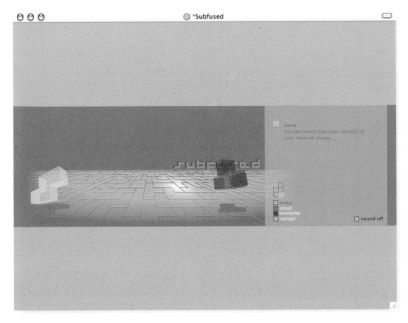

WWW.SUBFUSED.COM
D: MATTHEW ANNAL, **C:** ROBERT GIBSON
M: ROBGIBSON1983@HOTMAIL.COM

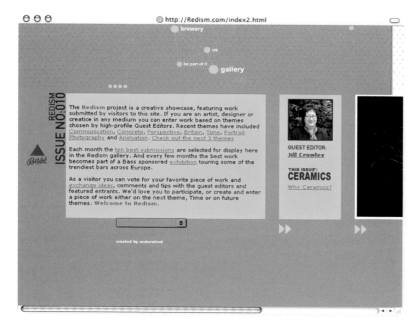

WWW.REDISM.COM
D: JASON HOLLAND
A: UNDERWIRED*, **M:** JASON@UNDERWIRED.COM

WWW.HELSINKIJAZZ.CO.UK
D: CHRISTIAN CHAMPAGNE
M: CHRIS@HELSINKIJAZZ.CO.UK

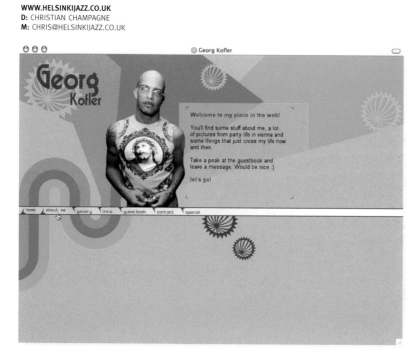

GEORG.MODELONE.AT
D: ALEXANDER KREMECEK
A: MODELONE, **M:** CONTACT@MODELONE.AT

WWW.NORVISTA.CO.UK
D: CHRISTIAN CHAMPAGNE, TIMO NEWTON-SYMS
A: W2S.NET, **M:** CHRIS@HELSINKIJAZZ.CO.UK

WWW.EH.CL
D: MAURICIO OLGUIN, MARCOS CORREA
A: EAGENCY.CL, **M:** CONTACTO@MAURICIOOLGUIN.COM

WWW.ALLMOTORS.COM
D: GEO HERNANDEZ
A: GEOGRAFIXX, **M:** GEO@GEOGRAFIXX.COM

WWW.ESQUEMALEY.COM
D: SANTI SALLÈS
A: TUNDRABCN, **M:** INFO@TUNDRABCN.COM

WWW.TABACAL.COM.AR
D: JAVIER PEREYRA
A: PROMINENTE S.A., **M:** JPEREYRA@PROMINENTE.COM.AR

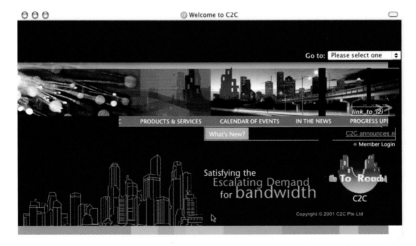

WWW.C2CCN.COM
D: KALINDA LOW, **C:** RAGHU, **P:** JOE CHUA
A: VOXMEDIA, **M:** JOE@VOXMEDIA.COM.SG

WWW.ELECTRICONLAND.COM
D: GIOVANI "AKIRA" FAGANELLO, **C:** GABRIEL "GORKA" GORSKI
M: DESIGN@ELECTRICONLAND.COM

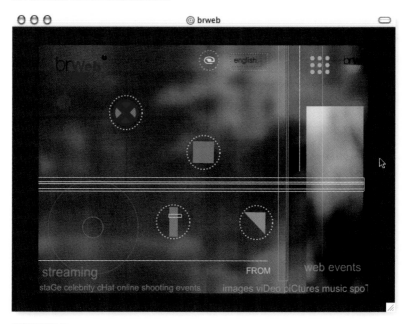

WWW.GROENEWEGE.COM
D: GUNTHER GROENEWEGE
A: G-DESIGN, **M:** GROENEWEGE@HOTMAIL.COM

WWW.BRWEB.IT
D: CATERINA AGUECI
M: CATE@MARKINO.NET

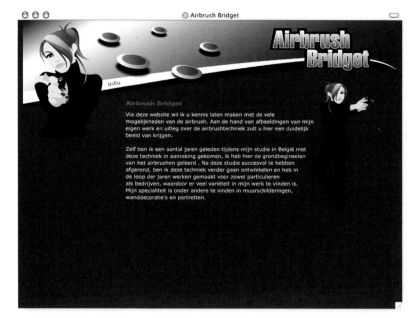

WWW.AIRBRUSH-BRIDGET.NL
D: DEBBY VAN DONGEN
A: CONK, **M:** INFO@CONK.NL

WWW.SCALAGROUP.COM
D: EMANUELE BERTONI, **P:** FRANCO GIOVANNINI
A: SCALA GROUP, **M:** EB@UNDERSCORE.IT

WWW.BIOPIGMENTS.COM
D: ABRAHAM ROIG, **C:** DANI AGUILAR
M: ABRAHAM@ROIG.NET

WWW.HDMDESIGNS.COM
D: HERMAN MALDONADO
A: HDM DESIGN + PARTNERS, **M:** HDMALDONADO@HDMDESIGNS.COM

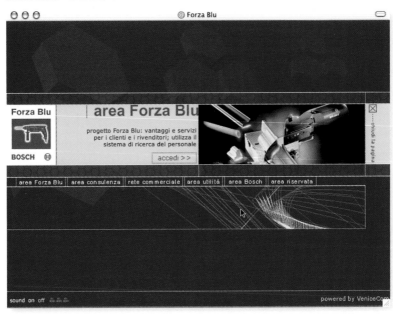

WWW.FORZABLU.IT
D: PACO ZANE, **C:** FRANCESCO GATTO, **P:** SANDRO LOVADINA
A: VENICECOM, **M:** PACO@VENICECOM.IT

WWW.GENXSPORTSINC.COM
D: STEVE GAUDER, **C:** CRAIG WELLER, **P:** RICK BROWN
A: DESIGN 2.0, **M:** STEVIEG@SYMPATICO.CA

WWW.SNOWCAT-ARCTIS.COM
D: MIRKO CAKANIC, **C:** DALIBOR SVER, **P:** ARCTIS D.O.O.
A: STUDIO IMAGO, **M:** STUDIO@STUDIOIMAGO.HR

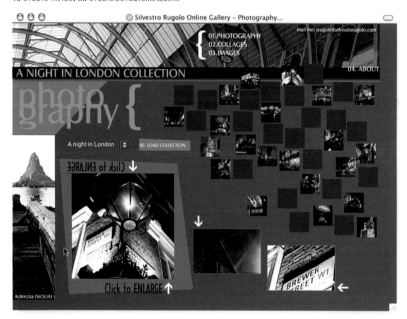

WWW.SILVESTRORUGOLO.COM
D: SILVESTRO RUGOLO
M: SRUGOLO@SILVESTRORUGOLO.COM

WWW.G-SCHLOSSER.AT
D: MICHAEL FARA
A: TEAM22, **M:** MF@TEAM22.AT

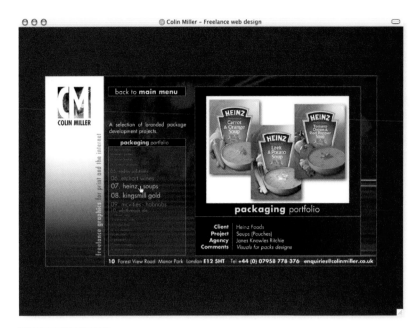

WWW.COLINMILLER.CO.UK
D: COLIN MILLER
A: FREELANCE GRAPHICS FOR PRINT AND THE INTERNET, **M:** POST@COLINMILLER.CO.UK

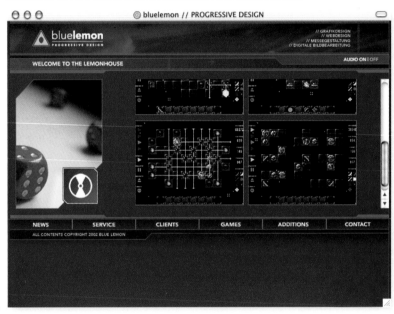

WWW.BLUELEMON.AT
D: BERNHARD AICHINGER
A: BLUELEMON // PROGRESSIVE DESIGN, **M:** OFFICE@BLUELEMON.AT

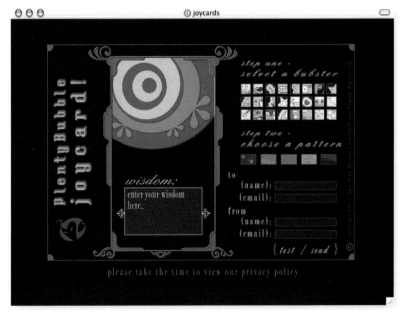

WWW.PLENTYBUBBLECRAZY.COM/JOYCARDS
D: DUNCAN WILSON, **C:** JAMES GRATTON, **P:** SAFFRON GROVER
A: ONE BAD MONKEY LIMITED, **M:** DUNCAN@ONEBADMONKEY.COM

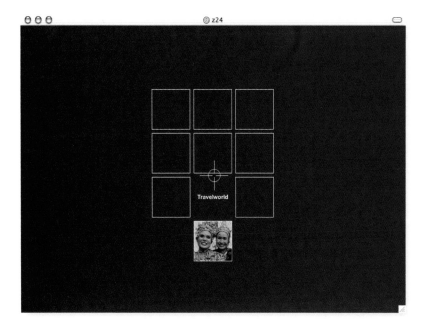

WWW.Z24.CH
D: ROBERT MASSE
A: SP-MULTIMEDIA, **M:** INFO@SP-MULTIMEDIA.CH

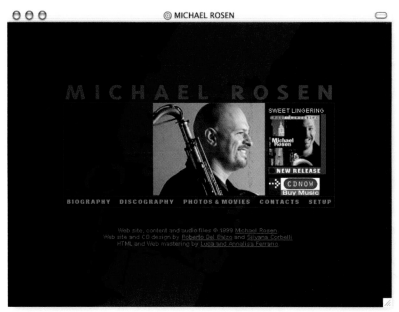

WWW.ROSENMUSIC.COM
D: ROBERTO DEL BALZO, **C:** ANNALISA FERRARIO, **P:** MICHAEL ROSEN
M: DBROB@LIBERO.IT

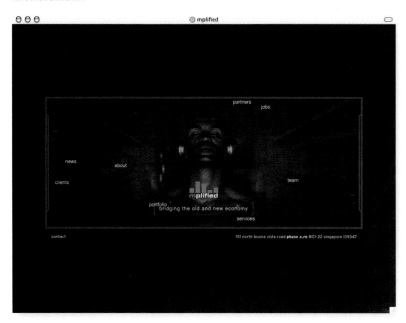

WWW.MPLIFIED.COM
D: CHARLIE TAY
A: MPLIFIED PTE LTD., **M:** CHARLIE.TAY@MPLIFIED.COM

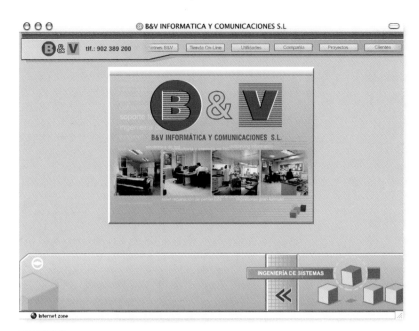

WWW.BYV.ES
D: LUIS ARMERO SERNA, **C:** JOSE MARÌA CARRATAL, **P:** ELISA HORNOS
M: LUIS.ARMERO@NUVOLBLAU.COM

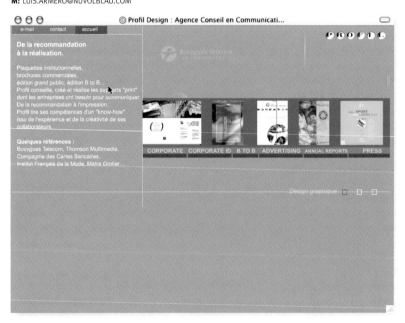

WWW.PROFIL-DESIGN.COM
D: FABRICE GRECO
A: PROFIL DESIGN, **M:** SN@PROFIL-DESIGN.CM

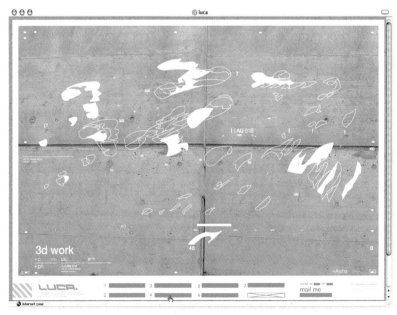

WWW.LUCA.ATRAX.WS
D: LUCA IONESCU
M: ACUL@OPTUSHOME.COM.AU

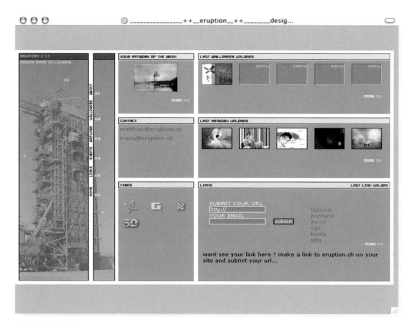

WWW.ERUPTION.CH
A: ERUPTION.CH, **M:** MATTHIAS@ERUPTION.CH

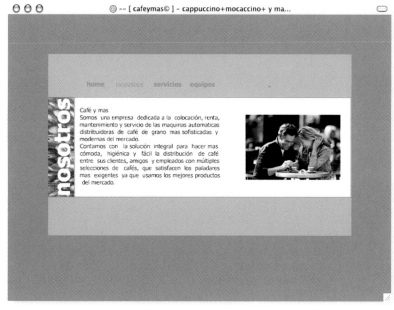

WWW.CAFEYMAS.COM
D: ROBERTO TEJEDA
A: ESFERA MULTIMEDIA, **M:** INFO@ESFERAMULTIMEDIA.COM

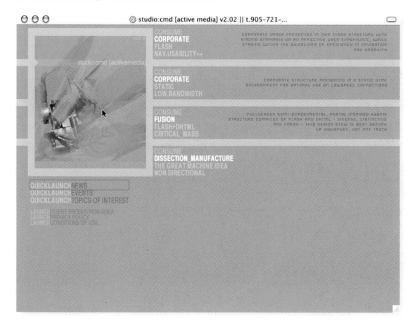

WWW.STUDIOCMD.COM
D: J. CHESEBROUGH
A: STUDIO:CMD [ACTIVEMEDIA], **M:** INFO@STUDIOCMD.COM

IMAGE.BEERFOTO.COM
D: WALTER MÖSSLER, **C:** PACO LA LUCA, **P:** BAMBOO PRODUCTIONS
A: TOUCHEE, **M:** MAIL@BEERFOTO.COM

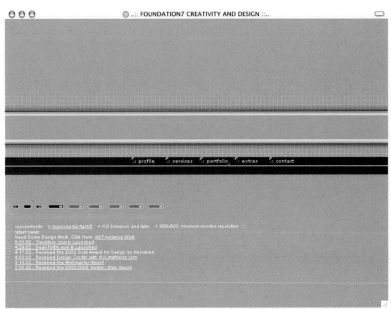

WWW.FOUNDATION7.COM
D: DOMINIC CURRENT
A: FOUNDATION7 CREATIVITY AND DESIGN, **M:** DOMINIC@FOUNDATION7.COM

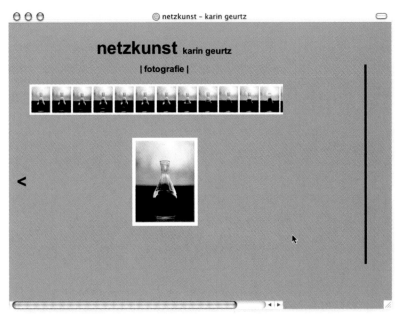

WWW.KARINGEURTZ.DE
D: TOBIAS HERRMANN
M: TOBIAS@ARTOBI.DE

WWW.INTUITIVE.NL
D: D. ZUIJDERLAND, **P:** B. VAN DE VOORT
A: INTUITIVE, **M:** DAAN@INTUITIVE.NL

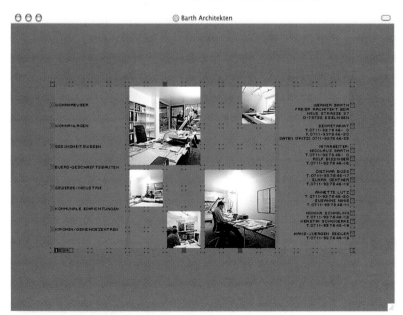

WWW.ALVEZEXPRESIONES.CJB.NET
D: ANNA MARIA LOPEZ
A: ANNA-ON-LINE INTERNATIONAL MULTIMEDIATIC DESIGNS, **M:** ANNANET@NAVEGALIA.COM

WWW.BARTH-ARCHITEKTEN.COM
D: HEINZ WITTHOEFT, **C:** [D-MIND] FUCHS/WEISS GBR, **P:** BARTH ARCHITEKTEN
A: ARCHITEKTURTAILE, **M:** HEINZ.WITTHOEFT@STATIONIST.COM

WWW.LUMINESSENCESTUDIOS.COM
D: CYNTHIA JOHNSTON
M: CLJ@LUMINESSENCESTUDIOS.COM

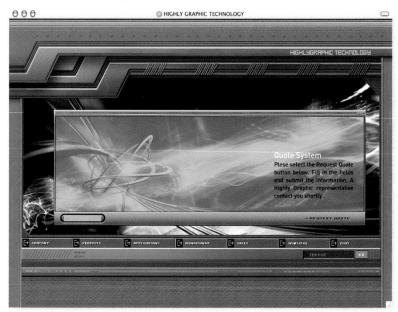

WWW.HIGHLYGRAPHIC.COM
D: JENS KARLSSON
A: CHAPTER THREE, **M:** SCOTT@CHAPTER3.NET

WWW.SCREENSCOUTS.COM
D: DAVID HUFSCHMIDT, **C:** MARCEL SCHADE, **P:** PHILIPP WIX
A: SCREENSCOUTS.COM, **M:** DAVID@SCREENSCOUTS.COM

WWW.BULLETFILMS.CO.UK
D: PETE CHAMBERS
A: BULLET LTD., **M:** PETE.CHAMBERS@BULLETFILMS.CO.UK

WWW.PERICON.DE
D: THILO VON DEBSCHITZ
A: Q, **M:** TVD@Q-HOME.DE

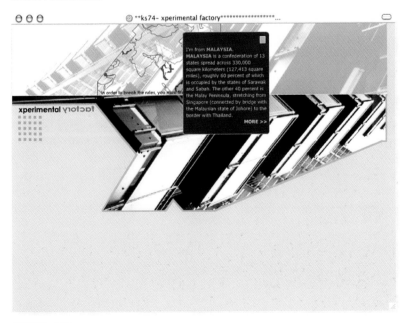

WWW.KS74.COM
D: KIM SENG
A: INTERACTIVE KNOWLEDGE SYSTEMS PTE LTD., **M:** KIMSENG@IKSONLINE.COM

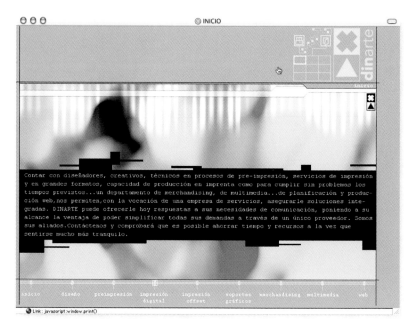

WWW.DINARTE.ES
D: JOSE MARIA JIMENEZ HERNANDEZ, **C:** EQUIPOXA
A: XAMEDIA S.L., **M:** DINARTE@DINARTE.ES

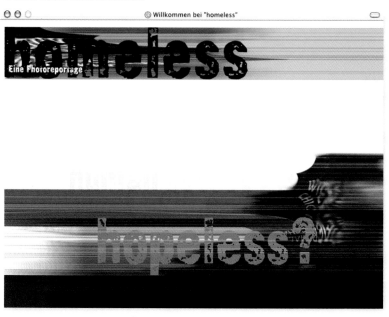

WWW.HOMELESS.DE
D: ANNE WITTHAKE
M: AWITTHAKE@WEB.DE

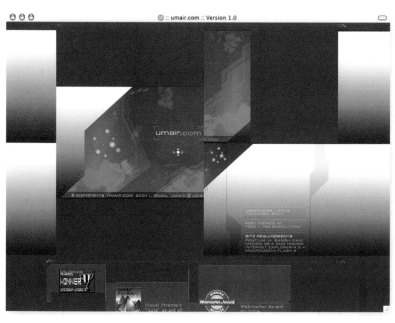

WWW.UMAIR.COM
D: SIDDIQUI UMAIR
A: UMAIR.COM, **M:** UMAIR@UMAIR.COM

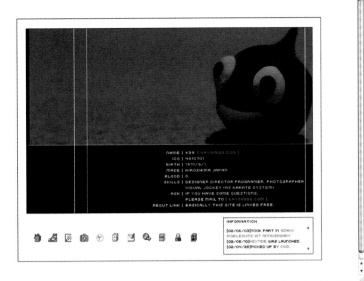

39.IMG8.COM
D: KAY-ICHI TOZAKI, **C:** +39
A: IMG8, **M:** KAY@IMG8.COM

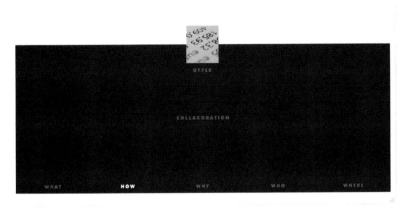

WWW.HOETETHOET.BE
D: VÈRONQIE HOET, **C:** ETIENNE FICHEROULLE
A: HOET&HOET, **M:** RONANE@HOETETHOET.BE

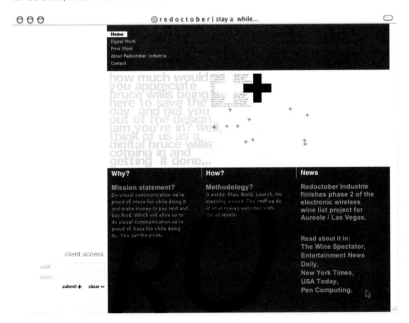

WWW.REDOCTOBER.COM
D: ANDI RUSU
A: REDOCTOBER INDUSTRIE, **M:** ANDI@REDOCTOBER.COM

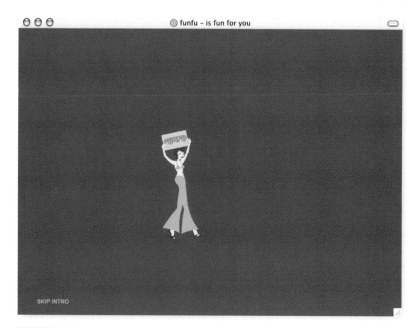

WWW.FUNFU.COM
D: STEFFEN OPPENBERG, **C:** SASCHA DEUTZMANN
A: 7T7, **M:** STEFFEN@7T7.COM

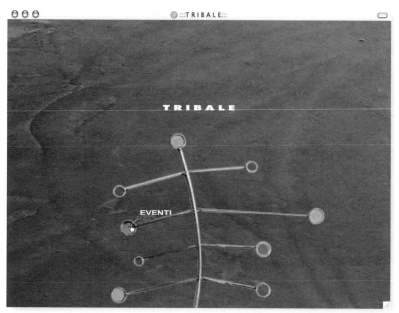

WWW.TRIBALE.NET
D: GIACOMO GIANCARLO, GIUSEPPE TOLO
A: KYNETOS, **M:** INFO@KYNETOS.COM

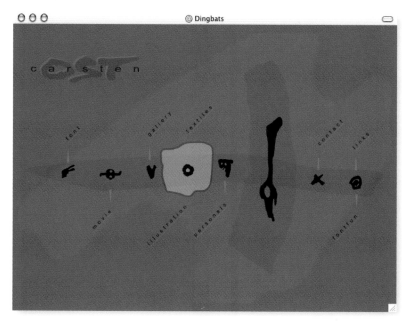

WWW.OSTSIGNS.DE
D: KARIN GEURTZ
M: KARIN.GEURTZ@T-ONLINE.DE

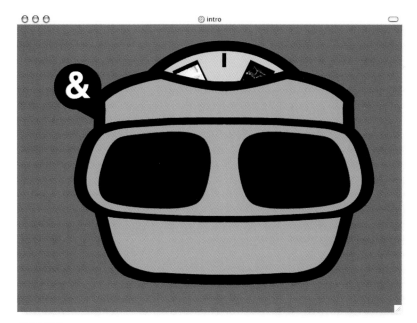

WWW.PIX.BE
D: INES VAN BELLE
A: PINKER, **M:** INFO@PINKER.BE

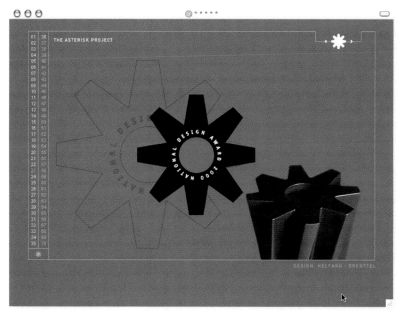

WWW.JHWD.COM/ASTERISK
D: WILLIAM DRENTTEL, JEFFERY TYSON, **P:** COOPER-HEWITT NATIONAL DESIGN MUSEUM
A: HELFAND|DRENTTEL STUDIO, **M:** WILLIAM@JHWD.COM

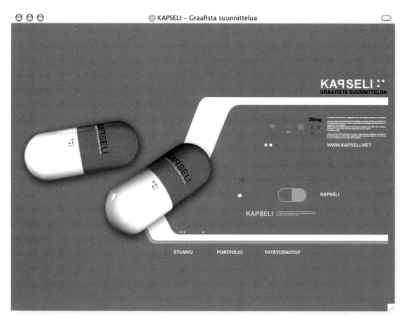

WWW.KAPSELI.NET
D: ARTO KETOLA
A: KAPSELI, **M:** ARTO@KAPSELI.NET

WWW.LOUISELATRAVERSE.CA
D: LYNDA GAGNON
A: CRÈATIONS WEB, **M:** INFO@LYNDAGAGNON.CA

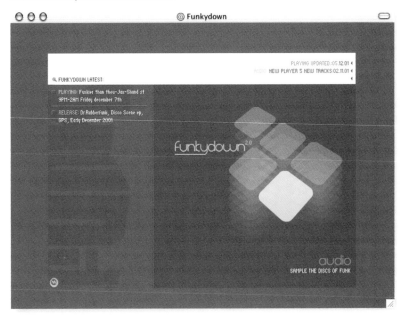

WWW.FUNKYDOWN.CO.UK
D: JIM MORGAN, **C:** NICK LAND, **P:** SIMON WARD
A: ACROYEAR DESIGN PROJECTS, **M:** INFO@FUNKYDOWN.CO.UK

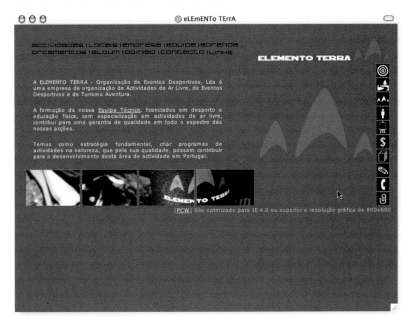

WWW.ELEMENTOTERRA.COM
D: ANA GRANJA
A: PCW, **M:** PAULA.GRANJA@LABOLIMS.COM

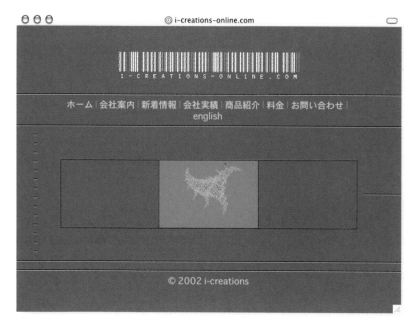

WWW.I-CREATIONS-ONLINE.COM
D: STEPHEN MILNE
A: I-CREATIONS, **M:** STEPH@I-CREATIONS-ONLINE.COM

WWW.NODE247.COM
D: TAKAYUKI NISHINA
M: TAKI@NODE247.COM

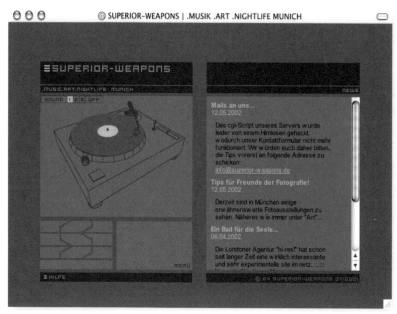

WWW.SUPERIOR-WEAPONS.DE
D: FRANZ VILSMEIER, SEBASTIAN POLLAK
M: FRANZ.VILSMEIER@FRESHGRAPHX.DE

WWW.MTGC.NET
D: ANDREA SCIARRETTA, **C:** ROBERTO SCIARRETTA
A: MT GLOBAL CONSULTING, **M:** ANDREA@MTGC.NET

WWW.NEOTRON.DE
D: MICHAEL ZALEWSKI
M: INFO@NEOTRON.DE

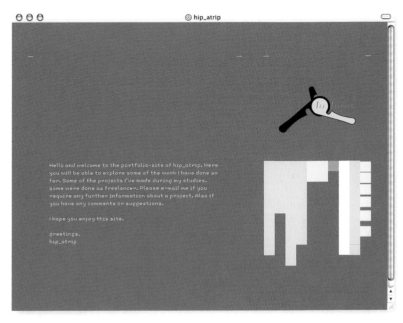

WWW.HIPATRIP.COM
D: JURGEN VANBRABANT
A: HIP_ATRIP, **M:** STYLE@HIPATRIP.COM

WWW.WEBBROTHERS.IT
D: STEFANO BALDUINI, **C:** MARCO DORONI
A: WEBBROTHERS, **M:** DESIGN@WEBBROTHERS.IT

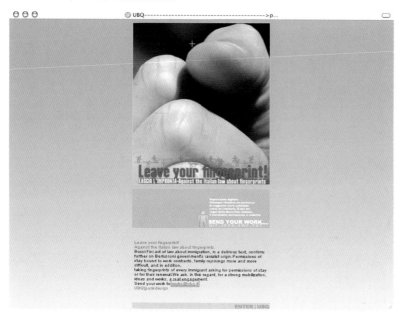

WWW.UBQ.IT
D: MIMMO MANES
A: UBQ, **M:** INFO@UBQ.IT

WWW.PIOGGIACIDA.COM
D: MAX BOSCHINI
A: FACCIA DA PIXEL, **M:** IO@MAXBOSCHINI.COM

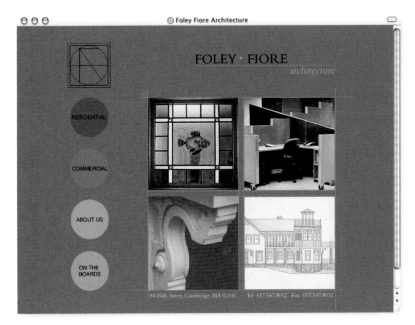

WWW.FOLEYFIORE.COM
D: MARY JO WOOTTON
A: MINDEX TECHNOLOGIES,INC, **M:** MARYJO@MINDEX.COM

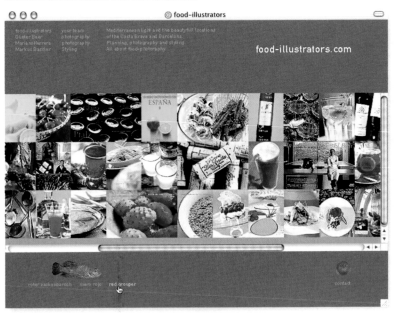

TOMATE@FOOD-ILLUSTRATORS.COM
D: MARKUS BASSLER, **P:** MARIANO HERRERA
A: INFINITE-LIGHT.NET, **M:** TOMATE@FOOD-ILLUSTRATORS.COM

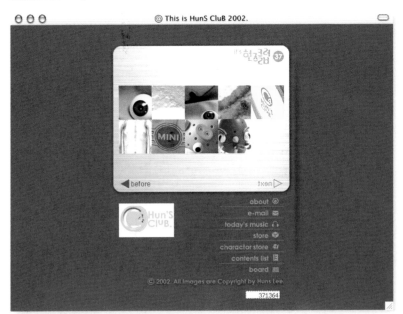

WWW.HUNSCLUB.COM
D: MYUNG-HUN LEE
M: GREGHUNS@LYCOS.CO.KR

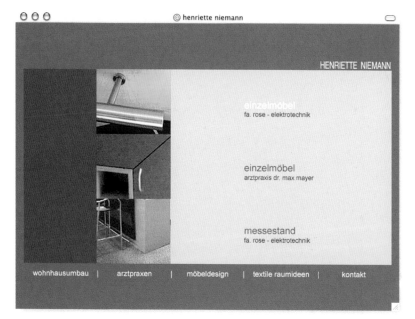

WWW.NIEMANN-H.DE
D: ANTJE WEBER, **C:** HANNO DENKER
A: DIE QUERDENKER, **M:** ANTJEWEBER2000@GMX.DE

WWW.DIDIER.GRAMMARE.FREE.FR
D: JEANNE DIDIER
M: JEANNE.DIDIER@LIBERTYSURF.FR

WWW.PARIND.COM
D: PARIND SHAH
A: PARIND ASSOCIATES, **M:** PARIND@PARIND.COM

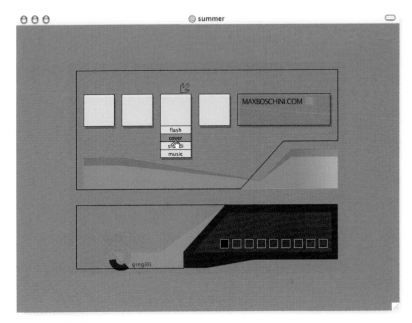

WWW.MAXBOSCHINI.COM
D: MAX BOSCHINI
A: GELATINA, **M:** IO@MAXBOSCHINI.COM

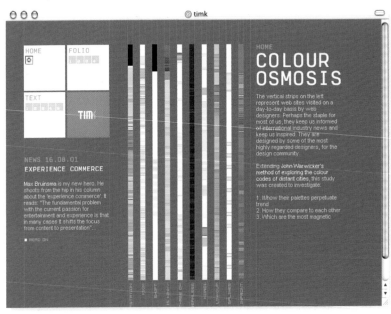

WWW.TIMKOTSIAKOS.COM
D: TIM KOTSIAKOS
M: TIMK@MINDLESS.COM.AU

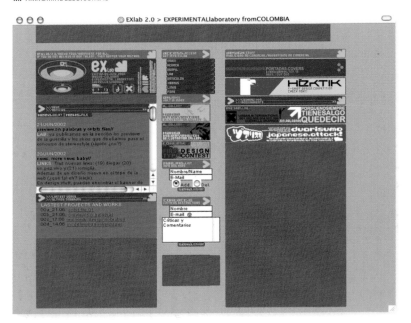

WWW.MEMBERS.TRIPOD.COM/EXLAB/HTML/INDEX.HTML
D: EDGARD IVAN GALLO PALMA
M: EXLABORATORY@HOTMAIL.COM

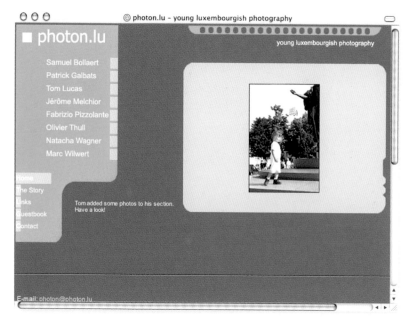

WWW.PHOTON.LU
D: TOM LUCAS
M: PHOTON@PHOTON.LU

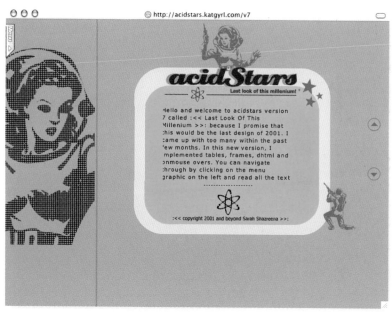

WWW.ACIDSTARS.KATGYRL.COM
D: SARAH SHAZREENA
M: EUPHORIA@KATGYRL.COM

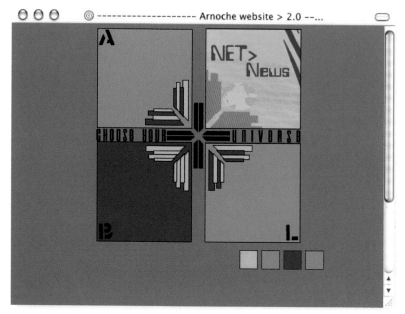

WWW.ARNOCHE.COM
D: ARNAUD LACOCHE
M: ARNOCHE@ARNOCHE.COM

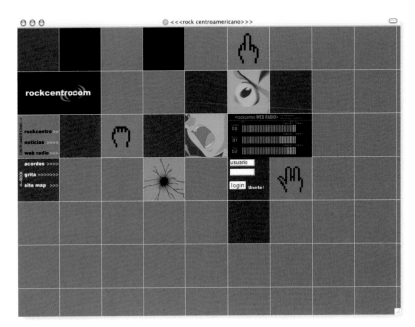

WWW.ROCKCENTRO.COM
D: CARLOS MURILLO
M: CARLOS@ROCKCENTRO.COM

WWW.HESPELER.COM
D: STEVE GAUDER, **C:** JOHN GOODWIN, **P:** STEVE GABANY
M: STEVIEG@SYMPATICO.CA

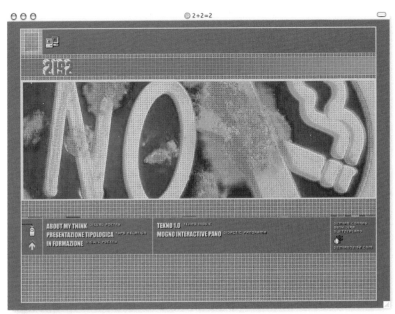

WWW.2IS2.COM
D: CONRAD DEMIAN
A: POINTPIXEL | COMMUNICATION DESIGN, **M:** INFO@POINTPIXEL.COM

WWW.REDWHITE.CH
D: CONRAD DEMIAN
A: POINTPIXEL | COMMUNICATION DESIGN, **M:** INFO@POINTPIXEL.COM

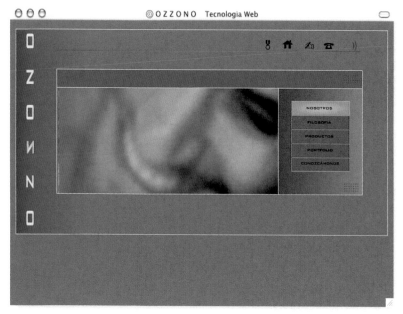

WWW.OZZONO.COM
D: FRANCISCO JAVIER SANCHEZ FERNANDEZ
A: OZZONO, **M:** OZZONO@OZZONO.COM

WWW.WEBAGENT007.COM
D: JAMES BEGERA
A: WEBAGENT007, **M:** INFO@WEB

279

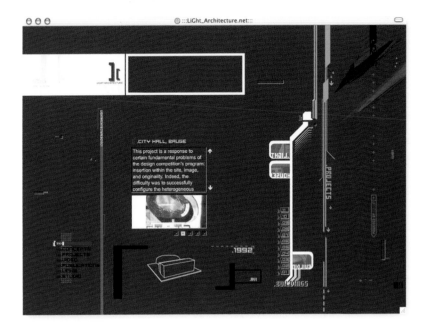

WWW.RANAULO.COM
D: STEFANO PEDRETTI
A: PULP, **M:** INFO@PULPIT.IT

WWW.MOLOMUCHO.COM
D: RICARDO CABELLO, **C:** JAN CARLO MITYORN
M: THEBOY@P1X.ORG

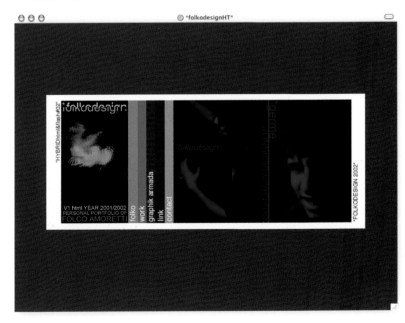

WWW.FOLKODESIGN.COM
D: FOLCO AMORETTI
A: *FOLKODESIGN*, **M:** FOLKO@LIBERO.IT

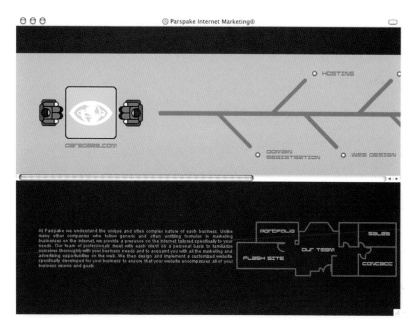

WWW.PARSPAKE.COM
D: MR. A. HAMSHEMI, H. HARANDIAN
A: PARSPAKE CO, **M:** SUPPORT@PARSPAKE.COM

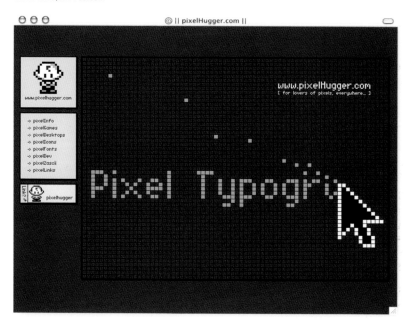

WWW.JUXTAFLO.COM
D: JUSTIN ADLEFF, CHAD CROSS
M: INFLUX@JUXTAFLO.COM

WWW.PIXELHUGGER.COM
D: PETE EVERETT
A: PLAYERTHREE, **M:** PETE@PIXELHUGGER.COM

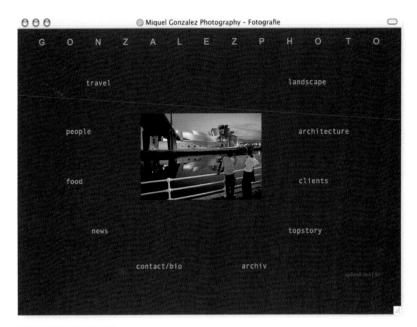

WWW.GONZALEZPHOTO.COM
D: MIQUEL GONZALEZ
A: GONZALEZPHOTO, **M:** MAIL@GONZALEZPHOTO.COM

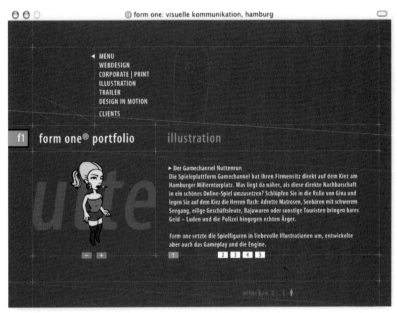

WWW.FORM-ONE.DE
D: CARLO KRUEGER, **C:** CHRISTOPHER GLAUBITZ
A: FORM ONE - VISUAL COMMUNICATION, **M:** INFO@FORM-ONE.DE

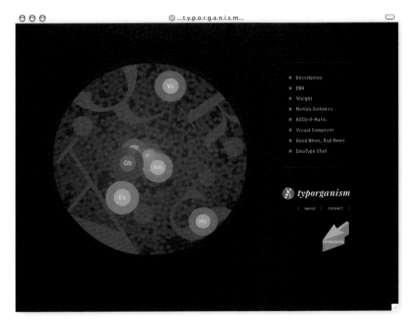

WWW.TYPORGANISM.COM
D: GICHEOL LEE
A: STUDIOTIMO, **M:** CAMEO@STUDIOTIMO.COM

WWW.UNDERCAST.COM
D: REG HERYGERS, **C:** CHRISTIAN AMMAN
A: UNDERCAST GRAPHIC & WEBDESIGN, **M:** REG@UNDERCAST.COM

WWW.CEROUNO.COM.AR
D: BRUNO COPPOLA, **C:** SERGIO CIARAVINBO, **P:** PABLO CAROU
M: PABLO@CEROUNO.COPM.AR

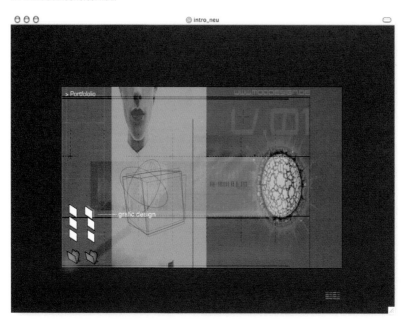

WWW.MODDESIGN.DE
D: MIKE JOHN OTTO
A: MODDESIGN, **M:** INFO@MODDESIGN.DE

WWW.COCACOLA.NL
D: HENK-JAN BERKHOFF
A: CLOCKWORK, **M:** HENKJAN@CLOCKWORK.NL

WWW.PRIMERAPERSONA.COM
D: ANNA MARIA LOPEZ
A: ANNA-OM-LINE MULTIMEDIATIC DESIGNS, **M:** ANNA@FASHIONMAS.COM

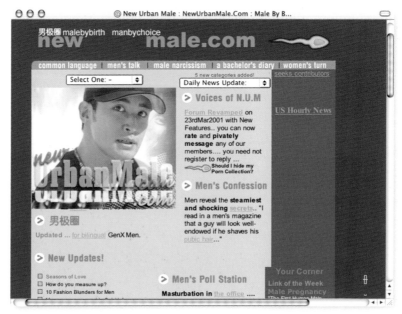

WWW.NEWURBANMALE.COM
D: SHENZI CHUA
A: MBMC INTERNATIONAL, **M:** SHENZI@MBMC.NET

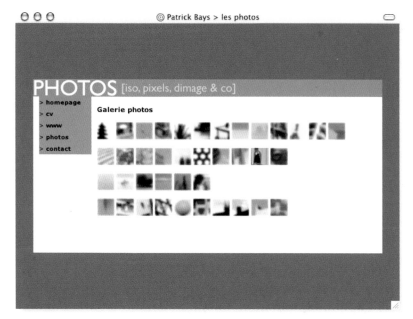

WWW.PATRICKBAYS.CH
D: PATRICK BAYS
M: PATRICK.BAYS@EPFL.CH

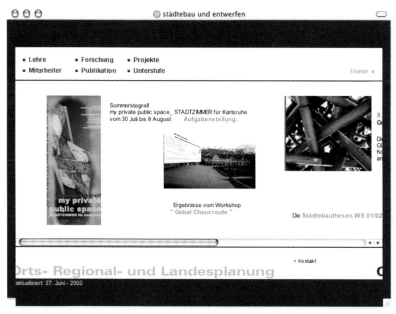

WWW.UNI-KARLSRUHE.DE/~STBA
D: MATTI WIRTH
A: STBA, **M:** MATTIWIRTH@WEB.DE

WWW.QUADRADISPLAY.COM
D: PICCARDA DI MONTEREALE
A: PRISMA S.R.L., **M:** SUPERPIC@LIBERO.IT

WWW.2ADVANCED.COM
D: ERIC JORDAN
A: 2ADVANCED STUDIOS, **M:** TNOVAK@2ADVANCED.COM

WWW.FASE2.DE
D: SEVERIN BRETTMEISTER
A: FA-RO MARKETING, **M:** SEVERIN@FA-RO.DE

WWW.HANSLOEFFEN.NL
D: GREA VAN VLERKEN, **C:** MASCHA VAN KEMPEN
A: OPLIJN, **M:** GREA@OPLIJN.NL

WWW.PIXELSURGEON.COM
D: JASON ARBER
M: JASON@PIXELSURGEON.COM

WWW.ANGEL-ORFEBRE.COM
D: RAFAEL REVIRIEGO
A: EQUIPO I-PEL E A2, **M:** RAFAEL@REVIRIEGO.COM

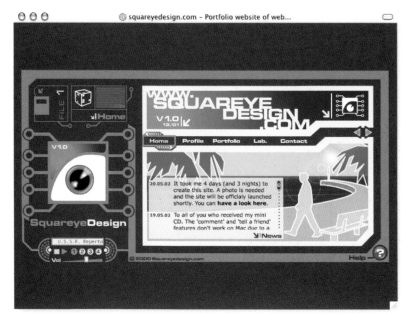

WWW.SQUAREYEDESIGN.COM
D: FRÈDÈRIC CAUNANT
M: CONTACT@SQUAREYEDESIGN.COM

WWW.IWDPRODUCTION.COM
D: JONAS LUNDBERG, **P:** JOAKIM HOEGSET
A: I.W.D. PRODUCTION, **M:** JLUNDBERG@IWDPRODUCTION.COM

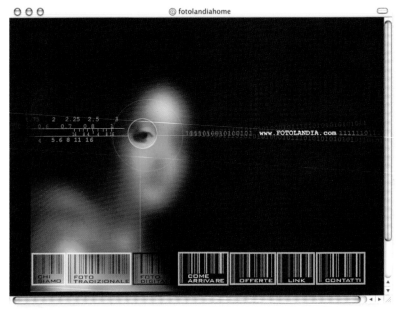

WWW.FOTOLANDIA.COM
D: GABRIELE CAVAZZANO
A: THE FORGE GROUP, **M:** CAVAZZANO@TISCALI.IT

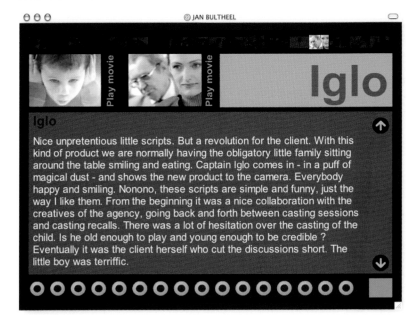

WWW.JANBUL.BE
D: INES VAN BELLE
A: PINKER, **M:** INFO@PINKER.BE

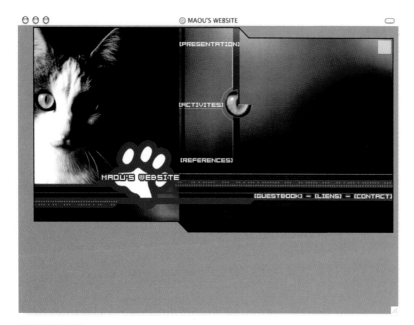

WWW.MAOU.FR.FM
D: ANTHONY THIBAULT
M: ANTHONY@GRAPHISMEDIA.COM

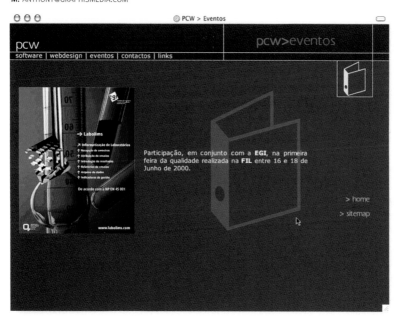

WWW.LABOLIMS.COM
D: ANA GRANJA
A: PCW, **M:** PAULA.GRANJA@LABOLIMS.COM

WWW.202OK.DE
D: UWE SKRABS
A: 01 DIGITALES DESIGN GMBH, **M:** SKRABS@01DIGITALESDESIGN.DE

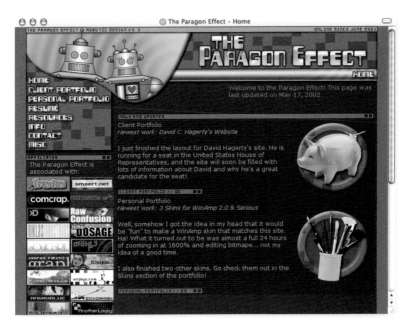

WWW.PARAGONEFFECT.COM
D: BRANDEE WARD
M: PARAGON@PARAGONEFFECT.COM

WWW.ULTRAWHEELS.COM
D: STEVE GAUDER, **C:** JOHN GOODWIN, **P:** STEVE GABANY
M: STEVIEG@SYMPATICO.CA

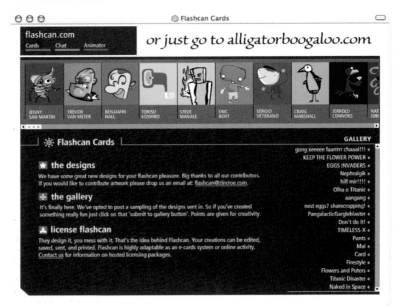

WWW.FLASHCAN.COM/CARDS
D: JASON KROGH
A: ZINC ROE DESIGN, **M:** INFO@ZINCROE.COM

WWW.RADIOREPUBLIC.COM
D: LIAN HO
M: GUYBOSS@SINAMAN.COM

WWW.BLACKLEMON.COM
D: NICOLA BELLOTTI, **C:** GHITA PASQUALI
A: BLACKLEMON S.R.L., **M:** INFO@BLACKLEMON.COM

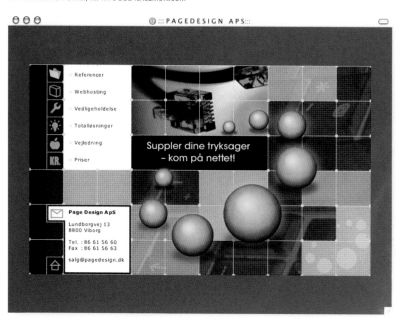

WWW.PAGEDESIGN.DK
D: MICHAEL ELKJÊR
A: PAGE DESIGN, **M:** MICHAEL@PAGEDESIGN.DK

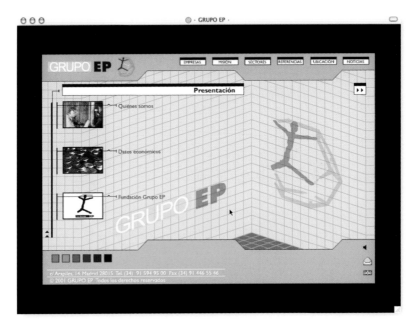

WWW.GRUPOEP.ES
D: JUAN JOSÈ PALACIOS VALDECANTOS, **C:** DIEGO PINILLA
A: BINDAR, **M:** JUANJO_P@YAHOO.COM

WWW.ZONEDESIGN.CJB.NET
D: JOE FAIZAL RIZA
A: ZONEDESIGN, **M:** ZONEGUNS28@HOTMAIL.COM

WWW.ANDRAWEBDESIGN.NL
D: RUDOLF FEHRMANN
A: ANDRAWEBDESIGN, **M:** SALES@ANDRAWEBDESIGN.NL

WWW.KIFI.BE
D: HANS VAN DE VELDE
M: HANS_VANDEVELDE@YAHOO.COM

WWW.STREAKERMAN.COM
D: BEN HIBON
A: UNIT9, **M:** UNIT9@UNIT9.COM

WWW.INICIA.ES/DE/ESCUELAARTESEGOVIA
D: JOSÈ LUIS GILARRANZ LEONOR
A: ESCUELA DE ARTE DE SEGOVIA, **M:** ESARTESEGO@INICIA.ES

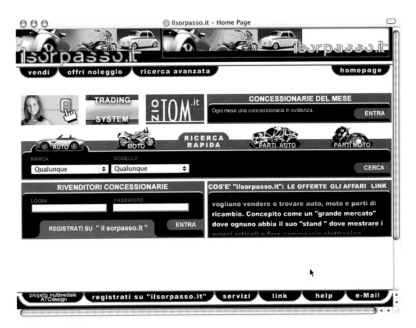

WWW.ILSORPASSO.IT
D: ALBERTO BARTOLI
A: ATO DESIGN SRL, **M:** ALBERTO@ATODESIGN.IT

WWW.VIPSRL.IT
D: SIMONA SCACCO, **C:** MATTEO FIORELLINI
M: SIMONA@LINKNET.IT

WWW.THEEXPAT.COM
D: HAIKAL LIM
A: NA, **M:** HAIKAL.LIM@ASIAONE.COM.SG

WWW.ARS3.COM
D: FERRAN SENDRA
A: ARS3, **M:** FERRANSENDRA@HOTMAIL.COM

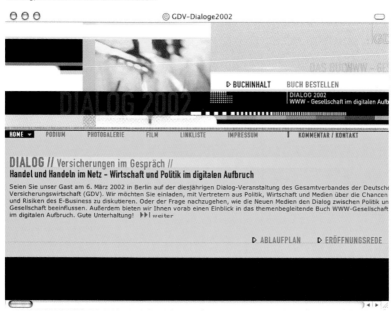

WWW.GDV-DIALOGE2002.DE
D: KATRIN BRACKMANN, **P:** GESAMTVERBAND DEUTSCHER VERSICHERER
A: ECC ONLINE RELATIONS, **M:** KA@OZ-ZONE.DE

WWW.NUOVEMODELLE.COM
D: NICOLA BELLOTTI, **C:** GHITA PASQUALI
A: BLACKLEMON S.R.L., **M:** P.GAMBAZZA@KI-WI.NET

WWW.UPSO.ORG
D: DUSTIN AMERY HOSTETLER
A: UPSo . oRG, **M:** UPSODESIGN@HOTMAIL.COM

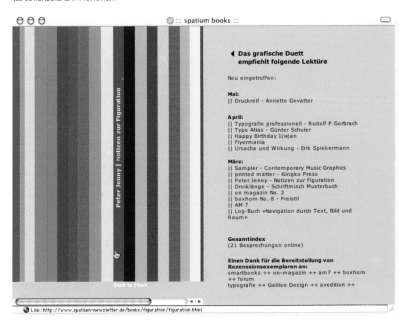

WWW.ACME.IT/LALATTA
D: LORENZO LALATTA
M: LORENZO.LALATTA@ACME.IT

WWW.SPATIUM-NEWSLETTER.DE
D: PETER REICHARD, CHRISTOPHER LINDLOHR
A: TYPOSITION, **M:** TEAM@TYPOSITION.DE

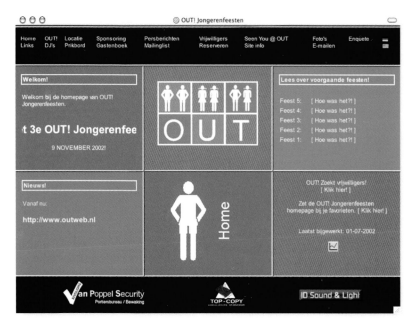

WWW.OUTWEB.NL
D: P.J.H.M. HENDRIKX
M: EMAILEN@HOME.NL

WWW.ELVISJACKSONPLANET.COM
D: MIANI ROBERTA
M: INFO@ELVISJACKSONPLANET.COM

WWW.TOKIDOKI.IT/CONTENT.HTML
D: SIMONE LEGNO
M: SIMONE@TOKIDOKI.IT

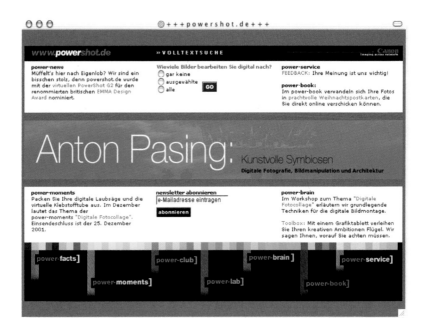

WWW.POWERSHOT.DE
D: MARIA TOMECZEK, **C:** WAGNER
A: TWMD GMBH, **M:** MT@TWMD.DE

WWW.GISGELATI.IT
D: ALBA BERTOLINI, **C:** SONIA FIGONE, **P:** DARTWAY
M: ABERTOLINI@DARTWAY.COM

WWW.MW091280.COM
D: MARK WONG
M: HIBIKI21@INFOSEEK.JP

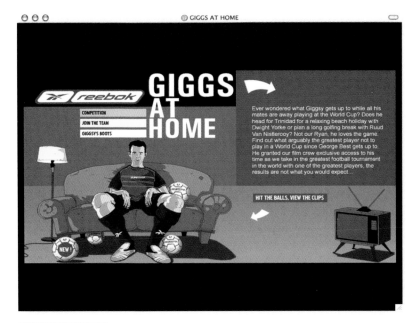

WWW.GIGGSATHOME.COM
D: BEN HIBON
A: UNIT9, **M:** UNIT9@UNIT9.COM

WWW.TRIUMPH-INTERNATIONAL.COM
D: MARINA SHTATLENDER, **C:** MARIO KLINGEMANN, **P:** COLLIN CROOME
A: COMA2, **M:** WWW.COMA2.COM

WWW.NEXTOPEN.IT
D: ALESSIO PAPI
A: NEXTOPEN MULTIMEDIA, **M:** ALESSIO@NEXTOPEN.IT

WWW.INSANITY.CA
D: BRIAN LARTER
A: INSANE DESIGNS, **M:** KAYLENN@CANADA.COM

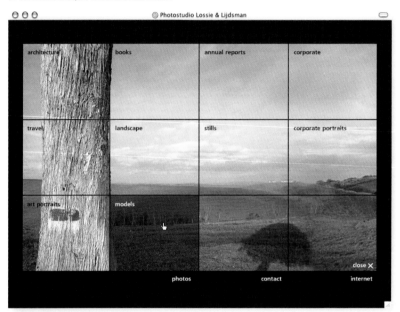

WWW.FOTOSTUDIOLOSSIE.NL
D: EUGENE YUSUPOV, **P:** HUGO LOSSIE
M: MLOSSIE@NAVITAS.NL

WWW.GOINGONSIX.COM
D: SEAN DONOHUE
M: SEAN@GOINGONSIX.COM

WWW.LICHT-BILD-TON.DE
D: NIELS BUENEMANN
A: FORM ONE - VISUAL COMMUNICATION, **M:** INFO@FORM-ONE.DE

WWW.YARDNYC.COM
D: STEPHEN NIEDZWIECKI
A: YARD, **M:** CURTIS@SOFIERCE

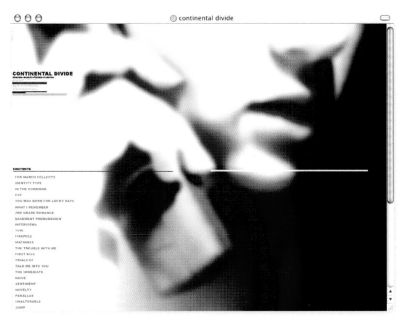

WWW.CONTDIV.COM
D: MIKE HEADLEY
M: MIKE@CONTDIV.COM

WWW.4SCREEN.NET
D: RAY CHUE
A: 4SCREEN GRAPHIC, **M:** RAYCHUE@4SCREEN.NET

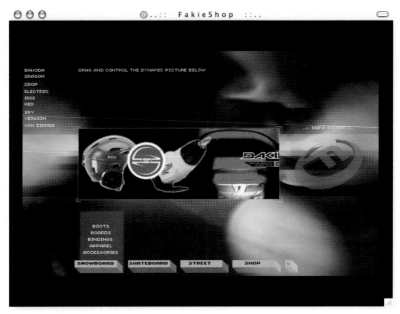

WWW.FAKIESHOP.COM
D: MARCO FORNASIER, **C:** RUDY PIO
M: TTRONKO@NEA07.ORG

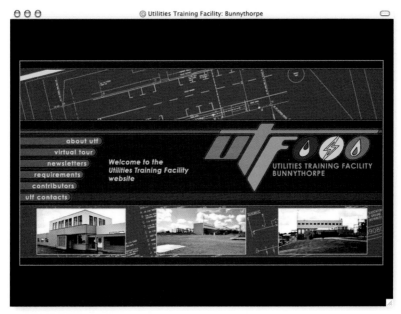

WWW.UTF.CO.NZ
D: RONALD STALLMACH
A: TEXTUS DESIGN, **M:** INFO@TEXTUSDESIGN.CO.NZ

WWW.IBMEN.COM
D: GEORGE THOMAS
A: OGILVY INTERACTIVE WORLDWIDE, **M:** GEORGE.THOMAS@OGILVY.COM

WWW.SULTANA.NL
D: GIJS VAN DER SCHOOT, **C:** FORTUNATO GEELHOED, **P:** GERARD DE BOER
A: DBK OGILVY & MATHERS, **M:** MARK@WEBINZICHT.COM

WWW.ALANCHANDESIGN.COM
D: PETER LO, **C:** JUMBO DREAM, **P:** ALAN CHAN
A: ALAN CHAN DESIGN COMPANY, **M:** CHANFAI@MAC.COM

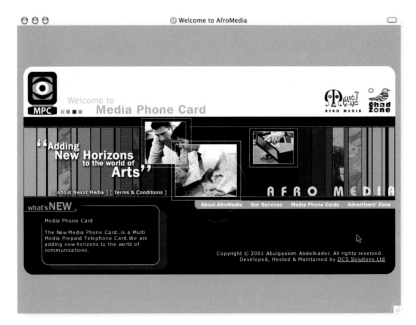

WWW.MEDIAPHONECARD.COM
D: JIMMY TEO
A: VOXMEDIA, **M:** JIMMY@DCSSOLUTIONS.NET

WWW.SIZE-VLC.COM
D: VOLKER SCARPATETTI
A: o A LA IZQUIERDA, **M:** VOLKER@CEROALAIZQUIERDA.COM

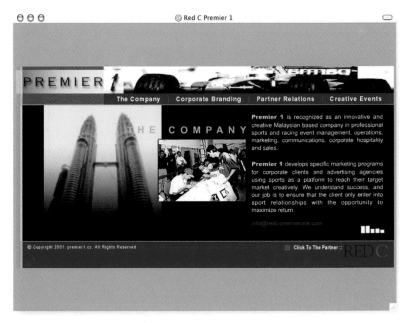

WWW.REDC-PREMIERONE.COM
D: CHARLENE SUMMERS
A: INGENISYS SDN BHD, **M:** EVIE@ASIA1.COM

WWW.2METHODS.COM/SECONDMETHOD
D: VITALIY ONISHENKO
A: 2METHODS.COM, **M:** VITALIY@2METHODS.COM

WWW.GATZANIS.DE
D: SONJA HÖLZLE
A: BEAUFORT 8, **M:** HOELZLE@BEAUFORT8.DE

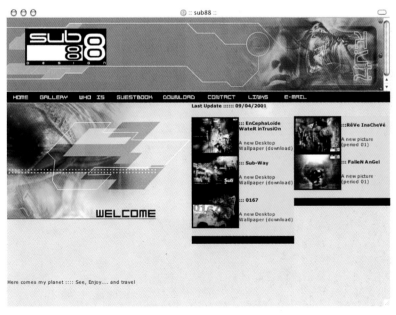

WWW.SUB88.COM
D: DAVID VINEIS
A: SUB88, **M:** DAVID@SUB88.COM

WWW.SICKONINETEEN.COM
D: RAFAEL RUIZ CASARES
M: RAFAEL@SICKONINETEEN.COM

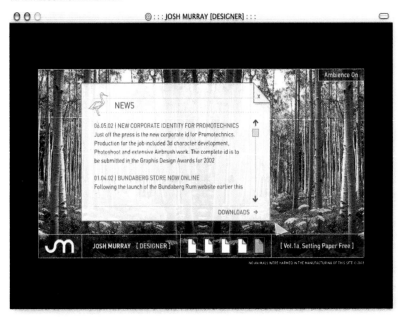

WWW.JOSHMURRAY.COM.AU
D: JOSH MURRAY
A: JOSH MURRAY DESIGN, **M:** HELLO@JOSHMURRAY.COM.AU

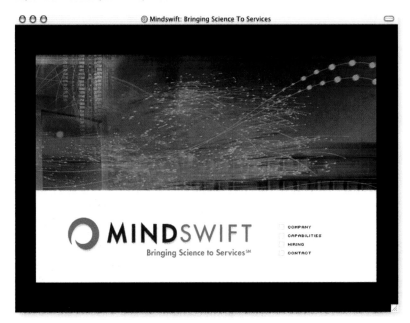

WWW.MINDSWIFT.COM
D: SHAWN SQUIRES
A: MARCH NETWORKS, **M:** SSQUIRES@MARCHNETWORKS.COM

WWW.PRACHTBOULEVARD.AT
D: RUDOLF HORACZEK
M: R.HORACZEK@PRACHTBOULEVARD.AT

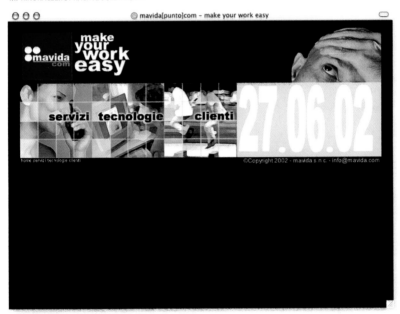

WWW.MAVIDA.COM
D: VIRGILIO VENEZIA
A: MAVIDA S.N.C., **M:** INFO@MAVIDA.COM

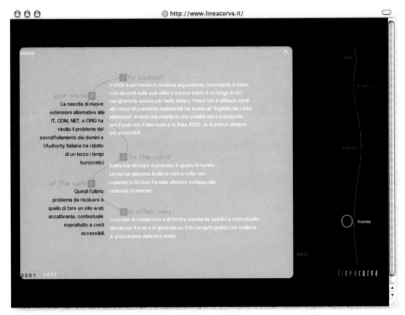

WWW.LINEACURVA.IT
D: DANIELE PODDA
A: LINEACURVA, **M:** INFO@LINEACURVA.IT

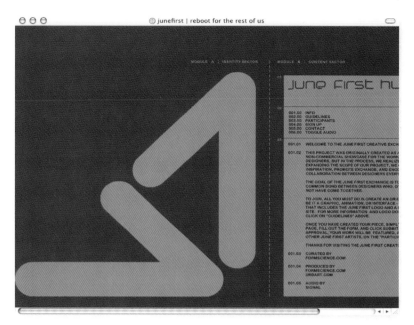

WWW.URBART.COM/JUNEFIRST
D: MIKHAIL PESCHAN
M: MISHA@FORMSCIENCE.COM

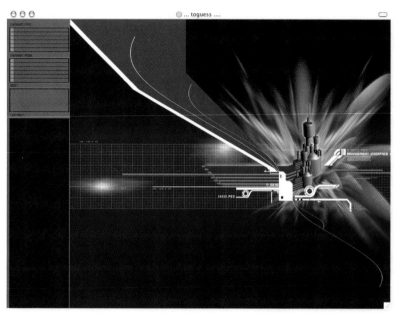

WWW.TOGUESS.NET
D: CYRIL POUTEAU
M: TOGUESS76@HOTMAIL.COM

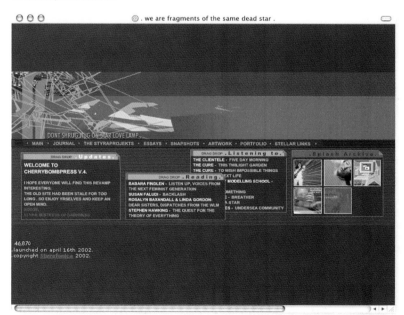

WWW.CHERRYBOMBPRESS.COM
D: GINETTE CHITTICK
M: STYRA@CHERRYBOMBPRESS.COM

WWW.RSMOBILE.DE
D: WALTER MÖSSLER, **C:** PACO LA LUCA, **P:** BAMBOO PRODUCTIONS
A: TOUCHEE, **M:** INFO@TOUCHEE.DE

WWW.LOCO-SHOP.COM
D: NICOLAS BARNABE, **C:** STEPHANE LEVY, **P:** JOHN HASSAN
A: WSCOM, **M:** ANJIE@NY.COM

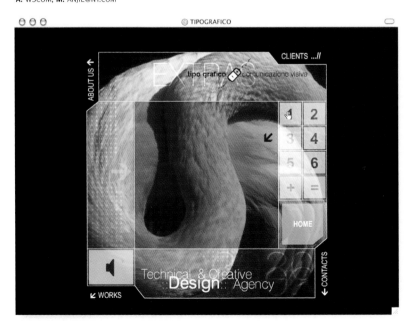

WWW.TIPOGRAFICO.IT
D: ANDREA GRECO
A: TIPO GRAFICO, **M:** RGB@TIPOGRAFICO.IT

WWW.HARRYWONG.NET
D: HARRY WONG
A: IDALE MEDIA, INC., **M:** HARRY@HARRYWONG.NET

WWW.MATTEOGANNA.IT
D: MATTEO GANNA
M: MATTEO@MATTEOGANNA.IT

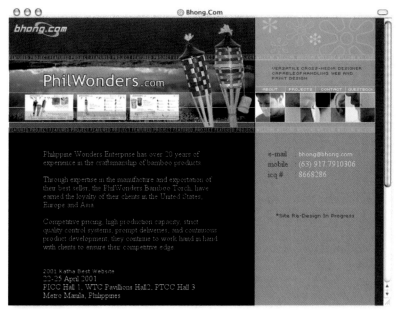

WWW.BHONG.COM
D: CAPIÒA BHONG
A: BHONG.COM, **M:** BHONG@BHONG.COM

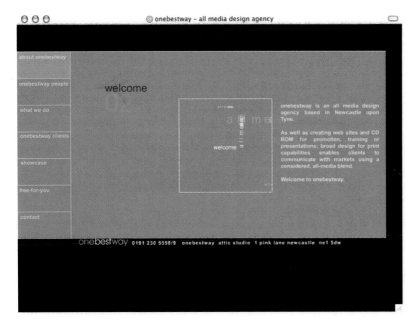

WWW.ONEBESTWAY.COM
D: JUSTIN COCKBURN, **C:** PHELIM CAVLAN
A: ONEBESTWAY, **M:** MIKE@ONEBESTWAY.COM

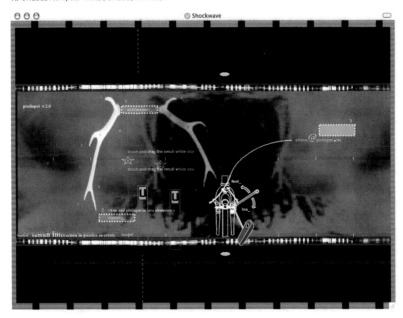

WWW.PINILOPEI.DE
D: TOMAS GARCIA GODINES
A: 3W4U , **M:** TOMAS@3W4U.DE

WWW.BUMCELLO.COM
D: SAMUEL ROUSSELIER
M: SAMUEL@BUMCELLO.COM

WWW.THEA-WEIRES.DE
D: RENE MARTIN, **C:** PETER GIERTZ
M: RECEPTION@VS42.COM

WWW.A12ARCHITECTEN.NL
D: JOOST KUIJPERS
A: RDBMC, **M:** INFO@A12ARCHITECTEN.NL

WWW.DIE-NEUEN-68ER.DE
D: KLAUS THEIßING
M: KLAUS.THEISSING@GMX.DE

WWW.BENFRANKDESIGN.COM
D: BEN FRANK
A: BENFRANK{DESIGN}, **M:** BENFRANK@BENFRANKDESIGN.COM

WWW.PURETOUCH.NL
D: JORIS KEESOM
A: ID-LAB, **M:** JORIS@ID-LAB.NL

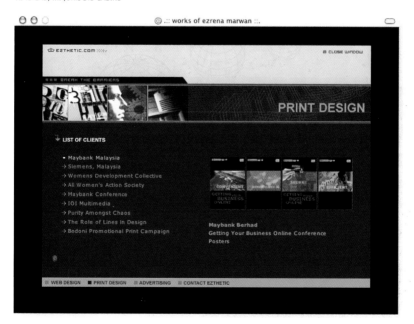

WWW.EZTHETIC.COM
D: EZRENA MARWAN
M: EZRENA@EZTHETIC.COM

WWW.AFLYINTHEWEB.COM
D: OSCAR ALVES
M: AFLYINTHEWEB@AFLYINTHEWEB.COM

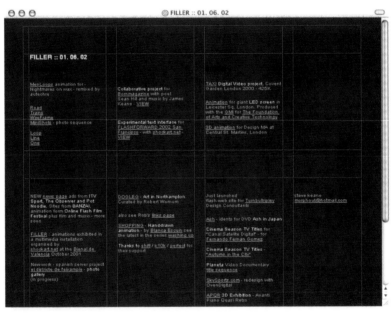

WWW.FILLER.DEMON.CO.UK
D: STEVE KEANE
M: MORPHOUT@HOTMAIL.COM

WWW.GMUNK.COM
D: GMUNK
M: BRADLEY@GMUNK.COM

WWW.TROYALVES.COM
D: DOMINIC CURRENT
A: FOUNDATION7 CREATIVITY AND DESIGN, **M:** DOMINIC@FOUNDATION7.COM

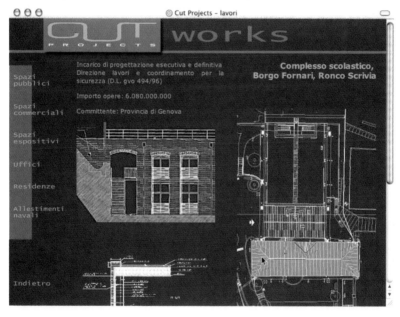

WWW.CUTPROJECTS.COM
D: SERGIO GIOVANNINI
A: DIGITALSTUDIO, **M:** SERGIO@DIGISTUDIO.IT

WWW.ELLINIKO-PANORAMA.GR
D: STEFANOS STEFANIDIS
A: WEB RELATION DESIGN, **M:** STEF@COMPULINK.GR

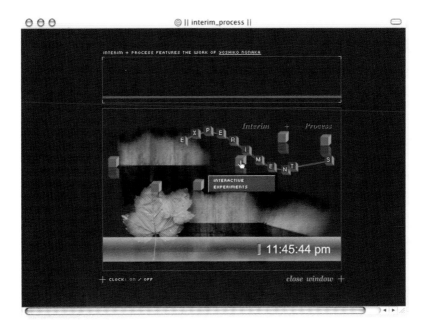

WWW.YOSHIKONONAKA.COM
D: YOSHIKO NONAKA
A: INTERIM+PROCESS, **M:** YNONAKA_BC@HOTMAIL.COM

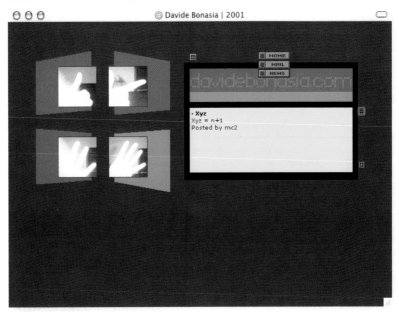

WWW.DAVIDEBONASIA.COM
D: MAX BOSCHINI
A: FACCIA DA PIXEL, **M:** IO@MAXBOSCHINI.COM

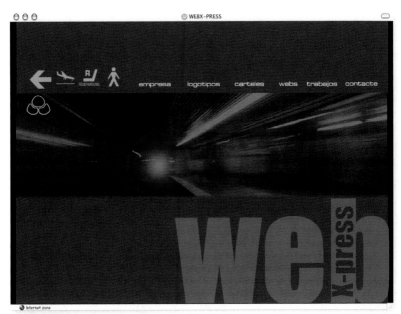

WWW.WEBX-PRESS.NET
D: GONZALO ESTEBAN
A: WEBX-PRESS, **M:** WEBX-PRESS@WANADOO.ES

WWW.STRUNYPODZIMU.CZ
D: RADEK VASICEK
M: RADEKV@YAHOO.COM

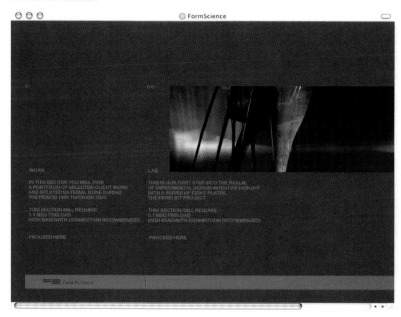

WWW.FORMSCIENCE.COM
D: MIKHAIL PESCHAN
M: MISHA@FORMSCIENCE.COM

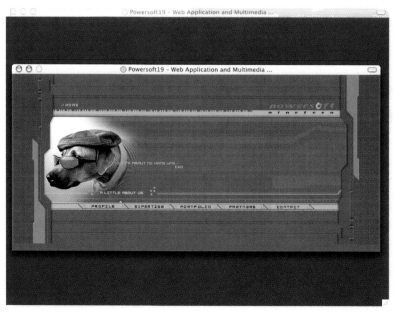

WWW.POWERSOFT19.COM
D: AIYAZ KIDWAI, **C:** TANYA ELAHI, **P:** ISRAR KHAN
A: POWERSOFT19, **M:** AIYAZ@HOTMAIL.COM

WWW.WOODWOODY.COM
D: NICOLAS CARACCIOLO, **C:** ANDRES ALONSO
A: FAHRENHEIT 451, **M:** NCARACCIOLO@451.COM

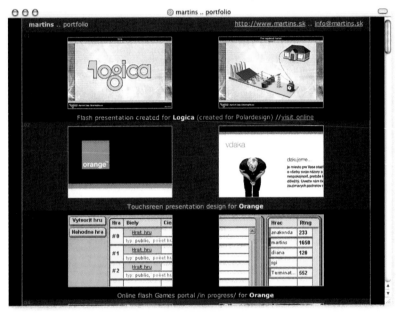

WWW.MARTINS.SK
D: MARTIN SOJKA
A: MARTINS, **M:** INFO@MARTINS.SK

WWW.FRANSMOLENAAR.NL
D: HALUK DEMIR, **P:** GLENN LEMING
A: CLOCKWORK, **M:** DEMIRHALUK@HOTMAIL.COM

WWW.WEPNET.TV/PRNET.HTM
D: RICCARDO IANNARELLI, **C:** VALERIA RIPPA, **P:** ANTONELLO CASTELLI
A: WEP SRL, **M:** RICCARDO@FORMATC.IT

WWW.KIRAGLUSCHKOFF.COM
D: KIMMO KUUSISTO, MISA KANNOS
A: AC-MAINOS, **M:** KIMMO@ACMAINOS.FI

WWW.SKRESLETADVENTURESERVICES.COM
D: GONZALO FREXAS, **C:** SEBASTIAN LUJAN, **P:** ALEJANDRA PALLAS
A: GOON DESIGN, **M:** INFO@GOONDESIGN.COM

WWW.COMMUNICASIA-ONLINE.COM
D: JOE CHUA, **C:** SIE LAY TIN, **P:** GOH JULIANA
A: VOXMEDIA, **M:** JOE@VOXMEDIA.COM.SG

WWW.LOMOSHOT.COM
D: CHRIS HORSTMANN
M: CHRIS@LOMOSHOT.COM

WWW.BEVODESIGN.COM
D: BEN VOOS
A: BEVO DESIGN, **M:** BEN@BEVODESIGN.COM

WWW.IN-BLEU.COM
D: GWEN BLUEMELS
A: SOLARSHELLNETWORK, **M:** BLEU@IN-BLEU.COM

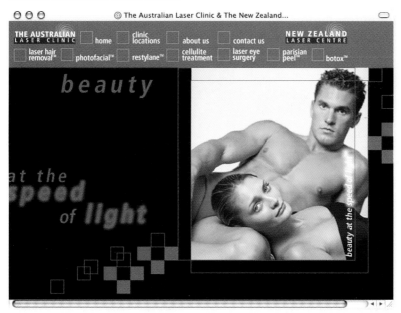

WWW.LASERCLINIC.COM.AU
D: TANIA TAN
A: WEBGIRL PRODUCTIONS, **M:** WEBGIRL@TODAY.COM.AU

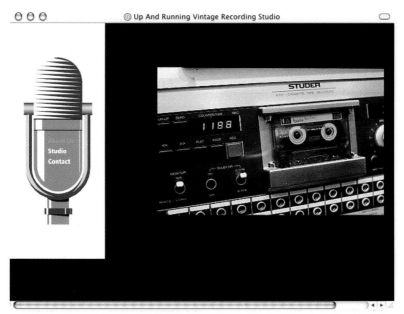

WWW.UP-N-RUNNIN.NET
D: CHRISTIAN CHAMPAGNE
A: CHRISTIANCHAMPAGNE.COM, **M:** CHRIS@HELSINKIJAZZ.CO.UK

WWW.AIR-ATLANTIS.COM
D: STEFANO ARGENTI, **C:** LORENZO GIOVANNINI, **P:** AIR-ATLANTIS
A: ATLANTIS SRL, **M:** M.BOTTI@AIR-ATLANTIS.COM

WWW.4PMEDIA.COM
D: YAGO DIAZ DIZ
M: MAIL@YAGODIAZ.COM

WWW.MJAU-MJAU.COM
D: KARL WARD
M: MJAU@MJAU-MJAU.COM

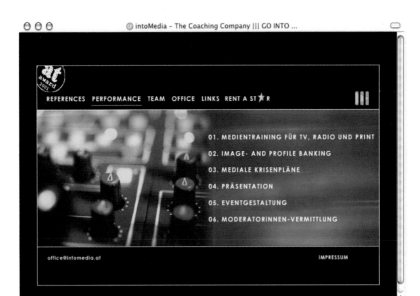

WWW.INTOMEDIA.AT
D: JOERG WUKONIG
A: WUKONIG.COM, **M:** OFFICE@WUKONIG.COM

WWW.LANDSCHAPSARCHITEKTEN.NL
D: KOEN HAUSPY, **C:** PASCAL IMMERZEEL
M: KOEN@FLUIDO.AS

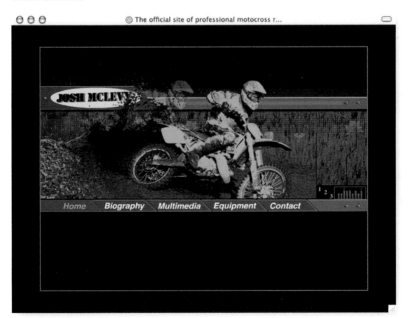

WWW.JOSHMCLEVY.COM
D: JOSH MARKOWITZ
M: JM@JOSHMARKOWITZ.COM

WWW.KREATIVMUHELY.HU
D: ZOLTAN CSORDAS, **C:** ATTILA PAL
A: MATAI ÈS VÈGH KREATÌVM"HELY KFT., **M:** PAL.ATTILA@CHELLO.HU

WWW.NAKAMILOUNGE.DE
D: BERND RÜCKER, **C:** M. FANDRÈ
A: NAKAMILOUNGE GMBH, **M:** B.RUECKER@NAKAMILOUNGE.DE

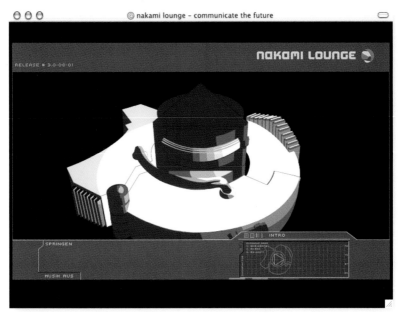

WWW.KATDESIGN.BE
D: TOON VAN DE PUTTE
A: VALORIS, **M:** TOON@KATDESIGN.BE

WWW.VOORDEELCOUPON.NL
D: RODOLFO ENGELEN
A: IDENTITY CONSULTANTS BV, **M:** KONING@IDENTITYCONSULTANTS.NL

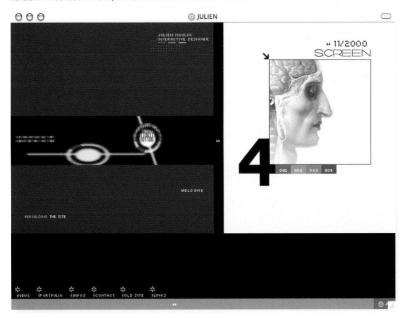

WWW.JULIEN.MOULIN.FREE.FR
D: JULIEN MOULIN
M: JULIEN.MOULIN@NOOS.FR

WWW.TALES.COM.BR
D: TALES SIMON
M: TALES@TALES.COM.BR

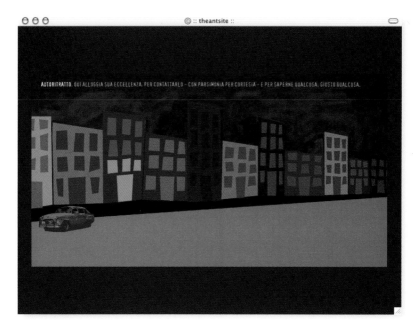

WWW.THEANTSITE.COM
D: ANTONIO CORNACCHIA
M: ANT@THEANTSITE.COM

WWW.BRITZONE.DE
D: VERENA JUNG
M: V_JUNG@GMX.DE

WWW.ZOZOPLANET.NL
D: CAROLINE VAN DEN BERG
A: CROWEB DESIGN, **M:** INFO@CROWEB.NL

WWW.UMBRIAMBIENTE.IT
D: ALESSANDRA COMPAROZZI
A: GRAFICHERO, **M:** INFO@GRAFICHERO.IT

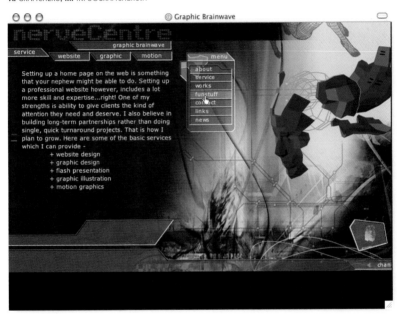

WWW.S8N.CJB.NET
D: SYAMLY RUSHDI
A: GRAPHIC BRAINWAVE, **M:** SYAMLY@MILLENNIUM-INTEGRA.COM

PLANETA.CLIX.PT/PLANETA2000
D: JOAO MARQUES
M: JOAOMM@HOTMAIL.COM

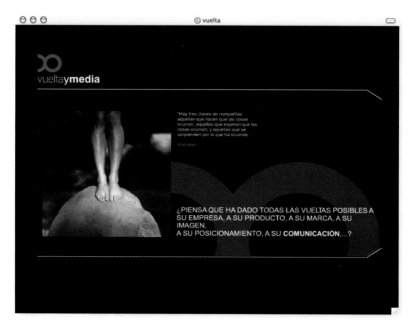

WWW.VUELTAYMEDIA.COM
D: VICENTE HERREROS, **P:** CARLOS BOSCH
A: VUELTAYMEDIA, **M:** VUELTAYMEDIA@VUELTAYMEDIA.COM

WWW.BATTILLOCCHI.COM
D: MASSIMO RISCA, **C:** ANGELO LAZZARI
A: SINTETICA SRL, **M:** RISCA@SINTETICA.IT

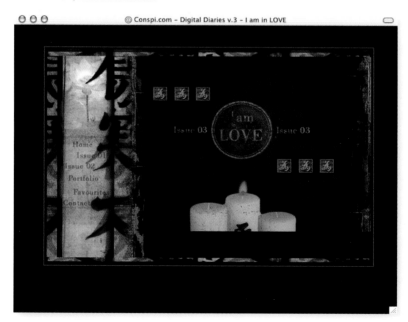

WWW.CONSPI.COM/ISSUE_03
D: VINCENT GHILIONE
M: M@CONSPI.COM

WWW.GIVEMETHE5.COM
D: FERNANDO MOSTACERO SERRA
M: MAKA_INA@HOTMAIL.COM

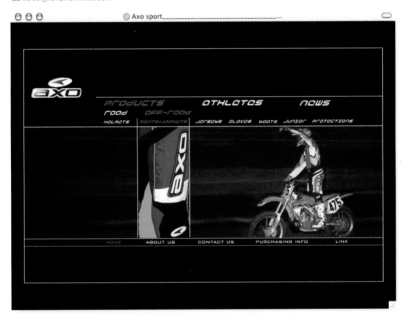

WWW.AXOSPORT.IT
D: CHIARA MUSSINI, LUCA BUSCAGLIA, **C:** PAOLO CHIESA
M: INFO@FACTORYGROUP.IT

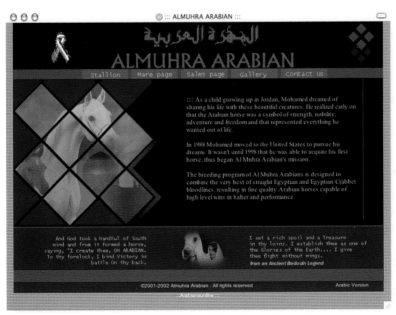

WWW.ALMUHRA.COM
D: EYAD ABUTAHA, **C:** TIM CHIPMAN, **P:** MUHAMAD ABDELKADER
A: WWW.EYAD.COM, **M:** INFO@ARABIANSONLINE.NET

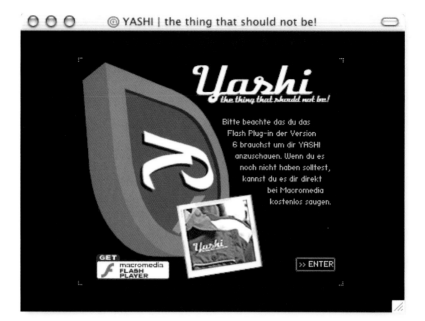

WWW.YASHI.DE
D: ULF GERMANN
M: ULF@YASHI.DE

WWW.BLOOMRIOT.ORG
D: JAN TONELLATO
M: WEBMASTER@BLOOMRIOT.ORG

WWW.KILLERLOOP.COM
D: JIM MORGAN, **P:** RICCARDO ZAMURRI
A: DEEPEND ROMA, **M:** WWW.DEEPEND.IT

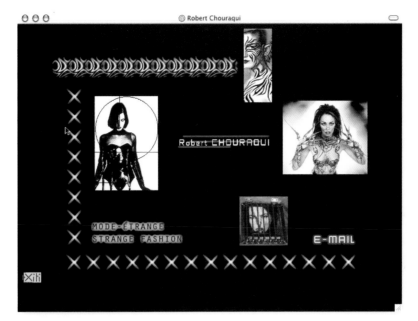

WWW.ROBERTCHOURAQUI.COM
D: ROBERT CHOURAQUI
M: ROBERTCHOURAQUI@ROBERTCHOURAQUI.COM

WWW.KUNGFOU.COM
D: DOC MORZY
A: KUNGFOU, **M:** PROD@KUNGFOU.COM

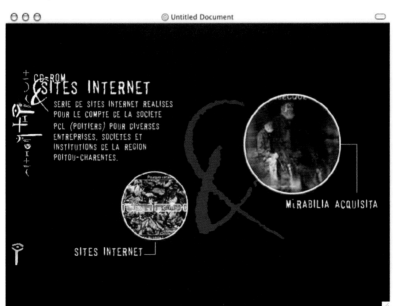

WWW.ANTHONY-THIBAULT.COM
D: ANTHONY THIBAULT
M: ANTHONY@GRAPHISMEDIA.COM

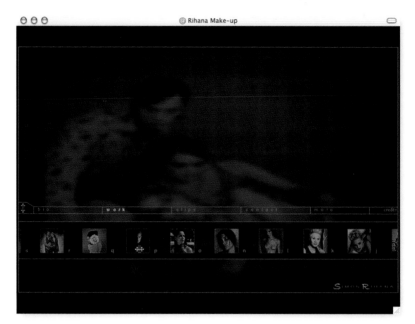

WWW.RIHANA.DK
D: MORTEN VILLADSEN, KIM VILE
A: ESTUPENDO INTERACTIVE I/S, **M:** MV@ESTUPENDO.DK

WWW.KREISLICHT.DE
D: SUSANNE STERNAGEL
M: SUSANNE.STERNAGEL@KREISLICHT.DE

WWW.SIMPLICITY.DOMAINVALET.COM
D: NUMAN PEKGOZ
M: NUMANPEK@HOTMAIL.COM

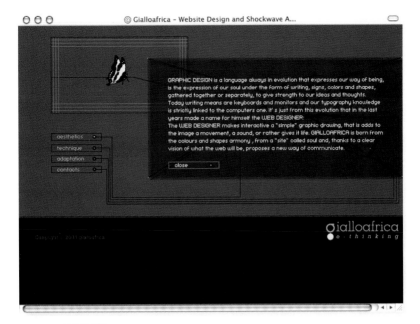

WWW.GIALLOAFRICA.COM
D: RICCI LORENZO
A: GIALLOAFRICA, **M:** INFO@GIALLOAFRICA.COM

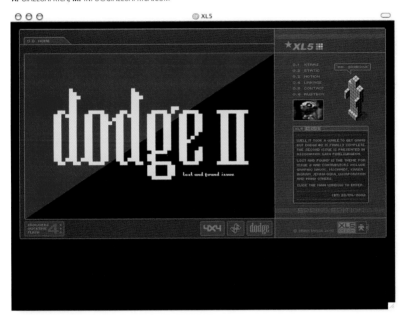

WWW.XL5DESIGN.COM
D: BRIAN TAYLOR
M: BRIAN@XL5DESIGN.COM

WWW.DESIGNHOLIC.COM
D: HIROYUKI KUROIWA
M: BLACK@DESIGNHOLIC.COM

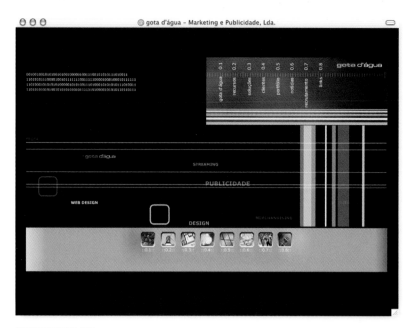

WWW.GOTADAGUA.COM
D: PEDRO MACHADO, **C:** PEDRO SANTOS, **P:** RUI GONZALVES
A: GOTA D'·GUA, **M:** PEDRO.MACHADO@GOTADAGUA.COM

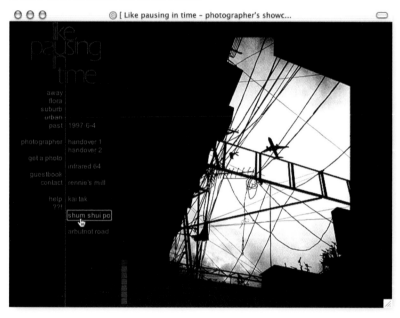

AN.THONY.NET
D: HO CHING KEE
A: LIKE PAUSING IN TIME, **M:** AN@THONY.NET

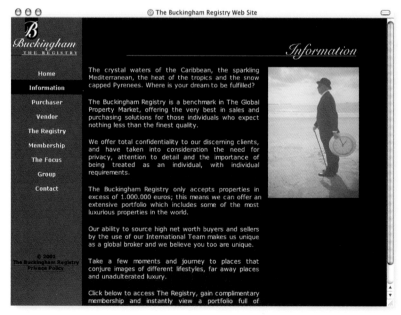

WWW.BUCKINGHAMREALTY.NET
D: BORJA BELLOD
A: IMAGEN CONSULTING, **M:** INFO@BUCKINGHAMREALTY.NET

WWW.ARTEH.COM
D: FABRIZIO RADICA
A: ARTEH, **M:** FABRIZIO@ARTEH.COM

WWW.A123.IT
D: ALESSANDRO DI LELIO
A: KORA S.R.L., **M:** ALESSANDRO.DILELIO@A123.IT

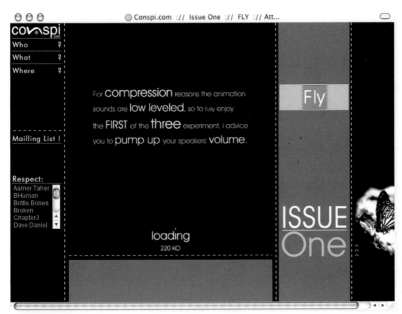

WWW.CONSPI.COM
D: VINCENT GHILIONE
M: CONSPI@CONSPI.COM

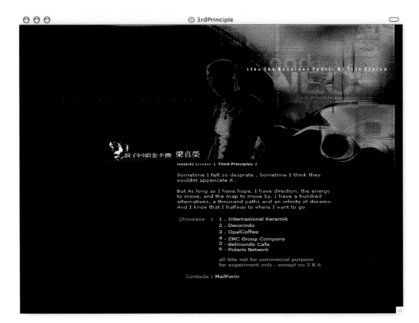

WWW.3RDPRINCIPLE.COM
D: LEONARDY GUNAWAN
M: GUNAWAN@3RDPRINCIPLE.COM

WWW.PEUGEOT.PT/206GTI
D: RAQUEL VIANA
A: EURORSCG CYBERLAB, **M:** RAKEL_V@HOTMAIL.COM

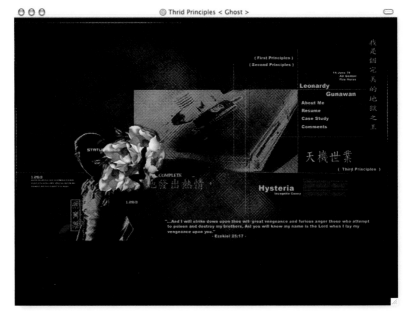

WWW.CASEYHYSTERIA.COM
D: LEONARDY CASEY
A: GUNAWAN, **M:** LEONARDY@CASEYHYSTERIA.COM

WWW.OSCARAD.COM.TW
D: JONATHAN HSU, **C:** JERRY LIN, **P:** SETTHA LEE
A: TYA STUDIO LTD., **M:** SETTHA@TYA.COM.TW

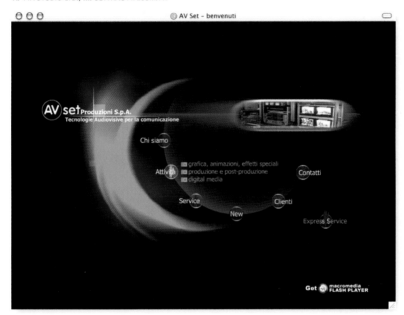

WWW.AVSET.IT
D: DANIELE GIARDINI, SARAH PENNISI
M: DANIELEGIARDINI@HOTMAIL.COM

WWW.PUDDINGBREZEL.DE
D: MICHAEL SCHÄFER
M: ZALS@GMX.DE

WWW.SOARTGROUP.COM
D: NICOLA DESTEFANO
M: EMPUSA@SOARTGROUP.COM

WWW.ICONIQUE.COM
D: CJ VAN GORSEL
M: JOOST@ICONIQUE.COM

WWW.DARKCLUB.DE
D: MARKUS MOHLBERG
A: DARKCLUB, **M:** MARKUS@MOHLBERG.DE

338

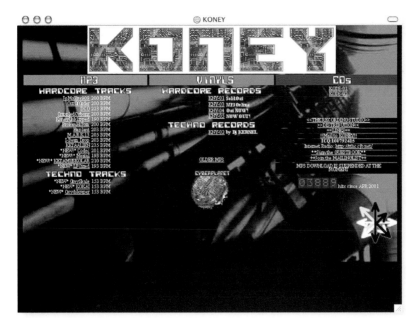

WWW.KONEY.ORG
D: STEFAN EGGER
A: TVB GROflARLTAL, **M:** INFO@GROSSARLTAL.CO.AT

WWW.SIR-OLIVER.COM
D: JOERG WUKONIG
A: WUKONIG.COM, **M:** OFFICE@WUKONIG.COM

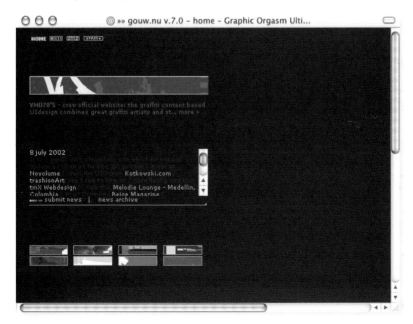

WWW.GOUW.NU
D: PASCAL GOUW
A: GRAPHIC ORGASM ULTIMATE WEBPORTAL, **M:** INFO@GOUW.NU

WWW.STEPAN.3AMP.COM
D: STEPAN HLUCHAN
A: 3 AM PRODUCTIONS, **M:** STEPAN@3AMP.COM

WWW.SUPERDEDO.COM
D: LUCA DRAGO
A: CYBERLABSQUAD, **M:** CYBLAB@TIN.IT

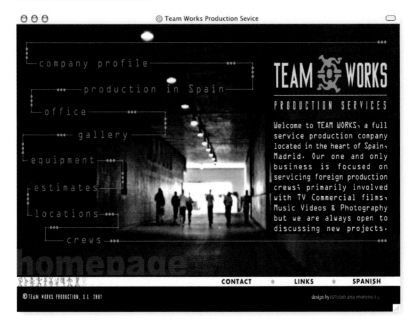

WWW.TEAMWORKSPAIN.COM
D: RICHARD TALUT
A: ESTUDIO ANA MORENO, **M:** RICHARD-STUDIO@MENTA.NET

WWW.GEOCITIES.COM/ELMORO1979
D: JORGE MORENO
M: ELMORO1979@HOTMAIL.COM

WWW.MAXIM.UK.NET
D: DAN SMITH, JIM MORGAN, **C:** NICK LAND
A: TW2, **M:** JIM@DEEPEND.IT

WWW.MANTRADIGITAL.COM
D: MANTRA
A: MANTRADIGITAL, **M:** MANTRA@MANTRADIGITAL.COM

WWW.ZUBIRIA.COM
D: JORGE ZUBIRIA TOLOSA
A: ZUBIRIA DISENO, **M:** JORGE@ZUBIRIA.COM

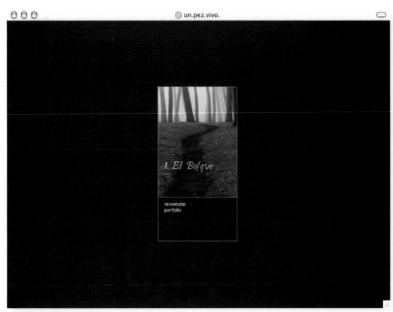

WWW.UNPEZVIVO.COM
D: JES'S DE LA PLAZA
A: UN.PEZ.VIVO, **M:** JESUS@UNPEZVIVO.COM

WWW.PUSHCANETWORKS.CC
D: PETRASCH MEINHARD
A: PUSHCA:NETWORKS*, **M:** M.P@PUSHCANETWORKS.CC

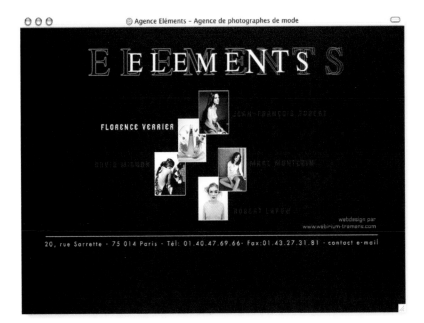

WWW.AGENCE-ELEMENTS.COM
D: SAMUEL BERNARD
A: WEBIRIUM-TREMENS, **M:** SAMUEL@WEBIRIUM-TREMENS.COM

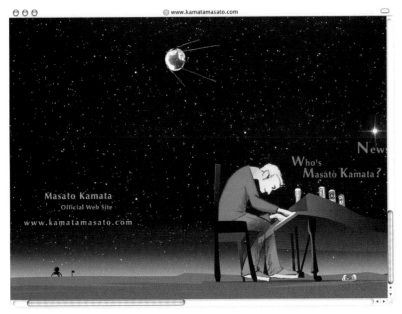

WWW.KAMATAMASATO.COM
D: KENJI ABE, **P:** NACRE STUDIO
M: NACRESTUDIO@MAC.COM

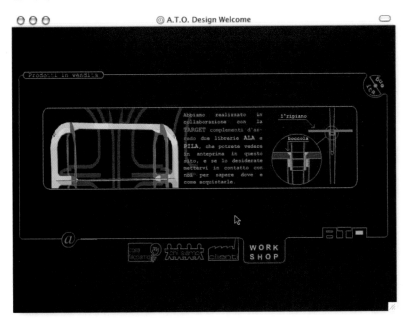

WWW.ATODESIGN.IT
D: TOMMASO MEONI
A: ATO DESIGN SRL, **M:** TOMMASO@ATODESIGN.IT

WWW.CUCKOOBOX.COM
D: CRISTIANO ANDREANI, **C:** MAURIZIO DELLA MARTERA
A: CUCKOOBOX, **M:** INFO@CUCKOOBOX.COM

WWW.ENFOCARTE.COM
D: LEONARDO VOLPE PRIGNANO
A: FVP DESIGN, **M:** QNLEO@HOTMAIL.COM

```
--------------------------------------------------
      Welcome to labellalola.com v1.05
--------------------------------------------------
labellalola.com is sited in the planet Earth and coordinated from Barcelona, Spain. (1)

The domain was registered in December/2000.
We aren't sure why we choose this name. (2)

We are young people but some of us have beard and long hair. (3)

We enjoy with the new technologys but we aren't indifferents with his responsibilitys (4)


But perhaps this is boring for you. (5)


--------------------------------------------------
Server: labellalola.com
Interface: Old Style
Version: 1.05
Author: de mikel

You choose:
```

WWW.LABELLALOLA.COM
D: MIKEL SEIJAS ALONSO
M: DE_MIKEL@LABELLALOLA.COM

INDEX